EMBATTLED SHRINE

EMBATTLED SHRINE
JAMESTOWN IN THE CIVIL WAR

BY
DAVID F. RIGGS

 White Mane Publishing Company, Inc.

This White Mane Publishing Company, Inc. publication
was printed by
Beidel Printing House, Inc.
63 West Burd Street
Shippensburg, PA 17257-0152 USA

In respect for the scholarship contained herein, the acid-free paper used in this book meets the guidelines for permanence and durability of the Committee on Production Guidelines for Book Longevity of the Council on Library Resources.

For a complete list of available publications
please write
White Mane Publishing Company, Inc.
P.O. Box 152
Shippensburg, PA 17257-0152 USA

Library of Congress Cataloging-in-Publication Data

Riggs, David F.
    Embattled shrine : Jamestown in the Civil War / by David F. Riggs.
       p.   cm.
    Includes bibliographical references (p.) and index.
    ISBN 1-57249-075-6 (acid-free paper)
    1. Jamestown (Va.)--History, Military.   2. Virginia--History-
-Civil War, 1861–1865.   I. Title.
F234.J3R54 1997
973.7'455--dc21   97-24185
                                              CIP

TABLE OF CONTENTS

ILLUSTRATIONS

MAPS

ACKNOWLEDGMENTS

Jamestown's Civil War history has been overshadowed by its fame as the first permanent English settlement in America. This book is intended to shed some light on the 1860s, and this objective was achieved with the assistance of numerous persons and institutions.

As always, my wife Susan provided support and assistance through her own research and knowledge of Virginia history. She also assisted with editorial matters and rendered invaluable guidance with a new word processing program.

My National Park Service colleagues at Colonial National Historical Park made contributions through their daily work as well as special assistance. This included extended loans from the park library; sharing of files, maps, and computer data; and methods for assimilating cultural resources. A word of special thanks is extended to James N. Haskett, Assistant Superintendent, Historic Interpretation and Preservation; Jane M. Sundberg, Cultural Resource Management Specialist; Diane G. Stallings, Jamestown Historian; Kirk D. Kehrberg, Interpretive Support Specialist; Diane K. Depew, Yorktown Historian; Richard D. Raymond, Yorktown Museum Curator; and Marge Shave, Volunteer Yorktown Curatorial Assistant.

The staff of the Virginia Historical Society graciously made their institution's fine collections available and provided guidance about these resources. Sara B. Bearss, Graham Dozier, Virginius C. Hall, Ann Marie Price, and E. Lee Shepard were especially helpful.

It was my pleasure to make extensive use of the Earl Gregg Swem Library at the College of William and Mary. Special recognition is due to Margaret C. Cook, Kay J. Domine, and Bettina Manzo.

Colleagues at other parks and offices of the National Park Service assisted in various ways. A special word of thanks is due to Robert K. Krick of Fredericksburg and Spotsylvania National Military Park for reviewing the manuscript, and to Donald C. Pfanz, also of

Fredericksburg, for providing a typescript of unpublished letters. Christopher M. Calkins and James Blankenship, Jr., of Petersburg National Battlefield suggested source material. Robert E. L. Krick of Richmond National Battlefield Park shared his personal research. Dale E. Floyd of the American Battlefield Protection Program offered guidance about earthworks.

Carol K. Dubbs of Williamsburg, Va., generously shared her knowledge of that town's Civil War history. Eve S. Gregory of Spring Grove, Va., pointed the way to several important documents about William Allen's prewar activities.

White Mane Publishing Company did more than merely place this work in circulation. Skillful editorial guidance by Martin K. Gordon improved the book's scholarship and readability, and the entire staff contributed to refining the final product.

Recognition also is due to George M. Brooke, Jr., Lexington, Va.; Ludwell H. Johnson, III, College of William and Mary; Dennis B. Blanton and Jared Bryson, Center for Archaeological Research, College of William and Mary; John Ingram and Del Moore, Colonial Williamsburg Foundation; Edward R. Crews, Richmond, Va.; Michael F. Geisinger, Vernon Hill, Va.; James H. Hutson, Library of Congress; Martha W. McCartney, Williamsburg, Va.; Blake A. Magner, Westmont, N.J.; John M. Coski, Guy R. Swanson, and Corrine P. Hudgins, Museum of the Confederacy; Michael P. Musick and Stuart L. Butler, National Archives; the Naval Historical Foundation, Washington, D.C.; Timothy A. Parrish, Greensboro, N.C.; Ervin L. Jordan, Jr., University of Virginia; Richard J. Sommers, Michael J. Winey, and Randy W. Hackenburg, U.S. Army Military History Institute; Diane B. Jacob, Virginia Military Institute; James I. Robertson, Jr., Virginia Polytechnic Institute and State University; William R. Massa, Jr., and Judith Ann Schiff, Yale University; and Preston Young, South Boston, Va.

My parents provided their usual encouragement plus a home for research trips to Fredericksburg and Washington, D.C.

Finally, a word of appreciation to our cat, Nittany, who spent countless hours with me while I was writing but never once placed her paw on the keyboard.

David F. Riggs
Williamsburg, Va.
July 1996

CHAPTER 1

A MILITARY HERITAGE

William Allen must have been astounded by events in the spring of 1861. At the age of thirty-three he was the wealthiest man in Virginia, and Jamestown Island was one of his many properties. Suddenly he found himself at Jamestown not in the role of proprietor but as an artillery officer, preparing to defend his land and his state against the United States Army. War changed lives so quickly in the Old Dominion that year.

The Confederates decided to fortify Jamestown shortly after Virginia seceded from the Union. This, however, was no sudden recognition of the island's military significance; rather, it was a continuation.

When English colonists settled at Jamestown in 1607, the site was selected for its strong defensive advantage. Although referred to as Jamestown Island as early as the seventeenth century, the "island" actually was joined to the mainland by an isthmus. By 1781 this narrow strip had eroded away, technically making Jamestown an island. The Englishmen found that the isthmus could be fortified against American Indians while their commanding view down the James River enabled them to watch for invaders from rival Spain. Furthermore, the water along the shore was so deep that it permitted boats to be tied near land, adding their guns to the defense. Because of their inland location, well removed from the Chesapeake Bay and the Atlantic Ocean, the settlers had more time to react against their European adversaries and to thwart any surprise attacks. The colonists chose well from a military standpoint, but the island itself was swampy. A hot, humid climate, marshland, brackish water, and mosquitoes combined for diseases which ultimately inflicted more losses upon them than Spaniards or warriors under Powhatan, who ruled the Indian chiefdoms of eastern Virginia.[1]

Fortification was a continuous concern. Shortly after the colonists landed on May 14, 1607, tree branches were placed in the shape of a

1

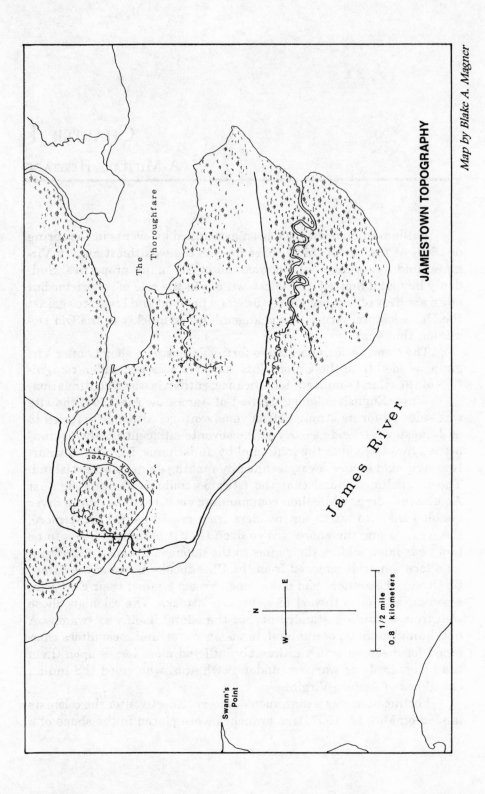

JAMESTOWN TOPOGRAPHY

James River

Back River

The Thoroughfare

Swann's Point

N
E
W
S

1/2 mile
0.8 kilometers

Map by Blake A. Magner

half moon as protection against several attacks by hostile tribesmen. Recognizing the inadequacy of this barrier, the Englishmen constructed a sturdy fort which was finished by June 15, only one month later. Triangular in shape, its three bulwarks were crowned by artillery.[2]

This second fortress, generally referred to as James Fort, enclosed about one acre upon which the fledgling newcomers built their makeshift houses, church, and storehouse. The long side of their isosceles triangle fronted the river while the two shorter sides guarded against land attack. Any sense of security was short-lived when most of the fort and its buildings burned in an accidental fire in January 1608. It was restored quickly and became the colony's third fort in less than a year. In September 1608 John Smith became president of the resident councilors who governed the colony. Smith, whose hallmark was discipline, instilled a military attitude in the settlers. He expanded the fortified area to three acres by establishing a pentagonal enclosure as the fourth fort, and the first of Jamestown's blockhouses was constructed in 1609 to guard the isthmus which joined the settlement to the mainland. This latter fort apparently was more substantial and survived for years to come.[3]

These first four fortifications were at, or very close to, what generally is called the fourth ridge on the western end of the island along the river. A turf fort was constructed along the river and to the east, about as far down as the eighteenth-century Ambler house. This four-sided earthwork might have been erected about 1663 and dismantled within less than twenty years. The last of Jamestown's colonial forts was authorized in 1667 and built between 1670 and 1676. Like its four earliest predecessors, it stood in the vicinity of the western bank's fourth ridge and in a nearby vale. Plans for the fort specified that it be made of brick with walls ten feet high and ten feet thick where it faced the river. Conflicting accounts say it was to have either eight or fourteen guns, and in 1701 this crescent-shaped structure was reported as having twenty guns. By 1716 it was deserted and in ruins, its fortunes declining with the town it defended.[4]

Despite this succession of forts, the Englishmen soon found it more effective with American Indian opponents to follow the maxim that the best defense is a good offense. In 1611 Sir Thomas Dale established an effective military system, which included offensive operations, and martial law prevailed from that date until its termination in 1619. Peace was caused only partially by the settlers' military prowess. Other factors included the marriage in 1614 of John Rolfe to Powhatan's daughter, Pocahontas, and the chief's advanced age. But a few years after Opechancanough became chief, he exploited the

Western End of Jamestown Island

National Park Service,
Colonial National Historical Park

settlers' complacency by launching a massive surprise attack on March 22, 1622, which inflicted great loss, although Jamestown was spared from assault thanks to a warning that alerted its defenders. The Englishmen soon rebounded and waged a ten-year war which ended in a truce in 1632. There was relative peace interrupted by raids and skirmishes until Opechancanough again startled the unwelcome settlers with a sudden assault on April 18, 1644. This short war concluded in 1646, virtually ending the threat from the Powhatan tribes.[5]

In the second half of the century the colonists became occupied with internal strife, world colonial wars, and American Indian tribes beyond the Tidewater. In 1652 the English Civil War led to Jamestown's peaceful surrender to a fleet dispatched by Oliver Cromwell. After the monarchy was restored, the colonists became participants in the second and third Anglo-Dutch Wars of the 1660s and 1670s, although ships from the Netherlands failed to penetrate as far as Jamestown. The last major military event to affect Jamestown started with a series of clashes with Indian tribes. These battles made settlers on the colony's western frontier feel unprotected and ignored, and this culminated in Bacon's Rebellion against the eastern Virginia based government where Jamestown served as capital. Although Nathaniel Bacon's mutinous followers eventually were defeated, Jamestown was besieged and burned by the insurrectionists on September 19, 1676, before order was restored. Jamestown was rebuilt, and ensuing treaties with the Indians again led to peace.[6]

It was fire which struck the mortal blow to Jamestown's prominence. Despite the English fears of Spaniards and Indians, of Dutch wars, and of rebellion like Cromwell's and Bacon's, this age old natural enemy plagued the colonists from beginning to end. Fire claimed James Fort one wintry night during the town's first year, it destroyed numerous buildings thereafter, and the conflagration of Bacon's Rebellion raised serious questions about rebuilding and keeping the capital there. Nonetheless, Jamestown recovered. After the statehouse fire of 1698, however, it was decided the following year to move Virginia's seat of government to nearby Middle Plantation, renamed Williamsburg. Ninety-two years of political dominance ended.[7]

Even before Jamestown lost its role as Virginia's capital, the fate of its aging fort near the statehouse was debated in the General Assembly. In 1694 the fort was considered ruined, its bricks decayed. For the remainder of the decade the legislators made divergent proposals either to repair it or to abandon it, and shortly after the legislature moved to Williamsburg in 1699 it considered the fort's ruins useless. The debate continued into the eighteenth century while the lawmakers continued to pay the salary of Edward Ross, the fort's gunner. A recommendation to spike the fort's guns was followed years later by a debate on the virtues of maintaining the site because it overlooked the James. By 1716 a visitor to Jamestown found only a ferry, a church, a courthouse, three or four brick houses, and a small rampart with embrasures "gone to ruin." Near the quarter-century mark there was no further reference made to the fort which formally was abolished in 1725.[8]

By the middle of the eighteenth century only a few structures remained at Jamestown. Even the church, which remained active until then, was abandoned. At this time the Ambler and Travis families completed their years of consolidation and became sole owners of Jamestown, each family having title to about half of the island. With the town a mere memory, suitable portions of the island were used as farmland.[9]

Military activity returned to Jamestown with the American Revolution. A ferry remained at Jamestown Island in the 1770s due to the river's reduced width at its western end, and it was this narrowing of the river which continued to provide strategic importance. Mary Ambler, widow of Edward, took her children to Hanover County in 1777 for greater safety, temporarily leaving Jamestown to the Travises and the military.[10]

Champion Travis was accustomed to protecting Jamestown's interests even prior to the revolution. He was in his early twenties when he first represented the corporation of Jamestown in the House of Burgesses in 1769, a position he retained into the war years. In 1774 he served in the Virginia Convention which met intermittently for several years, thereby affirming his alliance with fellow colonists who resisted British policy. A few months after the war began he was chosen colonel of the Elizabeth City District Battalion in September 1775, a unit composed of companies from Williamsburg and six neighboring counties, including James City County which contained Jamestown. The following year he was appointed a commissioner of the state's Navy Board which was entrusted with Virginia's naval preparations.[11]

Travis's duties frequently required that he be absent from Jamestown, and it was during one of these periods that some of the war's early excitement occurred. On the night of November 1, British vessels came up the James and exchanged shots with American sentinels stationed at Jamestown. Only minor damage was sustained when two or three cannonballs struck the ferry house. Then Virginia's royal governor, John Murray, fourth Earl of Dunmore, sent Captain James Montagu upriver with the schooner *Kingsfisher* and two sloops. After failing to destroy the crossing at Burwell's Ferry, Montagu continued to Jamestown and reached it on the fourteenth, joined by a reinforcing tender. Colonel William Woodford's 2d Virginia Regiment of Foot already was there, crossing the river. The Americans were so menacing along the riverbanks that the British elected to await nightfall before moving against the Jamestown ferry.[12]

Concealed by darkness, a ship's boat was sent toward Jamestown, which was guarded by about ten men under Captain John Green. Two sentinels who were posted along the beach detected the boat, challenged it, and received no answer. They discharged their muskets while the British were about fifty yards away and received return fire. One of the sentinels ran to summon Green while the remaining soldier fired three more rounds, the latter within about twenty yards of the approaching foe. Upon firing the third shot, he heard cries on the boat which turned back and was gone by Green's arrival.[13]

As the larger boats fired on Jamestown, Green's guards fired back. One of the vessels ran aground on a sand bar along the opposite shore at the small community of Cobham. Continentals on the Surry County side attacked in boats of their own, but several were distracted by a boat laden with oysters which was moving toward the *Kingsfisher*. During the exchange of fire, a British cannonball tore through the chimney of Travis's kitchen. Although this was the lone achievement for the king's forces at Jamestown, Montagu's boats hindered Woodford's movement long enough for the British to win a battle at Kemp's Landing, and temporarily solidify their position on the Southside.[14]

Several months later, in March 1776, a British tender ran aground opposite Jamestown one night. Unable to free their vessel, the crew threw the guns overboard and abandoned it. The next day colonists captured it and converted it for use in their own navy. There was a different kind of naval encounter the following month when two runaway slaves at Jamestown misidentified a rebel vessel and offered their services to Lord Dunmore. This costly error resulted in their execution.[15]

By April it was decided that Jamestown should be heavily fortified. Troops and cannon were sent to the island, although most of the artillery was transferred to boats. Infantry included three companies of Colonel Charles Lewis's 2d Battalion of Minutemen which were ordered to Jamestown in June. Within a month the climate and its associated illness took their toll. Two companies became unfit for duty and were sent home to recuperate.[16]

Ironically, it was during this period when Jamestown's strategic importance was again recognized that it lost its political clout. Throughout the eighteenth century it had been the British equivalent of a "rotten borough," retaining its own representative in the House of Burgesses, though without the necessary population base. The state's founding fathers who assembled for the Virginia Convention of 1776 changed this. The convention approved a new constitution on June 29 that denied Jamestown its own seat in the lower house. A second irony of the convention was a petition it received from Champion Travis. In it, Travis requested compensation for damage to his property caused not by British ships, but by the Virginia troops which occupied the island.[17]

By late 1776 through 1780 Jamestown served a variety of functions. Its wharf occasionally welcomed imports, and arms were stored at the island, reminiscent of its role during the seventeenth century. A battery with two guns and twelve men stood guard in 1777. Military activity was minimal during this period while attention was focused on colonies to the north and south. But in 1781 the opposing armies converged on Virginia as their main theater of operations. At first the main antagonists were the Marquis de Lafayette, commanding an American army, and General Charles, Earl Cornwallis. While the contestants skirmished and maneuvered that spring and early summer, Cornwallis and his former adversary, Major General Nathanael Greene, selected Jamestown as the site to exchange prisoners from their earlier campaign. The exchange occurred that July. Earlier in the month Jamestown became associated with a battle that bore the name of nearby Green Spring, originally constructed in the mid-seventeenth century as the home of Governor William Berkeley.[18]

On July 4 Cornwallis departed Williamsburg and headed for Jamestown. There he intended to cross the river and continue to Portsmouth, following Sir Henry Clinton's order to send part of his army northward to join Clinton in New York. Lafayette recognized the opportunity to strike the British army at this awkward moment when Cornwallis's forces would be on both sides of the river. Cornwallis, in turn, attempted to deceive Lafayette. He sent only a fragment of his army across the James and retained the majority of his men in concealment on high ground near Jamestown, just north of Glasshouse Point.[19]

In mid-afternoon Brigadier General Anthony Wayne's troops, who spearheaded the Continentals, advanced along a narrow causeway surrounded by marshland. They began skirmishing with British forces which withdrew in the manner of an outnumbered rear guard about midway between Green Spring and Jamestown. Not entirely convinced by Cornwallis's ruse, Lafayette personally reconnoitered, discovered the redcoats' deception, and returned to the battlefield late in the afternoon just as the combatants became hotly engaged. At this moment Cornwallis unleashed his army and quickly outflanked Wayne. Realizing that an immediate retreat might cause disastrous panic, Wayne tenaciously took the offensive to check the British, then withdrew. Upon reaching Green Spring and Lafayette's reserve forces, he reformed. Nightfall prevented Cornwallis from pursuing. The following day British dragoons and mounted infantry advanced several miles, renewed skirmishing, and returned to their lines. American casualties in the Battle of Green Spring were nearly double those of Cornwallis's 75, with more than 139 killed, wounded, and missing, plus the loss of two artillery pieces.[20]

On the night of July 6 Cornwallis moved his main army to Jamestown Island, and crossed the river to Cobham the following day. Lafayette sent troops under Brigadier General Peter Muhlenberg to the island on July 8. There he recovered nearly two dozen wounded Americans whom the British had abandoned during their river crossing. Lafayette established a hospital at Jamestown which operated for months under a flag of truce. One of its occupants in September was Wayne who, unscathed in the nearby fighting at Green Spring, was wounded by a colonial sentinel while en route to an appointment with Lafayette.[21]

It also was in September that Jamestown played a minor role in the Yorktown campaign which led to Cornwallis's surrender the following month. On September 2, the French started landing reinforcements for Lafayette at Jamestown under the Marquis de Saint Simon.

Some two weeks later additional Frenchmen disembarked at various points along the James River, including Jamestown, as George Washington and Comte de Rochambeau converged on Yorktown for the decisive victory of the American Revolution.[22]

For more than a quarter of a century thereafter the only reminder of war was the 1807 bicentennial observance of the founding of Jamestown, attended by Champion Travis and other members of the Virginia Convention of the revolutionary era. Then came the War of 1812 between the new American nation and the mother country. Following the British attack on Hampton on June 26, 1813, the governor appointed Brigadier General William Byrd Chamberlayne commander of Virginia militia between the James and York Rivers. Chamberlayne distributed his troops along necks of land that protruded into the James, but his disbursement was insufficient to thwart the invaders. British troops came upriver in barges and raided at numerous locations, including Jamestown where the Ambler property was plundered on July 1. The Virginians responded quickly and repelled the enemy. By early August the danger passed and the militia disbanded. Only in April of 1814 did Jamestown again receive attention during the war, this time from Colonel Decius Wadsworth of the U.S. Ordnance Department who issued the familiar assessment that the island was one of several potential sites for establishing a fort. When the war ended within the year, discussion of fortifying Jamestown ceased. It was relatively quiet for Jamestown's occupants thereafter, with the exception of the Virginiad of 1822 which was another observance of Jamestown's founding. The Travis home which survived two wars with Britain caught fire during the celebration.[23]

With over two centuries of military history, Jamestown was destined to become a significant site in yet another conflict.

CHAPTER 2

WILLIAM ALLEN PREPARES FOR WAR

Two seemingly unrelated events in 1831 had a profound effect upon Jamestown three decades later when civil war erupted. It was in this year that Jamestown's ownership passed entirely to David Bullock, thereby beginning the era when the island was the property of a single proprietor. Meanwhile, across the James in Surry County, William Allen of Claremont died. A boy in the Orgain family who celebrated his third birthday that year was the link between these occurrences.[1]

Named William Griffin Orgain, he was born July 29, 1828, probably in Petersburg. The son of Richard Griffin Orgain and Martha Armistead Edloe Orgain, he was the third of four children. His only brother, Montgomery Mackenzie, died in infancy in 1824; he also had an elder sister, Elizabeth, and a younger sister, Mary. Richard Griffin Orgain supported his family with several businesses in Petersburg, including partnership in a tobacco firm and the Exchange Coffee House (later Niblo's Hotel), and he owned an interest in the Petersburg Theater Company.[2]

There was a momentous change in the lives of the Orgain family after the death of William's great-uncle, William Allen. A wealthy bachelor, Claremont's owner left his estate to the three-year-old William Griffin Orgain "upon condition that he take the name of William Allen" to perpetuate the family name. In addition to Surry County's Claremont, the inheritance included the properties of Kingsmill in James City County and Curles Neck in Henrico County. The lands were bequeathed to the new William Allen for life only and bore the stipulation that upon his death he must transfer them to his eldest son.[3]

Young William was educated at Claremont by tutors until he concluded his formal education by attending Amelia Academy from the fall of 1844 to June 1847. Immediately thereafter he toured the northern and eastern United States with Dr. Philip Slaughter, an Episcopal minister from Petersburg, and in 1848–49 they toured Europe together.

10

Meanwhile, Allen's wealth had increased. After his father's death in 1837 his mother acted as guardian and expanded his holdings with the purchase of Jamestown Island in James City County, Berkeley in Charles City County, and Strawberry Plains in Henrico County. Soon after he reached the age of twenty-one, Allen received his estate on January 1, 1850. It included nearly 23,000 acres in five counties and over $52,000 in cash.[4]

From a financial standpoint no suitor in the state was as desirable as William Allen. As early as 1845 Sally Minge was betrothed to him, but the engagement was broken and Miss Minge later wed George E. Pickett, a future Confederate general. Ultimately Allen met Frances Augusta Jessup at Judge Thomas S. Gholson's home on Hinton Street in Petersburg while she was visiting the judge's daughter. High bred and gracious, Frances was the daughter of James and Catherine Shriver Jessup. The Allen-Jessup wedding vows were exchanged at the bride's home in Brockville, Canada, on December 22, 1852. This union brought the Allens six children but two daughters died young, leaving three sons and one daughter who reached adulthood.[5]

Across the James and down river from his Claremont home, Allen owned considerable land in James City County including Jamestown Island. Purchased in 1846, its 1,702 acres comprised one of several properties he had in the county, including Kingsmill, Neck of Land, Littletown, and Powhatan Creek. Although most of Jamestown Island was swampland, about 500 acres were used to raise such livestock as swine, sheep, cattle, oxen, cows, mules, and horses. Indian corn, wheat, and oats were the main crops, supplemented by Irish potatoes, sweet potatoes, and hay. After a decade of Allen's ownership the island's farm had a cash value of $40,000 with implements and machinery worth $1,600, livestock appraised at $4,650, and animals valued at $1,205.[6]

An overseer managed the Jamestown operation and lived in the old Ambler house. In 1860 overseer J. C. Gibson's labor force consisted of thirty slaves which apparently was the average figure throughout Allen's first decade of farming there. This was a small percentage of the blacks owned by Allen. At his major properties alone, Allen had over 500 slaves, and some of his contemporaries have estimated that he owned 700–1,000 slaves. Allegedly called "Marse Buck," Allen has been portrayed as a benevolent and respected master. This notion was substantiated to some extent by the blacks who made a special effort to attend their former owner's funeral in the postwar years. However, violence by blacks at Jamestown during the war years suggests that there was strong disaffection with the institution of slavery, if not with Allen's management.[7]

Allen used his plantations on both sides of the James for farming and related endeavors. At another of his James City County sites he had a gristmill. It was historical coincidence that in addition to Jamestown Allen also owned Curles Neck, whose seventeenth-century owner, Nathaniel Bacon, burned Virginia's first colonial capital. Allen allegedly permitted Cyrus McCormick to demonstrate his harvesting machine at Curles Neck. Yet Claremont remained the main farm and headquarters for other business ventures, including a partnership which Allen formed in 1854 with John A. Selden and Augustus Hopkins. Allen supplied the capital and bought land while his associates built a railroad, set up a sawmill, and sold timber from a wharf they constructed at Claremont. After three years they agreed to dissolve their partnership, and in 1858 Allen resumed the business with William A. Allen of Baltimore. This agreement lasted only two years at which time Allen foreclosed on his partner and operated the business independently. Allen's diverse interests also were evident by his investment in Selden and Miller, a mercantile firm in Richmond, and a fleet of schooners which he funded to carry freight on the James River. At least one early record indicates that Allen might have had difficulty managing the enormous wealth which he inherited, but the 1860 census records show improvement. By that time his real estate value had risen to $250,000 and his personal estate was listed as $1,000,000.[8]

Known as "Buck" Allen, or as Willie "Irish" Allen to his closest friends, Allen had a superb physique, a zest for the good life, and a

generous heart. He frequently hunted, sailed his yacht, *The Breeze*, and enjoyed an abundant supply of wine and cigars. A natural athlete and a fine horseman, he also was noted for his "craze for rare stock and pits," the latter being an allusion to cockfighting. His hospitality and parties were legendary, and he was "overindulgent to his own tastes for the best of solids and fluids," for this was a man who "made money flow like water." His social life extended not only to upper class planters along the James but to national and international dignitaries. Despite his love for revelry, Allen did not forget the downtrodden; he was recognized as a charitable man who donated generously to the needy.[9]

Captain William Allen
Virginia Historical Society

As owner of Jamestown Island, Allen sometimes found himself in an awkward situation. It could be difficult to farm on property which attracted visitors from the entire country because it was a national shrine. Benson J. Lossing visited Jamestown while writing his pictorial history of the American Revolution. Artist Robert Sully painted several pictures of the site based upon sketches he made while there in 1854. Pilgrimages were frequent and for a variety of reasons. Bishop William Meade inspected the site with several clergymen who came to pay homage to the ruins of the church tower there which dated to 1639. Still others came as Virginians and as other Americans, visiting the site where their state and their nation's English heritage began.[10]

When the 250th anniversary of the founding of Jamestown was approaching, Allen was confronted with a major dilemma. As proprietor of the island he could forbid the celebration from taking place on his land, averting the possibility of serious crop damage. Yet civic duty beckoned. As early as February 1854, three years before the Jamestown commemoration date, John Armistead visited Allen at Claremont to plead that the event should be celebrated on the island itself. Armistead hoped that if he and his colleagues appealed to Allen, he would consent and even join the effort "with much spirit," as had been the case with events on other property which belonged to the wealthy landowner.[11]

The Jamestown Society of Washington City, composed of Virginians in the northern part of the state, was founded at the time of Armistead's visit and was dedicated to achieving this goal. As the years passed the society did indeed persuade Allen to permit the celebration to be held on his historic island. The celebrants agreed to have the ceremony near the Travis family graveyard, about two miles east of the original settlement site, in order to afford some protection for the crops. Land around the church already was cultivated and, as one visitor commented, "Allen's wheat is everywhere." As the big day drew near it was noted that "Allen enters into it heartily."[12]

When the long-awaited day dawned on May 13, 1857, Allen was there to greet Virginia's Governor Henry A. Wise and accompany him on a visit to the ruins of Jamestown church. As agreed, the main event was farther east on the island where thousands of people gathered. There were specially constructed cabins, a 175-foot long refreshment salon, and a dining hall which seated 500 persons. A large fleet provided transportation to Jamestown for the crowd of civilians, and a large military encampment assembled there. Some of the soldiers had to perform guard duty at the original town site when church bricks and fragments of cemetery stones disappeared as souvenirs. *Harper's Magazine* publicized the event with drawings by David H. Strother. A former president and Virginian, John Tyler, delivered the main address which lasted about two to two-and-one-half hours, a speech which he assessed as "as brief as I could make it, and yet too long."[13]

Later that day the visitors who had arrived by boat returned to the flotilla of steamers from Richmond and Norfolk which patiently awaited them in the James River. There was a great dinner for the Jamestown Society aboard the *Powhatan*, followed by forty-three toasts. For one of them, glasses were raised in honor of "Wm. Allen—The proprietor of the site of Jamestown—May the pilgrims of 1957 meet with as hospitable a reception as we have." This grateful acknowledgment complimented Allen on his role as a proper host.[14]

Although life appeared normal at Jamestown with continued farming, construction of a causeway across the Back River swamp, and visits by occasional pilgrims, war clouds were on the horizon. A visit on April 21, 1859, was symbolic of both the national appeal of Jamestown and the sectional rift in America. Headed by Massachusetts Senator Edward Everett, the group planted ivy at the base of the church tower and listened to speeches by Everett and John R. Thompson, editor of the *Southern Literary Messenger*. Former President Tyler noted Everett's leading role in this act and wrote grudgingly that it "should have been done by some native born son of Virginia a century ago." Later that year John Brown's raid at Harpers Ferry stimulated Virginia's military preparation, prompting the formation of militia units, and renewing the dedication of those already in existence. This included the 71st Regiment Virginia Militia in Surry County, and by 1860 Allen was among its members with the rank of lieutenant. Allen was among the regiment's many members who were fined that year, his transgression being failure to attend training for officers on May 4. When the Civil War erupted in 1861 Allen was among the early enlistees. Returning to his native Prince George County, he assembled volunteers at Brandon Church on April 21, four days after Virginia passed its ordinance of secession, which coincidentally was the second anniversary of Everett's Jamestown visit. There he organized the Brandon Heavy Artillery. Although most of the unit's members were from Prince George and Surry counties, there also were volunteers from Dinwiddie, Charles City, and Chesterfield counties. Soon after the battery's formation, Allen's men crossed the James River and occupied Jamestown Island.[15]

Like many citizen-soldiers, Allen was a novice at war. It cannot be ascertained whether he occupied Jamestown Island by order or through his own initiative, but it proved to be good strategy. Conveniently, it was necessary to defend the James River against invasion from the south in order to cover Richmond's rear, and this in turn protected Allen's properties. Perceptively, Allen had his men begin constructing an earthwork for their battery before engineers issued the order. Major General Robert E. Lee, commander of Virginia forces, responded by expressing his desire that Allen take formal command of his battery and support Virginia's defense efforts at Jamestown. Accordingly, the artillerymen officially enlisted on May 10 with Allen as their captain, and the unit became Company E of the 1st Regiment Virginia Artillery.[16]

Similar to the English colonists who were wary of Spaniards more than two centuries earlier, the Virginians recognized the importance of defending the Peninsula situated between the James and York Rivers. At one end of the James was the vital industrial city soon to become the Southern capital, and some 120 miles from Richmond were the Virginia Capes and the Chesapeake Bay, which provided a Northern foothold by the Union's retention of Fort Monroe. With the Federals firmly entrenched at the tip of the Peninsula, it was impossible for Southerners to defend the coast, making the defensive positions along the James all the more important. Herein lay Jamestown's significance. The lower James was so wide that only its narrow points could be covered by artillery which sought to check Union advances, and the island's extension into the water offered this luxury.[17]

Jamestown Island Reduced the River's Width
National Park Service, Colonial National Historical Park

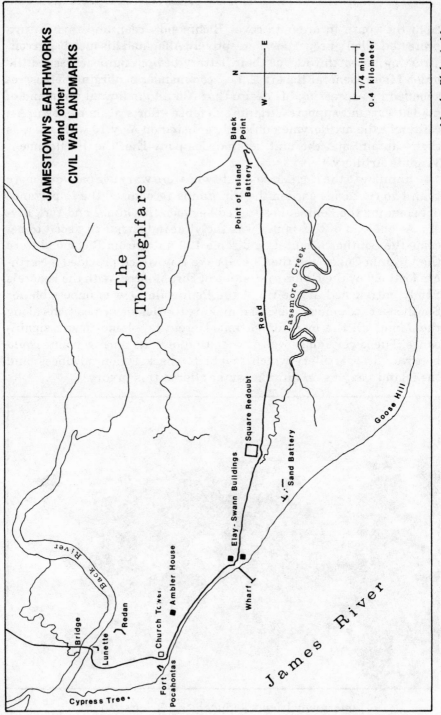

JAMESTOWN'S EARTHWORKS
and other
CIVIL WAR LANDMARKS

N
W E

1/4 mile
0.4 kilometer

The Thoroughfare

Black Point

Point of Island Battery

Passmore Creek

Road

Goose Hill

Square Redoubt

Sand Battery

Elay - Swann Buildings

Wharf

Ambler House

Church Tower

Fort Pocahontas

Cypress Tree

Lunette

Redan

Bridge

Back River

James River

Map by Blake A. Magner

As the James River rounded a bend at the eastern end of Jamestown Island it was three and one-quarter miles wide. In contrast, by jutting into the river the island reduced the James's width to one and one-eighth miles at its western end, enabling cannon and small arms to challenge passersby. Furthermore, the channel narrowed to 250 yards at a depth of four to ten fathoms and swung close to Jamestown, enabling gunners to anticipate the restricted route available to ships. Heavy naval guns and seacoast artillery could easily reach their targets. The island was about two and three-quarter miles long, one and one-quarter miles wide where it bulged to the east, and approximately 300 yards wide at its narrowest point to the west. Its 1700 acres, which already were eroding in the west, were bordered by the James on the east, south, and west. To the north it was separated from the mainland by the Back River which widened into The Thoroughfare. Four ridges were at the western end, as was the Pitch and Tar Swamp which extended eastward. Passmore Creek ran along the lower part of the island and joined the James to the east. Beneath Passmore Creek was a series of ridges that formed Goose Hill. Vessels moving upriver first encountered Black Point which was at the eastern tip of the island.[18]

In order to threaten naval vessels bound for Richmond on the James River, Jamestown itself had to be defended. Flank attacks had to be stopped to the north along Back River and The Thoroughfare. This eventually was accomplished by constructing earthworks on the mainland and on the northern edge of the northwestern end of the island. Passmore Creek, which flowed more than a mile into the island's southern interior and was navigable for vessels with a shallow draft, ultimately was guarded by an inland earthwork.[19]

When the Brandon Heavy Artillery arrived at Jamestown it found an island that had been cultivated annually amid seventeenth- and eighteenth-century ruins, the eighteenth-century Ambler mansion, and miscellaneous nineteenth-century structures. Crops and livestock had been profitable despite the ubiquitous swampland.[20]

Prominent among the earlier structures, the seventeenth-century Jamestown church tower still reached upward on the western end of the island. Remnants of a fort and powder magazine from the late 1600s were visible in the river, as was a cypress tree. Those sentinels engulfed by water bore silent witness to powerful erosion. The forces of nature also had destroyed the bridge that once linked Jamestown with the mainland. About one-half mile southeast of the church tower there was a T-shaped wharf with a few small frame structures at hand. This was the former Elay-Swann tract, proclaimed by a

Ruins of the Ambler House

Photograph by author

few persons in the twentieth century to be the site of the original settlement. Historical evidence and archeological excavations showed that habitation came there much later, with the nineteenth century being an especially active period.[21]

The finest structure at Jamestown was an eighteenth-century Georgian mansion known as the Ambler house. It was named for its owners who formerly shared proprietorship of the entire island with the Travis family. Made of brick, it had an elegant interior and a variety of furnishings which were admired by visiting Southern officers. Allen lived in the house during Jamestown's Confederate occupation, and he kept it stocked with liquor from several centuries. On special occasions he showed guests a musket he had unearthed from the town's historic ruins. Before the war, Allen's overseer was permitted to live in the main residence because the Allens' family home was across the river at Claremont. Numerous outbuildings and slave quarters were on the grounds, as well.[22]

One of the engineer officers assigned to Jamestown noted that the island was in a good state of cultivation. Recognizing that the army needed food as well as earthworks, Lee is attributed with voicing his regret that a promising wheat field had to be sacrificed for a redoubt. But this was war, and Allen's property, like him, was destined for many changes.[23]

While volunteers like William Allen flocked to defend Virginia, professional soldiers also answered the call. Robert E. Lee promptly accepted his governor's appointment as major general and commander of the state's military and naval forces in late April. He remained active in this capacity, organizing his native soil's defense, until Virginia transferred its army and navy to the Confederate States two months later.[1]

Lee relied heavily on the Virginia state engineer, Colonel Andrew Talcott. A northerner who hailed from Connecticut, Talcott celebrated his sixty-fourth birthday a few days after Virginia seceded. Like Lee, he was a West Point graduate and veteran of the Corps of Engineers where he rose to captain during the years 1818–1836. He demonstrated his creativity by using astronomy to develop what became known as "Talcott's method" as a means to determine latitude. Upon his resignation from the army, he became a prominent civil engineer working with railroads and navy yards, in river improvement, and in ascertaining territorial boundaries. Much of his career in both military and civilian service was spent in Virginia, where he grew fond of the state.[2]

Talcott had known Lee in the pre-war army. Three decades earlier they were assigned together

Colonel Andrew Talcott
Virginia Historical Society

at Fort Monroe where Talcott was Lee's immediate superior. They developed a close relationship, and now Lee turned to his friend and former colleague for assistance against the nation they formerly served together. Talcott would pay a price for this deed, even though his length of service to the Southern cause was brief. During the war he returned to Mexico to continue work he had started earlier on a railroad. In 1863 he ventured to New York City to purchase supplies for this project and was arrested as a spy. After four months of imprisonment the charges were dismissed and he resumed work in Mexico.[3]

On April 29, Lee ordered his old comrade to examine the James River and determine the best site to erect a battery for its defense. Talcott was directed to lay out the works, but have a naval officer complete them. Talcott then was to continue to Fort Powhatan, below City Point, to select additional fort sites. Fort Powhatan would be under naval Captain Harrison F. Cocke.[4]

Talcott started exploring the James on May 1 accompanied by a fellow engineer, Captain Edmund Trowbridge Dana Myers, and Lieutenant Catesby ap Roger Jones of the navy. Toward the conclusion of the trip's second day, the trio disembarked at Jamestown Island. They were greeted by Allen and his newly formed artillery battery which had started constructing a fortification. Like the English adventurers who preceded them by some two hundred fifty years, Talcott was impressed by the island's qualities as a defensive site. On Friday, May 3, he laid out a battery for eighteen guns near the ruins of the church tower. It is not known whether or not this was on the same site as the one started by Allen; regardless, Talcott's battery superseded it. Satisfied with his day's work, he left Jones and Myers to continue the work and proceeded on his way. For the time being Jamestown was the only location he recommended for fortification, making it Richmond's main defensive position along the James.[5]

Jones's assignment to oversee construction of the battery was in keeping with Virginia's policy of having naval officers command the river batteries. These works would be armed with large guns, many identical to those on seafaring vessels. Forty years of age, Jones was a native Virginian. The "ap" in his name was a Welsh idiom meaning "son of," hence, "son of Roger." His long naval career included experiments upon the Dahlgren gun with its inventor, John A. B. Dahlgren, which improved both the weapon and Jones's knowledge of ordnance. During his twenty-five years of service in the U.S. Navy, he rose to lieutenant, resigned upon the Old Dominion's secession, and was appointed lieutenant in Virginia's navy effective April 23, 1861. One of the Union's most prominent naval officers, Rear Admiral David Dixon

Porter, is attributed with the remark that Jones was one of only two fellow officers whose resignation he regretted. Prior to his Jamestown assignment, Jones participated in the capture of the Gosport Navy Yard near Norfolk when the Union abandoned it. He would survive the war only to be shot fatally years later in Selma, Alabama, in a disagreement with a neighbor.[6]

Lieutenant Catesby ap Roger Jones
U.S. Naval Historical Center

To augment his experience Jones had a commanding presence. Tall and well proportioned, his uniform was immaculate and clean, providing the appearance of an officer conscious of his rank. He abstained not only from alcohol and tobacco, but from coffee and tea, as well. When he walked a graceful limp was detectable, caused by a bullet wound to the hip years before.[7]

When Jones met Allen he was pleased with the wholehearted efforts that the young millionaire had made. In addition to his initiative to fortify the island, Allen had requested eight 32-pounders captured at Norfolk, although Jones feared that this appeal would be ignored. Allen also had provided a wide variety of supplies for the new garrison at his own expense.[8]

The importance of defending Richmond increased dramatically during those early days of occupation at Jamestown. Richmond's status as the state capital was noteworthy in itself. More important to the Southern states, however, was its industrial prowess, most notably the city's Tredegar Iron Works which offered the secessionists their main source of production for large machinery and heavy weapons. Recognizing the city's value, the Confederacy sent troops to its defense and engaged in negotiations to move the South's capital from Montgomery, Alabama, to Richmond. Richmond's selection as capital was intended to assure that Virginia would join the alliance of Confederate States. Agreement was reached in May, and President Jefferson Davis arrived before the month's end. Now Jamestown defended the capital of a new nation.[9]

Jones vigorously assumed command of the earthwork construction the day of Talcott's departure. He ordered, and erroneously expected to receive, 250 men to assist with the project within twenty-four hours. He also anticipated six guns, but he worried about where he would find the remaining twelve. A quick survey of equipment revealed that despite Allen's generous contributions, supplies were sorely lacking. Jones needed entrenching tools and wheelbarrows along with at least 1,000 pounds of meat and other forms of subsistence for his workers. Furthermore, once artillery did arrive he needed a means to transport and mount the guns.[10]

With the Union navy extending its blockade to include Hampton Roads and the mouth of the James River, Fort Monroe's garrison appeared even more menacing. The absence of infantry to protect his battery became another worrisome matter for Jones. When he assumed command no mention was made of this subject, but he raised it with his superiors frequently during those early days at Jamestown.[11]

The solution to the problem appeared to be only a few miles to the east at Williamsburg. There Major Benjamin Stoddert Ewell was assembling troops to defend the Peninsula by land while his counterparts in the navy like Jones busied themselves with water defenses. A West Point graduate, Ewell found the role of professional educator more promising. When the war began he was fifty years old and president of the College of William and Mary. In 1862 he left the area to serve on General Joseph E. Johnston's staff, then returned to Williamsburg after the war to resume his academic career. His brother Richard rose to lieutenant general and corps commander in the Confederate army.[12]

Upon contacting Ewell, Jones was informed that the major's volunteers had neither the training nor the numbers to meet his requirements. Furthermore, Ewell's Williamsburg garrison had received a simultaneous request to provide troops for Gloucester Point. Severely pinched, Ewell roughly divided his Williamsburg Junior Guard into thirds, ordering two segments to Jamestown and Gloucester Point while retaining the third contingent with him at Williamsburg.[13]

The Guard had drilled on the college campus since its formation in 1859 in response to John Brown's Harpers Ferry raid. Shortly after Virginia seceded, it had enlisted in state service. The college students, local officials, and merchants who composed the unit made a ponderous march to Jamestown and arrived on the evening of May 4. Each soldier was accompanied by a servant, and the column was further encumbered by carriages and wagons bearing extra food, clothing, and medical supplies. When Jones inspected this entourage he found that it included a grand total of seventeen soldiers. Some of the workmen at Jamestown were edgy with reports of minor skirmishing down river, and Ewell hoped that this meager force might at least offer moral support and restore confidence. Jones barely had time to enjoy this psychological boost because of events at Gloucester Point. Artillery there dueled with a Union vessel, the *Yankee*, and within twenty-four hours of its arrival the Junior Guard was recalled to Williamsburg.[14]

As earthwork construction continued that May 5, Lee ordered Allen to assume command of his company as an official Virginia force and remain at Jamestown. Lee intended to have Allen's unit mustered into service as soon as Allen applied. Jones was pleased with the assignment and formally invited Allen to join him the following day. Allen likewise was positive about the orders, but reminded Jones that he needed arms and uniforms. In response, Jones requested rifled guns for Allen's men whom he regarded as fine marksmen. Company E of the 1st Regiment Virginia Artillery officially enlisted on May 10 with Allen as captain. The unit also was called the Brandon Artillery, named for the site where it first assembled and organized. However, the company soon became more closely identified with the place it had rushed to defend and became known as the Jamestown Artillery.[15]

Despite the Junior Guard's departure on May 5, Jones was offered assistance that day not only with Allen's assignment, but also by Commander Matthew Fontaine Maury. Like Talcott, Maury was assisting Richmond in stabilizing its defenses and after visiting Jamestown, he went to Fort Powhatan in search of guns and troops. The renowned oceanographer and "Pathfinder of the Seas," who was serving on the Governor's Advisory Council, returned in the evening with four 32-pounders and twenty men from the Greensville Guard.[16]

The guns arrived without tackles or any means of unloading them. Jones had no alternative but to stop construction on the earthwork and assign everyone to unloading the heavy cargo. The following morning Jones supervised the guns' proper placement. Once this was accomplished he resumed writing volumes of letters in which he painted a dismal picture of Jamestown's tenuous position and his need for ordnance, manpower, and supplies. Determined to keep attention focused on his position as an outpost, he bemoaned the fact that he needed a larger command to operate the guns just received and that the expectation of additional artillery meant that still more men would be needed. Following Lee's suggestion, he again asked Ewell to send reinforcements from Williamsburg, realizing that there was little hope of obtaining them. Although he secured a tug, the *Raney*, to serve as a lookout along the river, his position was quite vulnerable. Cocke and

Fort Powhatan continually irritated Jones who complained incessantly about the preference Cocke gave to that safer, upriver site instead of sharing resources with Jamestown.[17]

Captain William H. Briggs commanded the contingent of the Greensville Guard which reached Jamestown with Maury. Briggs's men had enlisted just the previous day. Immediately after their arrival Jones asked that Fort Powhatan send the remainder of the company and, perhaps to his surprise, his wish was fulfilled.[18]

By May 8 Briggs's entire unit was present, such as it was. In addition to Briggs it included three lieutenants, four sergeants, four corporals, and seventy-three privates for a total of eighty-five men. Unfortunately, these recruits needed basic equipment. The company had fifty Enfield muskets and eighteen flintlock muskets which lacked flint; two of the muskets were missing ramrods, and thirty were so old and useless that they needed replacing. Thirteen soldiers had no gun of any description. Ammunition was in short supply, too. There were only two cartridges per Enfield and ten balls for each flintlock. Two of the officers needed swords. Furthermore, the company had no cartridge boxes, no knapsacks, no camp equipment with the exception of a few kettles, no tents—not even stationery for official reports.[19]

Another company was ordered from Fort Powhatan to Jamestown on May 10. Like the Greensville Guard, this unit had enlisted only one day prior to its transfer. Named the Charles City Southern Guards, the company dated to 1859. In short order the enlistees from Charles City joined with those from Greensville to form Companies A and B, respectively, in what was known as Waddill's Battalion. The battalion's namesake was George M. Waddill, captain of the Charles City troops. A native of Isle of Wight County, Waddill had just turned twenty-three but, despite his youth, poor health forced his resignation the following year. He later served the state as an attorney and legislator.[20]

In Richmond Lee recognized the need for an army officer to take charge of the infantrymen who were arriving to support Jones's battery. Accordingly, Major John Mercer Patton, Jr. was selected. When appointed, Patton was in Richmond training volunteers and he was ordered to Jamestown on May 7 to continue that work with the new arrivals there.[21]

Patton probably reached Jamestown by May 9 for the thirty-fifth observance of his birthday. Although he received martial training from his native state's Virginia Military Institute, he decided to practice law in Richmond where he also wrote several legal volumes. He revived his military activities by 1852 as captain in the Richmond Light

Infantry Blues. After the Civil War ended, he wrote reminiscences of his military service, and several theological works. A frail person, he was described by one Southern soldier as a pigeon-headed man with a mind "as narrow as any King's that ever tormented mankind." Like his brothers, George Smith and Waller Tazewell, he would rise to the rank of colonel in the Confederate army. Patton's colonelcy was with the 21st Virginia Infantry, from which he resigned in poor health in 1862, later to assume less strenuous positions in Richmond. A descendant of the Revolutionary War general, Hugh Mercer, he was great-uncle to General George S. Patton, Jr., of Second World War fame.[22]

While assembling infantry support and artillery, Jones also supervised the fort's erection. Construction virtually started upon his arrival at Jamestown and continued ceaselessly, even during that hectic first week. In accordance with Talcott's instructions the earthwork was to have five sides and eighteen guns.[23]

Surprisingly, Jones had a sizable labor force from the very beginning. As owner of Jamestown and several nearby plantations, Allen had a large work force on hand and volunteered his slaves. Other Tidewater slaveowners likewise contributed, and by May 5 there were over 100 blacks at work. Quantities of dirt soon were needed to raise and thicken the fort's walls. Much of Jamestown was cultivated while the majority of the island was swampy, so some soil was imported from the mainland in order to avoid scooping trenches in Captain Allen's farm. A shortage of equipment, rather than manpower, became the immediate concern.[24]

While constructing the earthwork the Virginians found evidence of the early English settlers. By one account the "curious relics" that were encountered included a fragment of armor, while another version referred to several pieces of armor. An additional writer mentioned two pieces of armor, sword hilts, a caltrop, and several coins. Yet it was the recollection of Southey Savage Hankins that was most enticing. As dirt was being removed for the moat, butts of timber were found which the soldiers speculated was part of the colonists' original fort. Although this latter discovery perhaps contains fanciful conjecture, the artifacts were additional confirmation that

Armor Found by Confederates
National Park Service,
Colonial National Historical Park

the Southerners were in the vicinity of the 1607 settlement, a theory that was validated later by archeologists. Little wonder that the Virginians called their new earthwork Fort Pocahontas.[25]

Second Lieutenant Emmett M. Morrison

Eleanor S. Brockenbrough Library, Museum of the Confederacy, Richmond, Virginia

It was amid this construction activity that Emmett M. Morrison arrived. A youth aged nineteen whose home was across the James, down river at Smithfield, Morrison had just graduated from the Virginia Military Institute. Upon graduation his military training made him valuable for instructing raw recruits, an assignment he and many of his classmates fulfilled at Camp Lee in Richmond. Soon he was commissioned a second lieutenant of engineers. He then was ordered to Jamestown by Lee in the same directive that sent Patton there. Together they were responsible for converting the enlistees at Jamestown into soldiers.[26]

Three things immediately caught Morrison's attention when he reached his destination. One was the fort, growing in stature beside the seventeenth-century church tower as the dirt piled higher daily. Jamestown's second characteristic was in sharp contrast: its flat, barren appearance which was described by Morrison as "a perfect desert." The soil was sandy and the landscape was devoid of trees. Only as one looked southeastward did a third feature, the Ambler house, rise into view. The house was situated on about an acre of beautiful grass, the only greenery in the area. Morrison soon would be among the officers who adopted the mansion as headquarters.[27]

Talcott returned to Jamestown on May 11 to inspect Jones's progress. Although he accomplished a considerable amount in only one week and one day, Jones was not in the best humor. Myers, who had remained at Jamestown to supervise construction needs, was "quite unwell." Jones felt that he desperately needed a steamer and mourned the loss of his lone vessel, the tug *Raney*, that had been recalled to Richmond. Worse still, Cocke had visited two days earlier and had taken Jones's side and train tackles from three of his guns. Jones was furious. Only with extreme difficulty had he managed to build temporary platforms for his guns. Cocke gave preference to Fort Powhatan despite the importance Talcott and Jones placed upon Jamestown. Jones argued in vain with Cocke, pointing out that Jamestown, which was farther downstream, would be attacked first; that Fort Powhatan's guns were lighter and could operate without tackles; and that Cocke already had more tackles than Jones. As if this were not enough, the welcome infantrymen under Waddill taxed the garrison's low provisions. Finally, incoming ammunition and supplies frequently were the wrong size or had parts missing.[28]

Still there was much on the positive side. The number of guns in the fort had increased to eight: two 9-inch guns and six 32-pounders. When Jones test fired the 32-pounders he felt that the breeching was unnecessary; otherwise he was satisfied. With earthwork construction under way, one artillery unit present, and infantry support, Jamestown was beginning to take shape as a fortification.[29]

Captain Samuel Barron appreciated Jones's difficulties and sought to encourage him. As head of Virginia's Office of Naval Detail and Equipment he was well aware of Jones's problems with Cocke and in obtaining supplies. He wrote a supportive letter saying that he "sympathized...fully in [Jones's] annoyance." Barron declared that if it were within his power he would give Jones entire control of the situation; meanwhile, he encouraged him to persevere.[30]

Citizens of nearby Williamsburg were interested in Jamestown's progress, too. Undoubtedly they recognized that the Jamestown Road, which linked the two colonial capitals, made them vulnerable to attack from that direction. Robert Saunders, who was a former president of the College of William and Mary, railroad president, and politician, visited Fort Pocahontas and wrote enthusiastically about its status. He was impressed by the guns that already were mounted and ready, and his spirits were buoyed by the soldiers' expectations that another ten to twenty pieces of ordnance were coming. He underestimated the manpower at 150, shy by about sixty men. Another voice from Williamsburg was less optimistic. Thinking from the long-range military perspective and remembering what Peninsula summers were like, Ewell doubted that a permanent Jamestown garrison was feasible. He knew the area well, and he warned Lee that the island, which was "exceedingly unhealthy," might make it impossible for its defenders to survive the summer there.[31]

Talcott made his third visit to Jamestown within two weeks, arriving May 15. This time he was accompanied by Lieutenant John M. Brooke, naval aide to Lee, and Captain Archibald Fairfax, ordnance officer at the Norfolk Navy Yard. The trio's assignment was to report on the rival fortifications at Jamestown and Fort Powhatan. With his veteran engineer's eye and the counsel of his colleagues, Talcott again examined the earthwork and inspected the island, then departed the following day at 10 A.M. Losing no time, Jones fired a letter to Barron that day with his own summary of what the officers had found. The two 9-inch guns had only seventy cartridges, seventy shells, and eight stands of grape. Ammunition for the six 32-pounders consisted of 396 cartridges, 498 shot, seventy-five shells, and twenty stands of grape. Available powder came to four barrels, or 400 pounds. One of the 9-inch guns was difficult to work since it had no sights, sight box, screw, screw plate, or roller handspike. In order to service the guns 128 men were required, and another ninety to 120 would be needed when the additional ordnance arrived—far more artillerymen than were present.[32]

The report filed by Talcott, Brooke, and Fairfax was gratifying to Jones. Highly critical of Fort Powhatan's location and construction, it recommended that the fort be moved down river. In contrast, Jamestown's Fort Pocahontas was praised for its construction which was approaching completion. Earthworks intended to protect Jamestown from attack by land had been designed and would be erected immediately. As a final touch, it was felt that a battery of two or three guns across the river at Swann's Point would improve the Jamestown artillery's chances of stopping Union vessels.[33]

View from Inside Fort Pocahontas

Photograph by author

A total of 214 men defended Jamestown by mid-May, including Waddill's Battalion and Allen's artillery, the latter still without arms and uniforms. But its wealthy captain remedied this deficiency by providing these necessities at his own expense. Patton busily engaged himself in the role of drillmaster but, like Jones and the artillery, arms and ammunition remained a troublesome matter for the infantry. The men received small arms of three different kinds and calibers. Enfield rifle muskets, which became popular during the war, were distributed to the troops as were two smoothbore musket types, flintlock and altered percussion. Two shipments of ammunition were received for the Enfields, but both were incorrect in that the balls were larger than the bore.[34]

Significant changes in high command occurred as both Federals and Virginians turned attention to the Peninsula. Anxious to maintain its foothold at Hampton Roads, the Union sent Major General Benjamin F. Butler to Fort Monroe. Butler's service there was brief, but he left his mark on early military activities in the region. His counterpart was Colonel John Bankhead Magruder, a native Virginian and West Pointer, who was appointed Southern commander on the Peninsula on May 21. Magruder was a dandy whose elegance and flamboyance won him the sobriquet "Prince John." Within a month he was a brigadier general, and in October was promoted to major general.[35]

Magruder surveyed the overall strategic picture and realized that Jamestown alone could not protect the Confederate capital. Jamestown, which was a considerable distance upriver, would be the first opposition that the Union navy would encounter along the James. Moreover, the York River was virtually open and there was little defense on land. Magruder felt that it was necessary to erect earthworks at Yorktown to guard the York and at Williamsburg to block the land route. These additions by themselves, however, were insufficient. Yorktown was twelve miles down river from Williamsburg, so the Federals merely had to sail up the James to a point below both Williamsburg and Jamestown, land, march to Yorktown, and take it from the rear. In order to prevent this, Magruder pushed troops farther down the Peninsula while he fortified the position behind them. When completed, he had what was known as the Warwick Line, a series of works behind the Warwick River that stretched across the Peninsula from Yorktown and the York River to Mulberry Island on the James, just below Jamestown. The line guarded both flanks with fortified positions along the rivers and would thwart naval efforts to pass unopposed. Still, this did not reduce the need to strengthen Jamestown. It controlled a strategic part of the James just beyond Mulberry Island, where it served as the next obstacle for vessels. Jamestown also remained the immediate guard of Williamsburg's flank. Furthermore, it was months before the defenses at Mulberry Island were completed.[36]

With little more than a week in May remaining, plans were being made for an additional battery at Jamestown to improve control of the river channel. The site was selected by Talcott, presumably on his visit during the middle of the month when he examined the entire island. Located along the river about midway down the island, the earthwork would be in the vicinity of Goose Hill, surrounded by marsh and situated on a sandy beach. It derived its name from this latter feature and became known as the Sand Battery. Five 8-inch army guns were intended for the battery. Jones would be commander of all batteries while Patton retained command of the infantry. Characteristically, Jones lost no time in pointing out that this new battery increased his need for an experienced gunner. By adding 8-inch guns to the 9-inch and 32-pounders already at Jamestown, now he would be dealing with three different calibers.[37]

Nor did Jones ignore his needs for Fort Pocahontas. He recited the status of his artillery again, this time even giving the markings for each gun. These guns, too, needed additional men, especially a competent gunner and a few seamen who were experienced with heavy ordnance. He tabulated his ammunition in his usual methodical manner, but he took a new approach to emphasize his shortage: in addition to citing his inventory by the quantity actually present, he also expressed it in the number of rounds per gun. Finally, Jones compiled a long list of miscellaneous supplies.[38]

Captain William Nelson
Eleanor S. Brockenbrough Library,
Museum of the Confederacy,
Richmond, Virginia

Around noon on May 24 a second artillery unit reached Jamestown. Commanded by Captain William Nelson, the Hanover Artillery arrived from Richmond aboard the steamer *Curtis Peck*. Nelson was a fifty-two-year-old bachelor and native of nearby Yorktown. He grew accustomed to serving his state in the legislature, and raised a military unit as soon as Virginia seceded. It was easy to recognize Nelson, who scorned the customary artilleryman's headgear and instead wore a high silk hat. In the war's final weeks he attained the rank of full colonel. His men sometimes were identified as William Nelson's Company Virginia Light Artillery, or the Hanover Light Artillery.[39]

Like many new units the men from Hanover were deficient in supplies, including tents. Accordingly, they were sent to the nearby mainland, Neck of Land, and made their quarters in a large barn. Neck of Land, like Jamestown, was the property of William Allen, and his slaves cooked supper for the newcomers. The following morning the artillerymen visited Fort Pocahontas, then proceeded down river to the wharf where they unloaded plank from a boat. Private Henry R. Berkeley recalled that the dinner they received for their labor included "some of the meanest bread and meat I ever saw." Around dark they returned to the barn and were favored with a fine dinner with the officers who had two servants to prepare meals that were more palatable.[40]

Sunday morning, May 26, was a culinary adventure: many of Nelson's men were "compelled to try [their] hand at cooking some breakfast." The coffee was deemed acceptable but not the dumplings, which one private said would have killed old Nick, the family horse. Later that day a member of the company, Private Henry Martin Stringfellow, conducted worship services. Perhaps there was a word of thanksgiving for having survived the morning meal. Regardless, the new soldiers obviously were in no hurry to improve their cooking skills. Immediately after the service they gathered some rations, proceeded to Allen's slave quarters, purchased some eggs from the blacks, and then persuaded them to make dinner. With considerable satisfaction, it was pronounced the best meal since leaving Richmond.[41]

The Hanoverians took turns performing various tasks. Monday was Private Berkeley's first day posted as a guard at Fort Pocahontas, and he found the late spring's sun to be punishing. He complained about his "little military cap" which gave inadequate protection, allowing the sun to burn the skin off his ears.[42]

While the Hanover Artillery was adjusting to its new assignment, Lee, Talcott, and Barron expressed apprehension about troops on the Peninsula. In an effort to increase the buffer between Fort Monroe and Jamestown, the army sent reinforcements and supplies below Jones's position. This was hazardous and naval authorities asked Jones's opinion about bringing them ashore at Jamestown where his guns offered protection. Simultaneously, there were problems with new guns that arrived at the island. Vessels that transported them drew so much water that it was difficult to bring them ashore, and one naval captain confided that he was "anxious about [the] island." The army, likewise, was concerned. Lee and Talcott both were adamant that Jamestown should receive more guns. As encouraging as this news might have been, Jones found no solace in a message received near the end of the month advising him that most of the supplies he recently had requested were not available. At this time Jones added a personal request that underscored the shortages when he asked, "Can I not be furnished with a revolver?"[43]

Amid this concern about Jamestown's safety came disturbing word from Newport News, down river. On May 27 Butler's troops from Fort Monroe had successfully established an outpost there. Three volunteer regiments, a detachment of regulars, and two 6-pounders secured the position which was named Camp Butler and fortified with four 8-inch Columbiads. Virginia's naval officials renewed their cry that Jamestown's safety be assured. They predicted that the Union undoubtedly would attack and that the assault would be by both land and water, but army defenses were inadequate at this time. Captain Barron sounded panic-stricken when he learned of Butler's incursion. He advised Jones that he must spike his guns and retire, if necessary.

Captain Samuel Barron
Massachusetts Commandery,
Military Order of the Loyal Legion,
U.S. Army Military History Institute

Should Federals advance on the river's right bank, Jones was ordered to use steamers, scows, and lighters which would be placed at his disposal to ferry the army.[44]

In contrast to this apparent fear, Barron responded forcefully to Butler's move. Barron restored a naval vessel to Jamestown by assigning the steamer *Teaser* to its waters on May 29. Among other duties it was to assist in transporting men and supplies between the island and the mainland. Barron also reported that President Jefferson Davis reached Richmond that day, a significant milestone in the city's rising stature as capital of the Confederacy. Barron reiterated to Jones why Jamestown was not being ignored. It was, and for some time would continue to be, the first major work along the James opposing the Federals. In Richmond the fortification at Jamestown was considered "the battery for the defense of the city."[45]

Lee also responded to Butler's action, sending the Bedford Light Artillery and the 14th Virginia Infantry to Jamestown on May 29. As with the Hanover Artillery a few days earlier, the *Curtis Peck* made the delivery. Barron also notified Jamestown that two companies of cavalry were en route, but there is no indication that they ever arrived. The artillery, in accordance with precedent, was under Jones's direction since he commanded the batteries. The 14th Virginia's colonel outranked Major Patton who continued as instructor for Waddill's Battalion while the new arrivals were independent of Patton.[46]

The Bedford Light Artillery had been organized back in January and enlisted May 8. Its captain, Tyler Calhoun Jordan, was in his mid-twenties. A Bedford native, he had attended the University of Virginia, and by war's end rose to major. In contrast, the 14th Virginia Infantry had organized only a few days earlier on May 23. The regiment's colonel, James Gregory Hodges, was from Portsmouth and in his early thirties. Prior to the war he was a physician and had served as Portsmouth's mayor. He was destined to number among the fatalities of Pickett's charge at Gettysburg.[47]

Jones was pleased with the quality of the troops he was receiving, if not the quantity. He now had about 1,000 soldiers, "not one too many." All three artillery companies were manning the battery at Fort Pocahontas, but even this was inadequate since he still lacked the strength for four guns. Although their numbers were insufficient, Jones was pleased with the spirit, intelligence, and zeal of the artillerymen. Once they were drilled properly he was fully confident of their ability. Jones personally drilled them when time permitted. Between earthwork construction, work that was about to begin on a new bridge, and training new volunteers, he felt that he "never worked harder than in the last week."[48]

Another reason for Jones to be weary was the arrival of additional guns. Five Columbiads were sent to Jamestown and, although intended for the Sand Battery, he lost no time in mounting four of them at Fort Pocahontas. Two platforms were built on each flank for barbette carriages which raised the guns over the parapet and enabled them to fire in any direction. One pair of Columbiads was mounted on May 27, and two more were in place by the night of the twenty-ninth. Lieutenant Jones refrained from mounting the last Columbiad when Richmond sent word that it should be saved for the Sand Battery, which was expected to be ready for guns in about a week. Jones, who preferred to keep all the Columbiads at Fort

Pocahontas, confessed his dread of mounting guns on the marsh and sand of the lower battery.[49]

In late May and early June the arrival of troops at Jamestown and elsewhere on the Peninsula increased the need for both supplies and ways to transport them to soldiers. Magruder ordered Ewell to undertake this effort by collecting wagons from local residents. Furthermore, the donors were instructed to send the wagons with black teamsters selected by their masters. Accordingly, Ewell issued a call "to the citizens of James City, York, & Warwick Counties" for both free blacks and slaves, equipment, and any spare laborers for a variety of military needs.[50]

At Jamestown the effort to secure more laborers already was under way. Waddill's Battalion was especially influential in obtaining assistance. One example of this is found in the person of Andrew N. Gill, an overseer for William Jerdone in Charles City County. Early in May, Gill reported to Jamestown with the Charles City Southern Guards which became part of Waddill's Battalion. May 28 found Gill back home with orders to obtain as many free blacks as possible and return with them in three days to Jamestown where they would work on the fortifications. Gill scoured the countryside and designated twenty-eight men, although there was resistance to their leaving. By May 31 most of the blacks had joined him, and he departed with them by boat for Jamestown.[51]

As May drew to a close there were signs of improvement as each new company settled in. The Hanover Artillery was able to leave the barn on the mainland that had been its home and settled into tents at Jamestown. This pleased Jones as well as the Hanoverians, for he considered them less useful at their earlier distance. After moving to the island the artillerymen built two plank shanties. As Private Berkeley noted, the passing of each day enabled the men to increase their comfort. This was especially true of Jack Cooke. Unwilling to accept one aspect of soldiering, he requested a cook from home. Despite improvements there still were shortages, some of them vital. This was illustrated well by a reminder issued to the commanders of river batteries that they should conserve ammunition since there were no live shells available from Richmond at the time. Hints of change were in the air, too. Barron informed Jones that he expected his antagonist, Cocke, to deal more exclusively with "his first love—[Fort] Powhatan" as a result of changes that were expected in the command system.[52]

Most significant of the changes was the transfer of Virginia's forces to the Confederate States. For nearly two months after the Virginia State Convention voted to secede in April, the Old Dominion raised

Major General Robert E. Lee

Massachusetts Commandery,
Military Order of the Loyal Legion,
U.S. Army Military History Institute

troops with the agreement that they would be transferred to the Confederacy. With that time approaching, Lee, as commander of Virginia troops, wanted assurance that the James and York River batteries were in satisfactory condition. He elected to make a personal inspection.[53]

On June 3 Lee was joined by Talcott, his engineer. After spending the night of the fourth below Fort Powhatan, they arrived there on Wednesday, June 5, and then continued to Jamestown the same day. Lieutenant Morrison was given the honor of commanding a 100-man strong escort to accompany the visiting dignitaries. Jones, who was on the verge of illness, joined the pair as they inspected Allen's battery at Fort Pocahontas and rode to other strategic points on the island. After three or four hours, Lee and Talcott departed for Williamsburg, then journeyed to Yorktown where they spent the night. The following day they examined Gloucester Point and West Point, and on the fifth day they returned to Richmond around 2 P.M. Shortly thereafter Lee visited Davis at his White House and sent several dozen wagons with supplies to Magruder's forces on the Peninsula.[54]

Even on the day of the inspection by Lee and Talcott, Jones dashed a letter to Barron. Almost overcome by illness, he pleaded for at least two reliable and intelligent officers to ease his work load. In addition to Fort Pocahontas, the Sand Battery required his personal supervision as did construction of the bridge, and another redoubt would be his responsibility once completed. His best officer was gone, and he now had two assistants who lacked experience, plus Lieutenant Beverly Kennon whom he regarded as intelligent and experienced but "entirely unreliable." Consequently Jones personally had to tend to everything but the most routine matters. He felt "nearly worn out."[55]

The day of Lee's visit was exhausting for men in the ranks, as well. In addition to preparation for the inspection, they arose at their customary time of 5 A.M. with roll call at 5:30. After a long day of formalities, the troops retired for the night, only to have their sleep rudely interrupted. A boat along The Thoroughfare ignored a guard's call to identify itself and was fired upon several times. The 14th Virginia responded to the alarm, only to find that the intruder was a fisherman.[56]

While Lee and Talcott were concluding their inspection tour, Governor John Letcher wrote his proclamation that Virginia's land and naval forces would be transferred to the Confederate States. The proclamation was published two days after Lee's return to Richmond. Officers' ranks were announced shortly thereafter. Jones, who was a lieutenant in the Virginia navy, was converted to the same rank in the Confederate navy on June 11. Virginia's military units did not make the formal change in status until July 1 in order to correspond with the new quarterly administrative and pay period.[57]

Accordingly, the garrison at Jamestown was transferred from the state of Virginia to the Confederate States of America. During its period under Virginia administration Jamestown was the main defensive unit on the James River, a status it retained until mid-summer under the Confederacy.[58]

CHAPTER 4
THE LEGACY OF CATESBY AP ROGER JONES

While the Confederates fortified the James River, the Union made similar efforts to strengthen Fort Monroe. This stronghold provided the North with a vital base for operations at the lower tip of the Peninsula. Ironically, Lee and Talcott were erecting defenses against the fort they helped build during their service with the United States Army Corps of Engineers. Each side viewed the other as an offensive threat. There were numerous minor encounters between the opposing forces in the opening weeks of the war, as well as the Federals' establishment of Camp Butler in Newport News. Union troops launched the first notable attack up the Peninsula at Big Bethel on June 10, outside Hampton. Outnumbered by about two to one, the Southerners emerged victorious. The sounds of battle could be heard at Jamestown, where word of the grayclads' triumph arrived at sundown and was greeted with cheers. It was a small engagement by Civil War standards, but it was the earliest significant effort between the armies in Virginia.[1]

From the Confederacy's perspective Big Bethel demonstrated the North's ability to take the offensive on the Peninsula. Army and naval officers both renewed efforts to strengthen the region by land and by water. Jamestown had twenty guns the day of the engagement at Big Bethel: three 9-inch guns, six 32-pounders, nine 8-inch Columbiads, and two 12-pounder guns. Cocke echoed Jones's complaint that the number of men to work these guns was inadequate and he implored Barron to send more. Two days later the navy sent buoys to better mark the channel. This indicated the increased usage anticipated for the river in the immediate future and assisted the gunners in learning where to direct their fire. The cry from Jamestown was that, although the markings were appreciated, a large variety of supplies still was needed.[2]

Big Bethel caused some excitement at Jamestown, but the atmosphere soon returned to normal. The military details of everyday life

37

The Ambler House

National Park Service,
Colonial National Historical Park

already were beginning to bore some of the new recruits. In the Hanover Artillery one private commented that "we had nothing to change the dullness of camp life, except to drill, to do guard duty, to work on our fortifications and have dress parade every evening." Fishing and bathing were cited as the most common pleasures in the unit, and Private Edmund Anderson was creative enough to make a kite which the artillerymen watched as it ascended on a long string.[3]

Typical of most wars, officers obtained the more comfortable quarters. At Jamestown this was epitomized by the Ambler house. While Lieutenant Morrison described the building in flattering terms, Captain Myers was less complimentary, saying that it was in disrepair but habitable. Regardless of the house's condition, it served one salutary purpose which was not disputed. The officers congregated there on summer nights to escape the mosquitoes which Morrison averred he would pit against their counterparts anywhere. Occasionally Allen had festive dinners there for his fellow officers, as was the case one June evening when he hosted a "sumptuous feast" with champagne in abundance. Although Allen made generous donations to the Southern cause, he also found it fiscally wise to receive some reimbursement for his goods and services. In keeping with this philosophy, he moved into the house and rented other parts of the building as officers' quarters. As another function, Morrison had an office there, although he did not indicate whether or not he paid a fee for the room.[4]

Some of the new arrivals in the 14th Virginia received a negative first impression of Jamestown. Sergeant William H. Phillips noted that for the initial two weeks each man in the regiment had only two crackers and a little meat for meals, a menu that caused much internal quarreling. The Ross brothers, who served in the same regiment, corroborated this. Even the 14th's officers were unsatisfied at times, one commenting later in the month about "tough bread and salt meat, and bad very bad coffee." There gradually was improvement with vegetables that were furnished by local citizens at a modest cost. Another source of good eating was the boat that docked almost daily at Jamestown and often brought foodstuffs sent to the soldiers by their families.[5]

Mosquitoes and other small creatures that flew and crawled about the island were a constant source of aggravation to the newcomers. Their annoying presence sometimes prevented exhausted men from sleeping, and the rare nights in which they were absent were noted with great pleasure. While one officer accepted his fate and allowed the insects to crawl and chirp about him at night, one of his tentmates, Second Lieutenant Henry S. Morton, showed "antipathy to all sorts of 'bug sects.'" He sprang from the straw that served as his bed, captured the intruders, and with "merciless cruelty & delight he smashes them."[6]

On June 8–9 the 14th Virginia moved to a new site. Hodges's regiment was assigned to a somewhat central location on the island, just behind the Square Redoubt which was a new earthwork. They settled in one of Allen's wheatfields, thereby destroying a considerable amount of it. Tents provided shelter, although they were small for the dozen occupants who crowded into each of them. Planks were acquired for flooring, the timber probably provided by Allen himself. In honor of their host, the site was called Camp Allen.[7]

As soon as the 14th Virginia finished moving to its new location, the men were asked to volunteer their services to work on the batteries that still were under construction. The response was overwhelming, and the progress was rapid. Private Nathaniel Ross wrote that he and his brother, Daniel, were busy "rolling dirt in wheelbarrows, digging dirt, and pitching it with shovels." Much of this effort undoubtedly was devoted to the Square Redoubt, which was adjacent to Hodges's camp. Captain Edward R. Young, however, was not able to participate in this activity. Although he was not the regimental surgeon, he was a physician before the war. His medical training now took precedence over military matters, for the illness that had incapacitated Catesby

The Square Redoubt

Photograph by author

ap Roger Jones was present in the 14th Virginia, as well. By mid-June eighteen members were sick in Young's company alone, and a diary that he kept is testimony to the poor health experienced by many soldiers at Jamestown.[8]

Construction efforts by Hodges's men soon were rewarded. About June 17 the Cockade Mounted Battery arrived at Jamestown, and this probably was the unit that occupied the Square Redoubt. Organized May 14, the company was from Petersburg with Captain Gilbert V. Rambaut as its commander. One member of the 14th Virginia who helped construct the square earthwork described it as a bank of dirt about six feet high surrounded by a ditch that was about fifteen feet wide and eight feet deep. Rambaut soon had four cannon on the walls facing in each direction. The artillerymen joined the 14th Virginia at Camp Allen and soon became the recipients of timber and nails to better their living standard, Allen most likely furnishing the supplies.[9]

In the middle of the month Lee sent some final observations to Governor Letcher concerning the state of Virginia's early preparations. He had the highest praise for the citizens who rallied to defend their state. Agreeing with Jones's most frequent complaint, he recognized that it was easier to find enlistees than it was to provide them with

CSS *Teaser*

Eleanor S. Brockenbrough Library,
Museum of the Confederacy,
Richmond, Virginia

instruction, supplies, and adequate transportation. He listed numerous defensive works that were in place throughout the commonwealth,
including Jamestown. The island's importance was evidenced by its
twenty guns, which comprised half of the heavy artillery along the
James River.[10]

Lee took further action to strengthen Jamestown on June 18 when
he directed Lieutenant Robert R. Carter of the CSS *Teaser* to join in
the island's defense. Ordered to report to Lieutenant Jones, Carter
was instructed to take an active role. The *Teaser* was to patrol below
Jamestown and gather intelligence of Union activity by water and by
land. It was especially important to watch for the landing of troops at
Grove's Wharf, on the same side of the river and below Jamestown, or
at Stonehouse Wharf on the opposite shore. After just two days Carter
reported that night watches below Jamestown were dangerous for the
Teaser, which was easy prey in the darkness near enemy vessels. He
felt safer operating during the day, and requested that a lighter of coal
be kept at Jamestown to save time refueling.[11]

The *Teaser*, which had served at Jamestown late in May, was a
wooden tug that dated to about 1855. It had two 32-pounders. Future

service would be at the Battle of Hampton Roads, as a balloon tender, and in laying torpedoes (later called mines). Damaged in combat with the USS *Maratanza* on July 4, 1862, it was captured, retained the name *Teaser*, and served the Union in the Potomac Flotilla.[12]

Carter would have felt safer if the entire James River Squadron was ready to join him in patrols. But two months passed before the second vessel, the *Patrick Henry*, was ready for duty, and the *Jamestown* joined the squadron still later. Captain John R. Tucker commanded the small fleet. The *Jamestown* and *Patrick Henry* were sister ships. Although renamed *Thomas Jefferson*, the *Jamestown* continued to be known by its original name. In contrast, the *Patrick Henry* formerly was called the *Yorktown* and went by its second name, forsaking the Virginia town for which it had been named. The vessels were virtually identical: both were built in 1853, displaced 1,300 tons, were 250 feet in length, and were side-wheel steamers. The *Patrick Henry* was provided with some armor plate for protection. The state of Virginia had seized both boats at the beginning of the war for its own use and, subsequently, the Confederacy's. With two guns, the CSS *Jamestown* was at the Battle of Hampton Roads in March 1862 and captured three ships at that location a month later. Despite this service, in May it was sunk by the Confederates to serve as an obstruction at Drewry's Bluff to assist in blocking that Federal advance upriver. The *Patrick Henry*, which had as many as ten guns, saw action near Newport News in 1861. Like the *Jamestown* and *Teaser*, the *Patrick Henry* was engaged at the Battle of Hampton Roads, where it was damaged. It was used by the Confederate States Naval Academy from October 1863 until 1865, when it was burned by the Confederates during the evacuation of Richmond.[13]

There were fringe benefits to having gunboats nearby, and Jones promptly capitalized upon them. He now had twenty-two naval officers and men to man his batteries, fifteen of them from the *Teaser*. This fulfilled one of Jones's fervent desires, for it was important to have artillerymen familiar with the large guns to operate them and to school the new enlistees. Meanwhile Jamestown continued to function not only as a key defensive site but as a wharf for supplies vital to the immediate area. Among its cargoes were cannon that were forwarded to the earthwork at Spratley's farm, a few miles down river on the mainland near the point where College Creek flows into the James. In yet another cooperative effort the navy examined the channel and landing areas at Jamestown Island, especially those within range of the gun batteries. This exploration continued into the next month under Lieutenant Kennon, who also was assigned to study the island's topography. This flurry of activity must have cheered Jones

Remains of the T-shaped Wharf

Photograph by author

who now was bedridden but showed signs of improvement, as indicated by his continued requests for more grape and canister. The severity of Jones's illness, which was caused by Jamestown's climate, was such that he needed assistance throughout the month in handling his correspondence.[14]

Late in the evening of June 19, Jamestown was alerted about possible combat. Word was received that the Federals had 10,000 troops on the road toward Yorktown and Williamsburg. It was expected that a feint would be made at Jamestown to divert the garrison's attention from the main effort. The men slept by their arms that night in readiness for a battle that never came, and the next day the reported Union advance was recognized as a false alarm. Two nights later Jamestown's defenders fought a real battle with the forces of nature. A gale joined by sheets of rain toppled many tents. This was the first of several disruptive storms at the island that summer.[15]

As June ended and all Virginia units were transferred to the Confederacy, Jamestown had a strong combination of artillery and infantry that was improving daily. There was Allen's Brandon Artillery which continued to bear the name "Jamestown Artillery" with greater frequency in identification with the island's owner, and the unit's distinction as the first occupants of Jamestown. The Hanover Artillery assessed itself at this time as having fine young men who were "well drilled at the Great guns," an accomplishment which the tutelage of Jones and his naval personnel had made possible. Members of the Bedford Light Artillery still were without uniforms but were "in fine discipline, and well drilled." The newcomers, the Cockade Mounted Battery, were firmly in place just two weeks after their arrival. In addition to the artillery, there were the infantrymen in Waddill's Battalion who were drilled by Major Patton, as well as Colonel Hodges's 14th Virginia Infantry. Magruder had formally placed Hodges in command of the infantry on June 20, while Jones retained charge of the batteries. Unbeknown to all, Jamestown was at its height in troop strength and in its role as the James River's primary guardian of Richmond. The island's manpower and significance both would be reduced as the year progressed. During the summer nights, the troops observed one of nature's spectacles which likewise was in full glory. Thatcher's comet shone brilliantly in the sky with its fiery head and long tail, adding a touch of awe and wonder.[16]

With July came Independence Day on the fourth. Its observance typified the mixed feelings of Northerners and Southerners which were caused by the nation's dichotomy. Americans from both sections of the country shared a common heritage. Now they were at war but with common heroes. Perhaps George Washington represented the situation best as father of the fractured country. Here was a man who was a national symbol, whose name was used for the nation's capital, and yet whose home was in the seceded state of Virginia. Jamestown was another example, for both the Union and Confederate navies had a vessel which bore its name. On the Peninsula there was division as to how this eighty-fifth anniversary of the Declaration of Independence should be observed. In Williamsburg, Ewell's soldiers had no ceremony, regarding July 4 as a Yankee holiday. In contrast, Jamestown's Rebels recognized the rebels of '76 as taking a step toward the independence they now sought.[17]

Preparations for the celebration started as early as June 17 when officers met one evening to discuss the event. Once they decided to observe Independence Day, local residents also joined in the festivities. When the Fourth finally arrived, there was much excitement. It was a beautiful day, and the 14th Virginia and Waddill's Battalion assembled at the wharf to welcome guests arriving by boat including John Tyler and family, who lived upriver. When the boats came into view, the soldiers could see that they were decorated for the occasion and the decks were crowded with passengers. A band struck up a martial air but the guard, although dressed in its finest, did not appear adequate. At least one officer felt that the uniforms acquired to date were not up to standard. Despite this deficiency, the troops escorted the visiting ladies and gentlemen to an attractively maintained grave opposite the Ambler house.[18]

The formal ceremony was conducted with the crowd assembled at the house, complete with a stage that had been constructed for the ceremony. A prayer was followed by an hour-long oration by Lieutenant Colonel David J. Godwin of the 14th Virginia. Former President Tyler then gave the main address which likewise lasted an hour. One Confederate recalled that Tyler spoke "in eloquent strains stirring up hot fighting blood in us all" and he was "vociferously applauded." When finished, he reviewed the troops. Everyone then moved to a table that awaited them for a feast and toasts. Captain Young gave one of the toasts which captured the spirit of the holiday:

> To the Rebels of 76 George Washington & his compatriots,
>
> the Rebels of 61 Jefferson Davis & his,
>
> the hopes of human liberty clustered around the one then,
>
> upheld & sustained by the other now,
>
> the first left us a "hope a flame"
>
> that the last "would rather die than shame."

After dinner the celebrants retired to Allen's large granary where there was an hour or two of dancing. The festivities ended at sunset.[19]

The only demonstration of military skill on the Fourth came when the artillery fired a salute at noon. One of the gunners demonstrated his marksmanship by sighting on a barrel as it floated down river and split it with one of the battery's large projectiles. Many of the officers and enlisted men were so involved with the main ceremony that day that they ignored the event and only a few civilians observed it.[20]

Note was taken, however, when sentinels at the bridge that joined Jamestown to the mainland opened fire four days later. The incident proved to be of no consequence. An order received that day from Magruder was more significant. The general wanted the earthworks finished, and every available man was detailed for the task. There was no cooperation from the weather as the men worked arduously under the intense sun, and the breeze which usually drifted from the river was absent on those brutal days of July 8–9. Soldiers laboring on the fortifications fainted in great numbers, as did sentinels at their posts. But the work continued.[21]

Jones, still recovering from a month of illness, soon was relieved of one burden. He had feuded constantly with Lieutenant Kennon, who was examining the island and the river channel. After their third altercation Kennon requested a transfer. Jones was visited on the eleventh by Cocke, who sought peace and was amenable to Kennon's detachment from Jamestown. Consequently Kennon was sent to northern Virginia to experiment with torpedoes. Cocke also reported that he nearly had "a pretty little fight" with a Union steamer the previous day. Shortly thereafter Barron replaced Cocke and became commander of naval defenses in Virginia and North Carolina, a selection that gave Jones a supportive superior. Cocke exaggerated his work for Letcher by declaring that the James River was well fortified "at every desirable point and the works nearly completed."[22]

Jones had yet another high ranking visitor, Magruder, who had been promoted to brigadier general a few weeks earlier. The Peninsula's army commander decided to inspect Jamestown's defenses for himself. Despite the heat an admiring crowd followed him around on the twelfth, so eager was everyone to see the hero of Big Bethel. Jones and several army officers dined with Magruder that evening at the Ambler house. Magruder remained at Jamestown the following day and then sent Lee his recommendations. Although pleased with what he found, he did not concur with Cocke's conclusion that the fortifications were virtually finished along the James. Magruder found four earthworks at Jamestown, of which Fort Pocahontas on the island's western end

Brigadier General John
Bankhead Magruder
*Massachusetts Commandery,
Military Order of the Loyal Legion,
U.S. Army Military History Institute*

was the first erected and most prominent. The Sand Battery now stood guard midway down the island near Goose Hill and, like Fort Pocahontas, faced the James River. Inland there was another large earthwork generally referred to as the Square Redoubt; this stood in the south central part of the island at the point of deepest penetration by Passmore Creek and along an interior road. There also was an earthwork that guarded a bridge and causeway recently constructed under Myers's direction. The bridge was at the northwestern end of the island, not far from the original isthmus, and spanned the Back River to join Jamestown with the mainland. A rifle pit which resembled a small lunette provided further protection for the bridge. But Magruder wanted an additional redoubt constructed with two guns at Black Point, the island's eastern tip. This became known as Point of Island Battery. Magruder saw several advantages in having this battery. In addition to preventing a landing at this remote location, its guns could defend the mouth of Passmore Creek. He also saw the potential for its guns to cover water to the south which the Sand Battery could not defend because of the island's bulge. Looking to the north, artillery could fire toward the mainland, assisting the battery on Spratley's farm in thwarting a landing there. Jones and engineers at Jamestown, including Myers, were consulted and endorsed Magruder's proposal. Magruder took additional steps by ordering that two of the four heavy guns at the Square Redoubt be sent to Black Point.[23]

Magruder wanted to redistribute still other guns. Recognizing that the defenses of Williamsburg and Jamestown were interdependent, he desired that the armament of Spratley's farm be strengthened in order to reduce its chance of capture, which would turn Williamsburg's flank and endanger its earthworks. He felt that one heavy gun, preferably the 8-inch Columbiad that defended Jamestown's bridge and causeway, should be transferred to Spratley's farm and replaced by a 6-pounder. This would give Spratley's farm two heavy guns having previously ordered a 32-pounder be sent there. Another 32-pounder already was designated for Kingsmill, still farther down river and vital to Williamsburg's flank. Magruder regarded Jamestown as the safest place on his present defense line and therefore was comfortable with these proposals. Accordingly, he forwarded his orders to Lee for confirmation.[24]

Two days later Talcott visited Jamestown for a personal assessment. He voiced no objections. Lee then approved Magruder's proposals on July 16, but he reminded Magruder that Jamestown's defenses were stable and vital, and that the entire strategic situation on the Peninsula had been calculated in Richmond. Although he did not oppose the new battery at Black Point, Lee also reminded Magruder that the Sand Battery was placed midway down the island to prevent spreading the Confederate position over so wide an area as to make it indefensible. Approval was granted for relocating the guns, but only after the defenses were completed, especially the new Point of Island Battery. Until then guns that were intended for defense of the channel were to remain in place. As for the importance of Spratley's farm and Kingsmill, Lee said that Day's Point and the projected battery for Mulberry Island would reduce Williamsburg's vulnerability. In a blatant hint that Magruder should curb his desire to provide comprehensive defenses and deal with the situation realistically, Lee tartly stated that there were not enough guns to cover every exposed position on the Peninsula.[25]

For the time being there was no threat to the James River defenses, regardless of their number or condition. Only minor disturbances interrupted the otherwise tranquil nights at Jamestown. One such incident occurred at 10 P.M. on the night of July 17 when a steam tug ignored the order to stop. To make their point the Confederates fired several guns and the tug stopped. David Lambert was visiting from Williamsburg and he, too, was impressed by the artillery's roar. He also found that the men had expanded their means of entertainment. Several of them formed a glee club which he rated as "delightful," and blacks on the island had formed a band.[26]

At 3:30 in the morning on July 21 the 14th Virginia was awakened by its pickets firing alarm guns. Moments later the regiment heard three consecutive booms from cannon. Companies that composed Hodges's left wing were ordered to move at the double quick to the sound of the shots which came from the Point of Island Battery at Black Point. Hurrying in the darkness from their camp near the center of the island, the men deployed as skirmishers upon reaching the Point. They waited there patiently, but nothing happened. Having responded to yet another false alarm, the troops returned to camp.[27]

The real action in the war that day was fought in northern Virginia at Manassas. In contrast, Jamestown's main event was another visit by Talcott who evaluated the latest work on the island's defenses. News of the Confederates' overwhelming victory at Manassas arrived the next day, and shout after shout was raised and cannon were fired to celebrate. Like the rest of the South, Jamestown's defenders were jubilant when still more details arrived in newspaper accounts. They also became apprehensive that the war might end before they played a more glorious role in it. The level of anxiety rose so high in the Hanover Artillery that many of its members signed a petition to the secretary of war, requesting that the company be transferred to the Confederate army at Manassas. Private Berkeley was one of the exceptions. He was satisfied with the routine at Jamestown, did not sign, and raised the ire of several of his comrades whom he described as "very indignant." Soon the frenzy subsided, though, and all returned to normal.[28]

One man did transfer, but it was not one of the anxious artillerymen. Patton was promoted to lieutenant colonel and assigned to the 21st Virginia Infantry. After weeks of vigorous instruction, the infantrymen he had trained were ready for combat and his work at Jamestown was finished. He reached his new regiment on July 30 at Huntersville. The new assignment was timely for the drillmaster who was known for his delicate health. A wave of summer illness, much like that which afflicted the early settlers, was engulfing Jamestown and would cause much misery, just as it recently had affected Jones and Myers.[29]

The 14th Virginia's Captain Young was increasingly busy with his medical skills, and he was distressed by the severe illness that gripped many of his friends. By late July the hospital was nearly full. Young observed that the fever "is a more fearful enemy than our Northern foe & more dreaded by the men." It was considered an inglorious way to die, especially before having the opportunity to prove one's self on the battlefield. On July 29, the 14th Virginia struck its tents and moved to a new location on the island. This enabled soldiers to spread their tents wider apart, be less congested, and hopefully reduce the fever's rapid spread. Two days later there was great rejoicing in camp when it was announced that the regiment would be leaving Jamestown.[30]

The unit's order to move was part of Magruder's effort to create a strong Warwick Line. Earlier, on July 24, Companies A, D, F, and I of the 14th Virginia had been ordered to Spratley's farm. Lieutenant Colonel Godwin was sent with them as commander. Godwin's wartime service would end the next year with a severe wound at Seven Pines, but he later contributed to recording the war's history as one of the compilers of the *Official Records*. Almost simultaneous with Godwin's departure, Magruder also transferred the 8-inch Columbiad from Jamestown's bridge to Spratley's farm. Allen, who was on ordnance duty, was directed to oversee the gun's transportation, which perhaps was coordinated with Godwin. On August 2 Hodges left Jamestown with the 14th Virginia's remaining six companies. A recent rain made the road slippery, but the men appreciated the farewell they received as the artillery fired its guns in salute. Their final moments at Jamestown were difficult ones as they crossed the bridge. The weight of so many soldiers loaded with equipment rocked the span back and forth, sending many men to the railing to keep their balance. When ordered to spread out, the structure stabilized and the march resumed. A few days later the unit participated in the destruction of Hampton, which Magruder believed was about to be converted to a haven for runaway slaves. Hodges continued to Mulberry Island and Land's End. He was joined there late in the month by Godwin's four companies from Spratley's farm. The 14th Virginia became part of the Mulberry Island defenses on the right flank of Magruder's Warwick Line.[31]

Yet another transfer totally depleted Jamestown of its infantry support. On August 1 Waddill's Battalion was ordered to Mulberry Island and departed that same day. Private Gill, remembering his civilian duties as a Charles City overseer, learned of the pending move a few days earlier. He successfully completed a business transaction for Jerdone, his employer, and sent him 246½ pounds of bacon. Upon reaching Mulberry Island, Gill found it similar to Jamestown: the temperature was in the 90s, much of the vegetation was dried up, and the mosquitoes were "dreadful."[32]

Waddill's Battalion was exceptionally fortunate, for it transferred from Jamestown without leaving anyone behind ill. In July and August, Ewell's prophecy of summer illness was fulfilled. Dr. George C. Starke, assistant surgeon on the island, was overwhelmed with hospitals filled to capacity by typhoid fever. The situation became so desperate that he called for volunteers to nurse members of the 14th Virginia who remained there, unable to accompany their regiment to Mulberry Island. Soldiers from the Hanover Artillery responded to the summons and performed this duty every other night for three weeks. Despite these efforts, some of the patients died. At least one of the Hanoverians likewise became critically ill and was furloughed to recuperate. Barron, sympathetic to the prolonged illness Jones had endured, recommended his transfer. Justifying the move because Jamestown's climate was "inimical to his health," Barron sought to have Jones placed in charge of the *Germantown* which would be converted to a floating battery. Barron pointed out that Jones's knowledge of ordnance made him suitable for the project. Perhaps the two officers discussed the matter when Barron visited Jamestown in August, but Jones's illness still made it difficult for him to perform his duties fully. Uncharacteristically, Jones even was unable to conduct Barron on a tour of the batteries. Little wonder that he was willing to accept another position. Furthermore, Jones was becoming dissatisfied with his assignment. His men were proficient with their guns and the construction of batteries down river gave Jamestown more security, thereby making Jones's job less challenging. But despite Barron's endorsement, the transfer to the *Germantown* was denied.[33]

Meanwhile, Jamestown's role as a place of debarkation increased as Magruder strengthened his position on the Peninsula. Troops that landed there immediately proceeded to their point of destination. One of the more raucous units landed just after Talcott made his final inspection. Talcott, who had visited on August 11, returned on a rainy August 16 and completed his work the following day. At about the same time the Louisiana Tigers arrived and terrorized the citizens they were sent to protect, killing livestock and making residents feel that the Peninsula was being invaded. Even the artillerymen at Jamestown were unable to contain the Tigers, especially the 10th Louisiana. In twelve hours the Louisianians ate "every living thing on the island, but the horses, and their own species." The gunners must have breathed a collective sigh of relief when the regiment continued on its way to Williamsburg.[34]

Incoming troops were symbolic of the increased concern over a Union advance upriver. A new commander, Brigadier General John E. Wool, was assigned to Fort Monroe. In his late seventies, Wool was a veteran of the War of 1812 and the Mexican War. Magruder was determined that any Union offensive should be as difficult as possible, even while he was completing his Warwick Line. On August 22 he ordered Jones to construct boats for the Jamestown and Mulberry Island batteries to provide mobility. Four days later Jones was ordered to work with yet another kind of boat: canal boats. Magruder wanted them filled with granite and sand and sunk where they could impede Union traffic in the channel of the James and Warwick Rivers. First priority was the swash channel between Mulberry Point and Harden's Bluff. By early September this route was blocked, and Magruder's congratulations were accompanied by orders to have additional canal boats, which had been floated from Richmond to Jamestown, sunk across the mouth of the Warwick River. This activity seemed timely from the Confederate perspective. As August ended there were warnings that ships were assembled at Fort Monroe, so all batteries along the James were ordered to prepare for action. However, it turned out that this expedition was bound for Hatteras Inlet, North Carolina.[35]

While Magruder turned more attention toward solidifying his Warwick Line, Jones was occupied with many of the familiar problems at Jamestown. Once again he had only a few hundred artillerymen to defend the island. Work continued on the fortifications which, although suitable to contest control of the river, needed refinement. Lieutenant Colonel Josiah Gorgas, Chief of Ordnance in Richmond, advised Jones to abandon his position if embattled before bombproofs were finished. Numerous slaves from Peninsula plantations continued to shuttle between their owners' farms and Jamestown to strengthen its works. Jones was relentless in his quest for supplies, many of which he was assured were being prepared for shipment or were en route. Even some of his artillery needed rudimentary attention. His 8-inch Columbiads were a prime example, still needing to be sighted. Most of these weapons lacked even the line of sight marked on the tube. Jamestown was in far better shape in those final weeks of summer than had been the case only a few months ago, but there were these glaring needs to be met. Anxiety was heightened even more by Richmond's warning that a Federal "dash up James River" was inevitable.[36]

For Jones there were fears greater than invasion. He fretted openly about his status in the navy. Although his knowledge of ordnance made him valuable in establishing Jamestown's batteries, he inquired about another assignment. He was keenly interested in the Confederacy's effort to convert the captured wooden vessel, *Merrimack*, to an ironclad. In July the Tredegar Iron Works in Richmond had agreed to roll armor plate for the *Merrimack*, which later was renamed *Virginia*, and Jones followed the project closely.[37]

Lieutenant Robert D. Minor, who kept Jones posted on naval matters in Richmond, shared Jones's enthusiasm and said he hoped to serve aboard the *Merrimack* with him. Jones went even further. He actively pursued his interest in the ironclad by performing tests at Jamestown with ordnance and armor and making recommendations based upon his findings. In late August he made a target that was planked over and whitewashed, and in early September he fired upon it. His experiments were made with different powder charges in a variety of guns. The target was a wooden floating battery covered with three inches of wrought iron, and every shot passed through the iron. After examining the results, he recommended charges and gun types that he felt were appropriate for the *Merrimack*. "I consider the *M[errimack]* the most important naval affair the country has to deal with," he told Minor, "and consequently am deeply interested in her success, and anxious that it may be complete." He hoped that the newspapers would contain their interest in the vessel and not publish reports of its progress, thereby making it more difficult for the Federals to follow the *Merrimack's* development.[38]

While pondering an assignment to the *Merrimack*, routine duties at Jamestown required Jones's attention, as well. One evening in mid-September he complained about random firing by the *Patrick Henry* which he regarded as a waste of ammunition. Still another source of irritation was the arrival of 8-inch shot designated for Williamsburg. Although it was customary for Williamsburg's ordnance supplies to land at Jamestown, Jones hated to send ammunition suitable for heavy guns to inland defenses, reasoning that it was better suited for service against ships. Jamestown's fortifications were inspected again later in the month, but in lieu of Talcott the visiting officer was Colonel George Washington Custis Lee of President Davis's staff. Lee found a new command system formally in place. With the infantry gone but army personnel continuing to man the fortifications, Jones now commanded the entire island.[39]

A modest number of reinforcements were assigned to the Bedford Light Artillery and arrived by boat on October 1. One of the privates,

Henry H. Wills, was surprised to find that he was "verry [*sic*] well satisfied" amid the marsh and marsh grass which grew six to eight feet high. Soon he was busy with camp life, making "biskits [*sic*]." Another new artilleryman, Private Lindsey T. Wills, enjoyed the meal of beef, bread, coffee, and sugar that awaited them despite the hard rain that night. Some of the company's veterans told him that the downpour was the hardest since their own arrival. The newcomer was impressed by the wide river and the flatness of the area which was "sight level." Still, Jamestown Island was "the pretyst [*sic*] place I ever saw." The new arrivals immediately learned that their captain was trying to obtain light artillery and that, if successful, the Bedford company would be moved farther down the island.[40]

Like many soldiers, Henry Wills was impressed with the history and solemnity of Jamestown. Some of the soldiers assembled for Sunday services at the cemetery adjacent to the church tower. Others, like Wills, visited in the stillness of the night. He prayed there in the darkness with one of his comrades and described it as "the most effectual place I have met with." He would have gone often, but it was difficult to pass the guard from Fort Pocahontas.[41]

Wills's companion one October night was Private Henry Martin Stringfellow, who had arrived with the Hanover Artillery in May. Stringfellow was a theology student who performed ministerial duties at Jamestown. Unlike Wills, he had lost his enchantment with the island and he showed other human qualities that appalled him. While in Williamsburg he visited with Ewell's daughter, Elizabeth, who was known as Lizzie. Upon returning to Jamestown and reflecting upon his actions he felt compelled to write to her and apologize for his "light & trifling conduct & conversation." He explained that after being "cooped up here for 3 months my spirits ran wild when I escaped from my prison." As further explanation he said, "You can't conceive Miss Lizzie what a wretched blank camp life is, & how terribly conflicting with the Christian life." As evidence of the problem, he noted that he was able to assemble only eighteen of 350 men to attend a recent Sunday service. Two years later "Miss Lizzie" was forgotten as Stringfellow married Alice Johnston.[42]

The mood of the Hanover Artillery contrasted sharply with that of the newcomers from Bedford. Protest was commonplace among these veterans who earlier had expressed dissatisfaction with their Peninsula assignment which caused them to miss the battle at Manassas. Dissension now was so great that the Hanover company resorted to petition again, this time demanding that Nelson resign as their commander. "We thought the Captain rather too strict and exacting," one private explained. But this was the military, not a political referendum, and Nelson refused to comply. Arguing that he could not resign in good conscience, Nelson stood his ground. Eventually the squabble quieted down and, with the passage of time, Nelson even won his company's admiration.[43]

Early in October, Magruder reminded Colonel Theodore Hunt in Williamsburg of his important connections with Jamestown. If attacked, Hunt was directed to telegraph Richmond for reinforcements; the capital, in turn, would provide one regiment that would land at Jamestown, report to Jones, and await Magruder's instructions. Jones did not object to this liaison role, but Magruder's suggestion that he immediately dispatch a naval officer to Hunt to provide instruction for a 42-pounder carronade was rebuffed. Jones pointed out that he had no naval officer under him at the time. He was the sole person with adequate knowledge of the ordnance, and the only possibility for instruction was that Jones himself might be able to provide it at intervals between his other duties. The proposal was irksome to Jones, who begrudged having Williamsburg's heavy artillery ammunition shipped via Jamestown when he coveted it for his own guns. Jones continued to remind Richmond of his own needs. Most recently, a painter with the engineers used his entire paint supply, left to replenish it, and never returned. Paint was needed immediately for shot that was in storage and required protection against the elements.[44]

Magruder, meanwhile, wanted Jones to assist him further in solidifying the Warwick Line and lower points on the James. Once again he ordered Jones to sink canal boats to block federal navigation. On October 4, Jones sent Lieutenant Junius A. de Lagnel to Mulberry Point to await the boats. When they arrived he proceeded by steamer to the mouth of the Warwick River and sank them.[45]

While delegating the army's canal boats to another officer, Jones turned his attention toward a naval concern that was dear to his heart, the construction of the CSS *Merrimack*. Lieutenant John M. Brooke, who had persuaded the Confederate government to construct the ironclad, entertained second thoughts that autumn about the thickness of the armor plate. When he recommended that Tredegar Iron Works double it to two inches, he was ordered to conduct tests to justify this change since it required additional cost and labor. Brooke could have done this in Richmond, but he wanted to maintain as much secrecy as possible in order to keep the Federals ignorant of his progress. The capital was watched closely by Unionists, and newspapers trumpeted all available war news. For his test to be valid he had to use heavy artillery comparable to that which would be fired at the *Merrimack*, and the assistance of an expert on naval ordnance would add greater weight to the conclusions. Jamestown, with its isolation and heavy guns, was an ideal spot, and Jones's reputation provided additional credibility. Accordingly, Brooke went to Jamestown.[46]

The iron plating was tested during the first or second week of October. In addition to Jones, Brooke was joined by several observers. Captain Tucker, Lieutenants Minor, David McCorkle, William P. Powell, and Robert D. Rochelle were present, as was Nelson Tift, a civilian who was supervising construction of the ironclad *Mississippi* in New Orleans. The target which Brooke and Jones used for their experiment resembled the casemate that was planned for the *Merrimack*. Built with oak and pine, it was 12 x 12 feet, about two feet thick, and inclined at an angle of thirty-six degrees. In the first test round, the wood was protected with three layers of iron plate, each being one-inch thick. An 8-inch Columbiad was fired upon the target about six times from a distance of some 300 yards using solid shot and ten pounds of powder. The shot penetrated the armor and entered the wood, showing that this arrangement of plating was inadequate. Brooke and Jones then placed two layers of two-inch thick iron on the wooden target, a

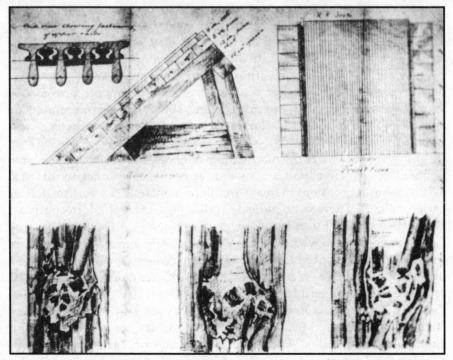

Target Used for CSS *Merrimack* T-iron Test

Virginia Historical Society

configuration that conformed with Brooke's revised recommendation. The experiment was repeated, this time using both 8-inch and 9-inch guns with ten pounds of powder, the 9-inch gun firing shells. This second arrangement of iron proved to be more effective as the outer plate shattered, the inner plate merely cracked, and the wood was untouched. Brooke had proved his point. Greater thickness was needed to protect the *Merrimack*.[47]

On October 12 Jones repeated the experiment on his own, this time with railroad T-iron instead of iron plate. Using ten pounds of powder, he fired six rounds of solid shot from an 8-inch Columbiad at a distance of 327 yards. Then, from a distance of 310 yards, he fired four unloaded shells from a 9-inch gun. The shots drove deeply into the wood, demonstrating that iron plate was superior to railroad iron, although Jones suggested that another test be conducted with the rails affixed better.[48]

Neither Jones nor Brooke indicated where these experiments were made at Jamestown. However, the need for an open field of fire of 300 yards and the variety of guns involved indicate that artillery at Fort Pocahontas probably was used. There were claims that the railroad iron in Jones's experiment was provided by Allen, which is possible since Allen operated a railroad at Claremont. Jones undoubtedly was pleased to play a role in the *Merrimack's* development. He probably took additional satisfaction in the government's effort to conceal its progress on the vessel, a position he had advocated earlier. The navy led the press to believe that the Jamestown experiments proved the iron plate to be "almost worthless," and the story was circulated in this guise for the benefit of Northerners who gleaned Southern newspapers for information.[49]

Toward the end of the month Magruder again was concerned about being attacked. He expanded his earlier request for Jones to instruct Williamsburg's gunners in heavy artillery to include the Yorktown batteries, as well. There is no indication that Jones complied. In contrast, the artillerymen at Jamestown were responding to threats from nature. A severe storm with flooding was especially damaging down river to the fortifications at Mulberry Island, and cooler temperatures hinted at the approach of a new season. Erection of winter quarters was started on October 28 as small lumber houses replaced tents. As for the danger from Unionists, a Bedford artilleryman confidently predicted that their opponents would have "a Jolly time of it" if they assailed the Confederate batteries. This spunky attitude prevailed despite the Southerners' latest reduction in numbers. Earlier in the month the Hanover Artillery, which probably occupied the Sand Battery, was transferred to Yorktown, thereby requiring the gunners to spread themselves thinner.[50]

A change of even greater significance occurred on November 6 when Jones was ordered to leave Jamestown Island and report to the Navy Department in Richmond, which he did three days later. His wish was fulfilled at last. Jones's new assignment was to test the guns for the CSS *Merrimack*, thereby associating him with the project that captivated his attention. Jones ultimately served aboard the *Merrimack*, but his longest assignment was at the Naval Ordnance Works in Selma, Alabama, where he served during the war's final two years, once again employing his knowledge of artillery. Yet it was at Jamestown, where he served for six months and labored with a host of difficulties, that he protected the Confederate capital. This was overshadowed by his later accomplishments. When he departed Jamestown its importance was being debated in some circles with the establishment of other batteries along the James. But there was no disputing that the island had stood strong and ready under his leadership, and that even with reduced troop strength it was a fortress to be reckoned with.[51]

Shortly after Jones's departure an accident took several lives at Jamestown. Lieutenant Thompson F. Waddill, who was detailed from Waddill's Battalion back in August to assume various quartermaster duties, had remained at Jamestown when his unit was transferred. On November 18, Waddill and three other soldiers were transporting the mail by boat when a severe storm arose on the James River and overturned their craft. Although they succeeded in clambering aboard the capsized vessel's hull, they were unable to right it. As darkness fell, exhaustion took its toll. Two members of the party dozed off and slipped into the river. Waddill "went crazy" and jumped overboard, apparently determined to save his comrades or perish in the attempt. The remaining soldier managed to pull Waddill back onto the boat, but he, like the first two men, had drowned. About 10 o'clock the following morning the boat reached Jamestown with its lone survivor. Lieutenant Morrison, who also had remained at the island when the infantry departed and served as adjutant, commanded the escort that took Waddill's body to his Charles City County home for burial. Morrison never forgot the grief of Waddill's mother and "his two interesting looking sisters." Shortly thereafter Morrison was named Waddill's successor.[52]

Jones's transfer brought changes in command and organization. In December the three artillery companies temporarily were reorganized as Lewis's Battalion, under Major John Redman Coxe Lewis. The Bedford Light Artillery became Company A, the Jamestown Artillery was designated as Company B, and the Cockade Mounted Battery was called Company C. Lewis, who was in his late twenties, had joined the U.S. Navy at an early age and accompanied Commodore Matthew Perry on his expedition to Japan in 1854. He resigned when the Civil War broke out, joined the Virginia navy, and was assigned to Jamestown around June 1861. He subsequently was appointed major in the Confederate army. Later in the war he served in both the Army of Northern Virginia and at Mobile, where he rose to lieutenant colonel in 1864, and he returned to Lee's army in 1865.[53]

Magruder sent the 52d Virginia Militia to Jamestown as infantry support for Lewis. In reality, it was a token force. Many members of the unit were struck from the rolls because they had enlisted in volunteer regiments or because they were exempted from service by a surgeon's examination or by proclamation of the governor. Originally consisting of four companies with a total of 700 men, their numbers were so greatly reduced that they were consolidated into two companies designated as A and B. Even so, their presence was welcome. With only a day's notice, the militia reported to Jamestown on December 12 in the tradition of their ancestral minute men. Their patriotic response was rewarded by granting an unusually high number of furloughs that allowed the men to return home and make the customary preparations for their families during their absence.[54]

The 52d Virginia Militia was commanded by Hill Carter, the sixty-five-year-old proprietor of Shirley plantation in Charles City County. A naval veteran of the War of 1812, he also had political experience as a member of the Virginia Senate. He was respected as a man "without fear and without reproach," and he had predicted civil war two decades earlier. His arrival at Jamestown meant resumption of the dual command system with Carter in charge of the infantry and Lewis commanding the artillery. A twist of fate awaited Carter and Allen. Both of them were wealthy Peninsula landowners who were joined in service at Jamestown, and although Allen was half Carter's age in 1861, both men would survive the war by only a decade and die on successive days.[55]

In mid-December attention returned to the endless endeavor to improve earthworks along the Peninsula. Lieutenant Charles T. Mason was the engineering officer assigned to Jamestown for this task. He was ordered to use whatever slaves were available to him to repair the road and to work on the fortifications as he saw fit. Soon he had thirty-two blacks from six different owners, the owners including two officers at Jamestown, Allen and Carter. Within a month he had done so well that he was granted a leave of absence. Former contributors

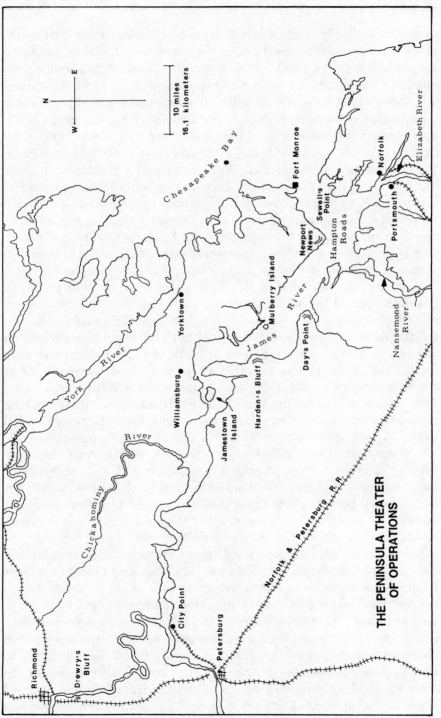

Map by Blake A. Magner

THE PENINSULA THEATER
OF OPERATIONS

of labor like Jerdone of Charles City County found their patriotism taxed by Magruder's new request for slaves and tools. Questioning Magruder's legal authority, Jerdone recalled that he had sent eleven blacks in the summer, received no compensation, and lost the spades and shovels that he sent with them. To compound his aggravation, his own plantation work was "completely out of sort." Just before Christmas another petition reached Charles City and New Kent counties. Issued by Magruder and signed by Carter, it requested slaves to strengthen the fortifications at Jamestown, Williamsburg, and Yorktown. On New Year's day Jerdone received yet another petition and he appeared to be softening, saying that he probably would comply when there were proper accommodations. But early in January Jerdone steeled himself. Concerned about his laborers' health and safety, he decided to resist until he was satisfied that conditions at Jamestown were adequate, a delaying action that he continued for two months.[56]

In the new year of 1862 Carter faced some of the same problems that had plagued his predecessors, including inadequate supplies and rumors of invasion. Ewell sent 100 muskets from Williamsburg for the militia, followed by a second shipment of thirty-two which arrived on January 7. Unfortunately, fifteen arms in the latter shipment were faulty. One day after the defective weapons arrived, Confederates at Norfolk, Yorktown, and along the James were advised that a large fleet was assembled at Fort Monroe. Three days later the vessels, which included troops under Brigadier General Ambrose E. Burnside, sailed in the opposite direction for North Carolina and the danger passed.[57]

Sometimes the rumbles of change from within were more disturbing than the threat of attack. On January 19 Carter felt compelled to protest Magruder's proposal to transfer guns from Jamestown to Mulberry Island. Carter conceded that if there were insufficient guns for all batteries along the river, then preference should be given to Mulberry Island and Harden's Bluff. He considered it bad policy to concentrate the artillery at a single point, such as Mulberry Island. If Jamestown were abandoned, Yorktown and Mulberry Island first must be made impregnable or the entire Peninsula would be seriously imperiled, but Carter had doubts that river defenses could be guaranteed anywhere. Therefore, he reasoned that the more obstacles there were to Union invasion the better. Carter apparently was not worried about immediate Federal attack. Late in the month he took leave to tend to personal business, a practice he continued with frequency. On January 31 Magruder, who was in a different frame of mind, warned of another fleet sighted at Fort Monroe. At that time Jamestown had 323 men present for duty with twenty pieces of heavy artillery. Like the month's earlier warning, however, this armada likewise failed to endanger the Peninsula.[58]

Early February was wet and dreary. Robert Carter, anticipating his father's mood at the island, wrote the colonel consoling words about the personal hardship caused by military obligations. "This rainy weather must be exceedingly irksome to you, at Jamestown," he sympathized, "for besides want of occupation, you are no doubt apprehending mismanagement at Shirley." In contrast, Allen, who always was watchful of his business ventures and was prone to take leave on occasion, seized the opportunity to expand his role in the war. On February 15 he wrote to Secretary of War Judah P. Benjamin and requested permission to raise a battalion of heavy artillery consisting of four companies plus one company of light artillery. He intended to have the companies defend the James River, and he pointed out that he already had one company under him at Jamestown. Permission was granted to raise the unit, and Allen instantly had representatives enlisting men in companies for the battalion.[59]

For the remainder of the month Jamestown was a subject for debate. While one faction recognized the island's importance and warned of its endangered position, the other belittled its significance. Support for Jamestown came from the CSS *Patrick Henry*. On February 12, the vessel had a Union prisoner who spoke authoritatively about an expedition with Jamestown as its objective. With assistance from part of Burnside's force which recently had captured Roanoke Island, the Federals supposedly planned to capture Jamestown and use this position to threaten operations against the York River and Petersburg railroads. This pressure was intended to nudge Magruder from his Yorktown defenses. Unlike previous occasions when Jamestown was targeted by Unionists, Magruder was not alarmed. Indeed, his regard for the island was diminishing. A week later he recommended that Jamestown's guns be transferred to Mulberry Island and Harden's Bluff if the heavy artillery needed for Yorktown and forts on the lower James could not be found elsewhere. He used Jamestown's narrow channel to justify his decision. He reasoned that heavy guns were not necessary to control the passage of river traffic at Jamestown. This was quite contradictory to his opinion of the previous summer when he felt compelled to increase the island's defenses. Perhaps his new strategic emphasis was caused by his frustrated efforts to secure additional artillery.[60]

Brigadier General Raleigh Colston, whose brigade was on the south side of the James at Smithfield, went a step farther in late February and challenged the concept that earthen forts alone could stop the Union fleet. He pursued the topic with the James River Squadron's detachment commander, Captain Tucker. To supplement the forts, Colston suggested that obstructions be placed in the river with Jamestown as one of the plausible sites, although he preferred one farther down river. Tucker was so enamored with the idea that he responded immediately. Agreeing in principle, he ruled out Jamestown and Mulberry Islands because he preferred the river depth above and below these two points. He recommended that a series of piles be used for obstructions and that, if necessary, they should be made even more formidable by using boats filled with stone to block the channel. A width of sixty feet should be left in the channel in order that the Confederates still could navigate the river.[61]

Questions about the James River defenses concerned politicians as well as members of the armed forces. On February 24, the Confederate Congress passed a resolution that President Davis should ascertain the strength of works along the James and at Richmond. Davis forwarded this request to the Engineer Bureau. The month ended in this uneasy atmosphere with Jamestown garrisoned by merely 169 officers and men. Their artillery had diversified by this time, with the heavy guns reduced to fifteen in number while four pieces of field artillery had been added. This change undoubtedly was welcomed by Jordan's Bedford company which preferred light artillery and was assigned to these guns.[62]

With spring on the horizon, efforts were renewed to improve Jamestown's fortifications. Magruder ordered local citizens to provide slaves for this task, a requisition that pitted farmers' patriotism against their desire to make a profit or, in some cases, merely survive. In Charles City County the Jerdone estate rudely received the word by courier on March 6 while he still was at breakfast. The Confederates wanted Jerdone to provide half of his male slave population to work along the James River or around Williamsburg. Nearly a week later he sent nine men. As the weeks passed he meticulously noted the date of each black's return and his physical condition. Some of the laborers were ill, and one even died of disease. The Selden plantation of Westover managed to stall the Confederate mandate a little longer. On March 13, the same day that Jerdone acquiesced, Selden sent his son Edward to Jamestown to make preparations for his chattels. The younger Selden was given money for a variety of expenses, including payment for a debt to Allen. Two days later, satisfied that he had done the best he could, Selden reluctantly sent six slaves to Jamestown. His own farming was woefully behind schedule, but what worried him more was the exposure suffered by his blacks on the island. Distressed, he warned of illness. A month later two slaves were returned to him, and he learned that two others who remained at Jamestown were ill.[63]

Meanwhile the weekend of March 8–9 was momentous not only for events on the Peninsula but for the course of the war. General Joseph E. Johnston's army, still guarding the Manassas Junction-Centreville position it had occupied since the previous summer's battle there, withdrew in anticipation of the Union army's advance. The Confederates halted behind the Rappahannock, thereby placing the river between themselves and their foe. Concurrently there was a different kind of activity at Hampton Roads that revolutionized naval warfare. The former *Merrimack*, now renamed the CSS *Virginia*, steamed from the Norfolk area toward the vicinity of Fort Monroe and the Union fleet at Hampton Roads. The *Virginia's* conversion to an ironclad warship was complete. It was joined by three vessels that assisted in Jamestown's defense, the *Jamestown*, *Patrick Henry*, and *Teaser*. On March 8, the *Virginia* tested Northern stamina by demonstrating that wooden ships were obsolete against its protective armor. Its guns and ram sank or ran aground several Federal vessels, despite its clumsy movement. The following day the USS *Monitor*, a newly constructed Union armor vessel, arrived from New York. For about two hours the *Monitor* and *Virginia* dueled to a tactical draw, initiating the era of combat between iron ships. As a consequence of this stalemate which left the iron warriors intact, the Union retained control of Hampton Roads while the Confederates remained masters of the James, Nansemond, and Elizabeth Rivers, as well as Norfolk. The result of the sound performance by both vessels was that each side stood in awe of what the other had accomplished. Both navies were anxious for the safety of their fleet of conventional warships.[64]

Jamestown was represented in the battle at Hampton Roads by more than the vessel that bore its name. Eighteen members of the 53d Virginia Infantry filled the manpower shortage on the *Patrick Henry*, participating in the fighting on March 8 and witnessing the *Monitor-Virginia* duel. They were members of what formerly was called Waddill's Battalion and had received their instruction in heavy artillery on Jamestown's guns. Private William H. Ware, who was in his teens in 1862, long remembered those fateful March days. His Confederate service included a wide variety of assignments, for in addition to artillery training at Jamestown, infantry service with Waddill and the 53d Virginia, and his naval detail at Hampton Roads, he later transferred to the 3d Virginia Cavalry. Another one of Waddill's men, Private George E. Webb, was among the fatalities in the naval engagement. But most notable of Jamestown's veterans was the temporary commander of

Looking Upriver at Jamestown Island

National Park Service,
Colonial National Historical Park

the *Virginia*, none other than Catesby Jones. When Franklin
Buchanan, the *Virginia's* captain, was wounded during the first day's
battle, Jones assumed command of the ironclad. Magruder was among
those who recognized Jones's role. He promptly sent Buchanan a letter of congratulations as senior officer for the "glorious and brilliant
victory" and expressed his delight that the commanding officers were
Buchanan and "my friend Lieutenant Catesby ap R. Jones."[65]

It was amid the excitement of the *Monitor-Virginia* confronta-
tion that President Davis received disturbing news. The report he had
requested on the James River and Richmond defenses was provided
by the Engineer Bureau. Although the James River defenses were
described as "rapidly improving" and as "good protection against
wooden fleets," ironclads were a different matter. The armored vessels
at Hampton Roads demonstrated that the heaviest ordnance available
should be used in conjunction with obstructions in the water, and perhaps torpedoes should be employed, as well. Unfortunately, one rami-
fication of making the river impassable was that the Confederates themselves would become reliant on land transportation, thereby losing
the swift interior lines provided by their own water system. Sites evaluated by the engineers included Drewry's Bluff, upriver from
Jamestown; Jamestown itself; and Mulberry Island, Fort Huger at

Harden's Bluff, and Fort Boykin at Day's Point, all below Jamestown. In compiling data on the defenses, the engineers miscounted Jamestown's armament, listing only four 9-inch Dahlgrens, four 8-inch Columbiads with two more en route, and five 32-pounders. This list probably included only the artillery at Fort Pocahontas since another Confederate, Corporal Randolph H. McKim, visited Allen's battery during early March and reported the same number and types of guns. As evidence of the Confederacy's concern about the *Monitor* coming upriver, Davis considered moving Jamestown's guns to Fort Huger in hopes of containing the new warship farther from Richmond.[66]

At mid-month Magruder contacted Davis about an entirely different matter that was troubling him. Recently the president had declared martial law in several areas of the state to solidify control for commanders in the field. His proclamation did not include James City County. Magruder considered this a serious omission, especially since it denied him total authority at Jamestown and Williamsburg where he had important garrisons. He cited the sale of spirituous liquors as an occasional source of great disorder in the county and implored Davis to give him the expanded control he needed. Within a few days the president granted Magruder his wish.[67]

Northern operations likewise were affected by Johnston's withdrawal to the Rappahannock and the battle of the ironclads at Hampton Roads. Major General George B. McClellan, commander of the Army of the Potomac, was compelled to modify his strategy for the spring campaign. He had planned to sail the Chesapeake to the Rappahannock River and land troops at Urbanna, thereby placing his army between Johnston and Richmond, but Johnston's new position foiled this move. There also was concern that the *Virginia* might venture out again and isolate the Federals since there was no nearby army or naval support. So McClellan looked farther south and chose Fort Monroe and the tip of the Peninsula as his base of operations. Inadvertently, Jones's strong demonstration with the *Virginia* had helped shift Union attention toward the Peninsula, which included his former command at Jamestown.[68]

CHAPTER 5

THE PENINSULA CAMPAIGN

General McClellan launched his Peninsula campaign on March 17. During the next three weeks about 400 vessels made numerous round trips and carried his mighty army via the Potomac River and Chesapeake Bay to Fort Monroe. The fleet's military cargo included some 100,000 men and thousands of horses and mules, cattle, wagons and ambulances, plus artillery and other military equipment. In contrast, Magruder's Army of the Peninsula awaited him with about 10,000 defenders. One day after McClellan's expedition was under way, the Jamestown garrison was forced to acknowledge the impact that attrition caused upon its strength. So many members of Carter's militia had transferred to other units that it was forced to reorganize and reduce its size again, this time from two companies to one. The new company became known as Charles Carter's Consolidated Company with Hill Carter still colonel of militia.[1]

During the weeks that McClellan transported his army, Magruder speculated about his opponent's course of action. "Prince John" shared his opinion with Lee, who recently had been appointed military advisor to President Davis. From his vantage point on the Peninsula, Magruder predicted that the *Monitor* would ascend the James with part of McClellan's army, thereby shielding Fort Monroe. He expected that another contingent simultaneously would contain the *Virginia* at Norfolk and occupy Major General Benjamin Huger's troops there. Jamestown was one of Magruder's main concerns. Located a short distance upriver from the right flank of the Warwick Line, the island might fall and make his position vulnerable. Both Jamestown and the mainland needed to be strengthened. Furthermore, Magruder renewed his proposal that the lower James River should be obstructed, this time recommending that it be blocked as far up as Jamestown. From Jamestown upward the river needed to remain open for supply ships with Jamestown as the receiving station.[2]

Contrary to most of Magruder's forces, Major Lewis had one artillery unit at Jamestown that was faced with the unusual situation of having more men than it could handle. Allen's recruiting efforts of the past few weeks had been a remarkable success. His enlistees surpassed the number he needed for his new artillery battalion, and Lewis hated to lose the potential manpower. He suggested that Magruder have the secretary of war permit Allen to raise six companies of heavy artillery and four regiments of infantry. Any surplus artillery and the infantry could be placed where most needed in Magruder's army. Meanwhile, as the month drew to a close, Carter reported Jamestown's strength as 520 soldiers. This was an improvement over the winter but less than intimidating. About 400 men were in the heavy artillery. The Bedford Light Artillery, now preparing for action elsewhere on the Peninsula, gave its strength at about 100 but needed thirty horses to be effective in the field. Carter's militia was down to a trifling figure of about twenty soldiers, who had eighty percussion muskets and 4,000 cartridges. Despite this excess in small arms, he requested 120 more in order to distribute them among the gunners to compensate for the inadequate infantry support.[3]

While McClellan's army was in transit, Lee had to ascertain where the Federals intended to strike so that he could direct reinforcements to the proper location. The Peninsula and Norfolk both were potential objectives. Late in March the picture cleared, and Lee sent troops to Magruder and ordered Johnston's army to join him. Magruder's numbers were bolstered to around 15,000 and, upon Johnston's arrival in April, the defenders' total was raised to about 55,000. Harmonious with Magruder's earlier concerns, Lee advised Magruder to guard against Union attempts to pass his batteries on the James and York Rivers and land in his rear at Williamsburg and Yorktown. Magruder quickly responded by issuing General Orders No. 168 to his army. He reiterated the importance of the Warwick Line, his fourteen miles of defenses that stretched across the Peninsula behind the Warwick River, anchored on the York River by Yorktown and Gloucester Point, and on the James River by Mulberry Island. Jamestown, just upriver, protected the Williamsburg and Yorktown positions from flank and rear attack. "The enemy is at length advancing," he announced. "We shall fight him on the line of Warwick River."[4]

On April 4, McClellan's army marched from Fort Monroe. Word of the movement was sent immediately to Carter at Jamestown. Carter also was alerted that the island was one of two points designated to receive the Peninsula army's sick soldiers; from there they would be carried by boat to hospitals in Richmond. Jamestown's own soldiers had a high incidence of measles and mumps, and several deaths were caused by "typhoid pneumonia" that month. The following day, in a downpour that lasted several hours and turned the roads to mud, McClellan reached the Warwick Line and elected to take the main Confederate position at Yorktown by siege.[5]

McClellan was reluctant to attack Yorktown for several reasons. Unfortunately for McClellan, he accepted faulty intelligence which stated that he, not Magruder, was outnumbered. This illusion was reinforced by Magruder's deceptive actions when he skillfully marched and countermarched his troops in a manner that made them appear to be everywhere in the bluecoats' front, and in great strength. Upon arrival at Yorktown McClellan's numerical advantage was overwhelming, but he lost this within days when Johnston's army arrived. After Johnston joined Magruder, the Army of the Potomac outnumbered the Confederates by a ratio of about two to one. The size of McClellan's army varies in contemporary reports and modern estimates according to the date and source used. Like any military unit, it also depends upon whether or not one tabulates the army's total size or its effective combat troops; if total size is used, then this figure includes the sick and wounded, soldiers detailed for other duties, and various excused and unexcused absences, thereby inflating an army's combat size. The ratio of two to one is about correct for the two armies' effective combat strength, but a ratio of three to one generally was the required formula for success for an attacking army. In addition to the army confronting him, McClellan was concerned that the CSS *Virginia* would take the offensive again. Its mere existence helped protect Norfolk and occupied the Union navy's attention, thereby depriving McClellan of support along the York River.[6]

Nature was one of McClellan's strongest opponents during the campaign. The Peninsula's clay soil and marshes could hinder a large army's movement any time, but the spring rains made the region even more impassable. Furthermore, the spring of 1862 featured the heaviest rainfall in twenty years. McClellan's initial advance toward Yorktown on April 5 was stymied by a deluge. A few days later it rained for twenty-eight consecutive hours and mud became knee-deep. Confederates likewise suffered, although as defenders they were spared the Union's agony of attempting to maneuver or to advance their artillery. By mid-April one Virginian described his camp as "desolate dreary and horrible" amid the lowlands, its soil always wet or partly submerged in water. Three days in the trenches with heavy rains soon had soldiers in water to their knees. Late in the month another graycoat wrote that he spent an entire day and night knee-deep in flooded breastworks, often lying in the muck to avoid sniper fire. Undoubtedly he was not alone in complaining of "a very bad cold."[7]

Like Jamestown's defenders, many of the Confederates who defended Yorktown were inspired by the history that had preceded them there. A Mississippian who was able to visit the town "found it [to] be a very old and dilapidated place." Still he was keenly interested in what he saw, including the site of Cornwallis's surrender and the church cemetery with tombstones that far pre-dated his native sod's statehood. Yorktown was equally impressive to a Virginian who was "in awe-struck silence" as he explored the "ancient little village" with "narrow streets" and "houses of antique style." He made special note of the Nelson house, the Swan Tavern, and the remains of Cornwallis's earthworks.[8]

As McClellan's mighty army settled into its second day of siege, Jamestown still was plagued by a supply shortage. Lewis sent word to Williamsburg that he had only fifteen cartridges per man and that 1,000 of them were damaged and unfit for use. He requested that 4,000 cartridges be sent immediately. The following day, April 7, the first units of Johnston's army reached Yorktown, but this did little to quiet some of the excitement and confusion at Jamestown. Captain Rambaut of the Cockade Mounted Battery was quite distraught. Two of his lieutenants had decided to raise new companies and were recruiting within the battery, a competitive act that caused great demoralization within the Petersburgers' ranks. Rambaut finally appealed to the secretary of war to restore order. Meanwhile, Carter misunderstood orders he received and prepared to abandon Jamestown. Lee promptly notified Magruder that he fully intended to defend Williamsburg and the batteries along the James and York Rivers, and he reiterated a warning to guard against Federal forces landing in the Confederate rear or flank, which included Jamestown.[9]

On April 12, Johnston attended a critical conference with the president in Richmond. He was accompanied by Major Generals James Longstreet and Gustavus W. Smith; Davis was joined by Lee and Secretary of War George Wythe Randolph. Johnston was appointed commander of the Army of Northern Virginia, which included his own army merged with Magruder's and Huger's, although usage of the new army's name did not become common practice for several weeks. Johnston had prepared himself for the conference by inspecting Magruder's lines on the Peninsula during the previous day, and based on this visit his perspective differed from that of Davis. Johnston felt that his position on the Peninsula was weak and that it should be abandoned in order to concentrate his army near Richmond for one great battle with McClellan. But Davis was not persuaded, and he ordered that the Peninsula should be defended.[10]

For Jamestown, continued defense meant reorganization. The island had 750 men, and Magruder was confident that he could reassign part of the garrison. Jordan had finished training his gunners for field service. While the *Virginia* remained near Norfolk and kept the Union navy in check, Magruder believed it was safe to move Jordan's field guns to the front. Consequently, the Bedford Light Artillery left Jamestown on April 15. The transfer appeared even more justifiable the following day when the Federals made their only assault of any consequence during the siege of Yorktown.[11]

Still other changes occurred at Jamestown. On April 16 an act of the Confederate Congress was approved which, among other things, stipulated that company, battalion, and regimental officers should be elected by members of their respective units. There was great haste to comply with this measure even though it meant that strict disciplinarians who were good officers might be replaced with popular, less capable leaders. Unlike units that had seen little change during the war's first year, there had been so much recent reorganization at Jamestown that the measure was almost meaningless. Allen's winter recruiting already had resulted on April 4 in the organization of the 10th Battalion Virginia Heavy Artillery, which consisted of five companies. These were Company A, the Metropolitan Guard; Company B, Captain James O. Hensley's Company; Company C, the Allen Artillery; Company D, the Jamestown Heavy Artillery which was the company Allen had organized in 1861 called the Brandon Artillery; and Company E, Captain Thomas Ballard Blake's Company. Allen was elected major of the new battalion on the day that it was organized. By the end of April there were 500 artillerymen under Allen, and Carter's 52d Virginia Militia supported them with thirty infantrymen. Allen, in fact, had thirty-two men above the prescribed maximum in Company D, which was an unusual problem for commanders. Captain Thomas Jefferson Page, Jr., on the other hand, lacked sufficient manpower in the Magruder Light Artillery because so many of his soldiers were ill from work in Yorktown's trenches. Page lost no time in requesting Allen's surplus.[12]

At the end of April, Johnston still considered his army's position hopeless, his opinion unchanged since his conference in Richmond two and one-half weeks earlier. "We are engaged in a species of warfare at which we can never win," he wrote Lee. "It is plain that McClellan will...depend for success upon artillery & engineering. We can compete with him in neither." The following day, May 1, he announced that he would abandon Yorktown and retreat toward Richmond. McClellan's siege artillery was almost entirely in place, making the graycoats' position more unbearable. It was imperative that the Southerners' withdrawal be stealthy since the opposing armies' lines were practically touching. Johnston was greatly outnumbered, and McClellan might be emboldened to attack the Confederates in this vulnerable moment. There was little that could be done at Jamestown until the order to withdraw was issued. Heavy artillery and its cumbersome equipage were not easily limbered and horse-drawn like field guns, so the wait was agonizing. There were personal matters to tend to, as well. On the date that Johnston decided to withdraw, Carter paid six weeks' rent to Allen's overseer for board provided both to himself and his servant at the Ambler house. Perhaps the date of payment was coincidence, or Carter might have received word of Johnston's plan with an admonition to keep it confidential, as was the practice in the Yorktown retreat.[13]

Johnston sent orders to Tucker and the James River Squadron on May 2 concerning the evacuation of Jamestown. The island's garrison, which he listed as 500 to 600 men, was ordered to Richmond via the James River. Tucker was instructed to inquire the following day about the island's transportation needs. If necessary, Tucker's vessels were to assist Lewis, especially in removing the heavy guns and ordnance stores. Whatever could not be removed was to be destroyed.[14]

Heavy rains on the first two nights of May further saturated the Peninsula and complicated Johnston's withdrawal. One local resident believed that he had never seen so much rain. Carter's 52d Virginia Militia, consisting of some two dozen men, easily abandoned Jamestown when orders to do so arrived on the night of May 3, but it was far more complicated for Lewis and his batteries under Allen and Rambaut. A member of Allen's battalion said the order to evacuate was "unexpected," indicating the movement's secrecy had been kept. Furthermore, Tucker's squadron, which was ordered to assist with Norfolk's evacuation, apparently did not reach Jamestown in time to help or was woefully inadequate when it did. Lewis complained about a "want of transportation" during the operation. It proved to be a long, frustrating night. The success of the Confederates' withdrawal from Jamestown rested largely upon the shoulders of the man who first occupied the island, Allen himself. Since the James River fortifications were being abandoned almost as far up as Richmond, Allen was in an uncomfortable position. He knew that he had this night, and this night only, to evacuate both his troops at Jamestown and his home upriver at Claremont. Lewis was deeply gratified when Allen offered all means of land and water transportation at his disposal, which included light-ers, arks, and schooners. Even so, it was impossible to remove every-thing in the allotted time. With such heavy and unwieldy cargo, only ammunition, three 9-inch Dahlgrens, and six 32-pounders were re-moved. Early on the morning of May 4 the improvised fleet sailed toward Richmond, arriving there at 11 A.M. on May 7. The following day Allen and Rambaut were ordered to place their commands in Camp Winder and the city defenses. There was plenty of work for the artillerymen as the officers mounted the 32-pounder guns on ship carriages at strategic points around Richmond. It was a different story, though, for Carter's militia. A lone lieutenant was discharged, "there being no men left to form a company." With the sudden orders of a single spring night, it was over. After more than a year of Con-federate occupation, Jamestown was abandoned to the Federals hav-ing never fired a shot against the foe. However, the garrison's men-acing presence had contributed to the Union's reluctance to test the James River batteries until a massive offensive could be organized.[15]

Even as the Jamestown artillerymen moved up the James to-ward Richmond that Sunday, May 4, word of their retreat traveled quickly down river. The news reached General Wool at Fort Monroe that day, and he, in turn, sent word inland to McClellan that both Jamestown and Mulberry Islands were ripe for the taking. In his dis-patch Wool cracked, "It would seem that the bird has flown."[16]

However tempting the abandoned posts might be, McClellan had other business with Johnston. The Federals pursued him in a rainfall that started on the evening of May 4 and continued for thirty hours. It was in this unpleasant weather that the armies clashed in a rear guard action at Williamsburg, and then Johnston resumed his withdrawal. Coincidentally, Allen's property was involved in this phase of the cam-paign, too. Union cavalry threatened the Confederate right flank at Williamsburg on land known since colonial times as Kingsmill, which was owned by the wealthy artillery major.[17]

On the day of the Battle of Williamsburg, Magruder explained the severity of Jamestown's loss to the secretary of war. With its for-tifications in their possession the Federals no longer needed gun-boats for safe passage upriver toward Richmond. But it was not until the following day that the USS *Monitor*, afloat at Hampton Roads, received word of Johnston's retreat. Still unaware that the Confeder-ates had abandoned the entire middle Peninsula, one crew member, Acting Assistant Paymaster William F. Keeler, predicted that "it can-not be that they will passively see our gun boats go up the river to destroy their fleet & shell out their batteries on Jamestown island."

He looked excitedly toward the departure of the *Galena* the next day, to be followed by other vessels. When the entire Union fleet made its move he expected the *Virginia* to attack, at which time the battle of the ironclads would be renewed with the *Monitor* defending the wooden ships. The "Big Thing," as the *Monitor's* crew called the *Virginia*, would be trapped between the shallow channel of the James, which prevented the *Virginia's* movement toward Richmond, and the *Monitor* herself.[18]

As the *Monitor's* crew awaited orders, the Union high command assessed the situation and prepared to act. McClellan sent cavalry to Jamestown on May 6, the day after the Battle of Williamsburg. The horsemen returned with news that the battery was abandoned, the magazines and gun carriages were burned, and, finding some artillery, they erroneously assumed that all the guns had been left behind. Incredibly, Johnston was less informed on this matter than was McClellan. Two days after the Nationals made their reconnaissance, Johnston pondered having Tucker and the navy remove guns from Jamestown and Mulberry Islands as if the river remained open. A day later he conceded that this opportunity was lost.[19]

Meanwhile President Abraham Lincoln, who had traveled to Fort Monroe, received a telegram from McClellan on May 7 about the cavalry's discovery at Jamestown. Grasping the need for action, Lincoln immediately interceded for McClellan, who had requested that gunboats be sent up the James, by contacting Flag Officer Louis M. Goldsborough. He conveyed McClellan's request and urged compliance on the condition that the *Virginia*, ever a concern, posed no threat. At noon on May 8, McClellan dispatched cavalry to Jamestown again, this time to monitor river traffic. The Federals stayed past sunset, their most noteworthy sighting being three vessels described as Confederate side-wheel steamers headed upriver. Another party of Union horsemen who were down river likewise reported the trio, all flying the South's flag. The soldiers at Jamestown erroneously reported the vessels as the *Yorktown, Patrick Henry*, and an unidentified steamer. Since the *Patrick Henry* was actually the new name for the *Yorktown*, it is probable that the observers actually saw the *Patrick Henry* and its sister ship, the *Jamestown*. This might have been Tucker making his examination of Jamestown and Mulberry Islands, as requested by Johnston.[20]

Some accounts of alleged Union army visits to Jamestown are erroneous. The 40th New York Infantry, known as "the Mozart Regiment," made numerous marches in the area after the Battle of Williamsburg. John H. B. Jenkins, a private in Company F who was in his early twenties, wrote a letter describing "James 'City,'" or "Jim's

City," as he said local people called it. At first one gets the impression that he was referring to Jamestown, although the name "James City" was used only in the seventeenth century and "Jim's City" was unheard of. He counted four dwellings, a post office, a store or factory, two smokehouses, half a dozen quarters for blacks, and one shed over a dry well. What is more peculiar about Jenkins's account is that it does not contain references to the prominent features at the island's western end which the New Yorkers would have seen after crossing the bridge, such as the church tower, the Ambler house, and the Confederate earthworks. Most military and civilian visitors used the island's roads, and this course required them to pass by these familiar sites. It is more likely that the regiment, which subsequently marched northwest through New Kent Court House, actually passed a cluster of buildings called James City, which was a dot on the map just northwest of Williamsburg. Two churches on the Old Stage Road to Richmond were known by this name, as well. There is another incident involving Union troops which is confused with Jamestown, this one by foragers at Amblers on the James. Amblers on the James was property located on the mainland that was owned by David Spencer Cowles. It was confused with Jamestown because of the name "Amblers" which mistakenly was identified with the island's Ambler house.[21]

In compliance with orders from Lincoln and McClellan, the Union navy moved up the James. At 4 P.M. on May 10 several steamships anchored off Jamestown. The USS *Galena*, an experimental ironclad, quickly checked the deserted batteries. Around 6 A.M. the following day, the entire fleet halted at Jamestown's wharf. Once again it was the *Galena* that reconnoitered, this time with two officers aboard a

cutter. Their first discovery was a schooner sunk at the wharf, possibly one of Allen's boats. They explored the island by water and by land until they located all five batteries. Only one of them was examined closely, and it contained four 8-inch Columbiads, all spiked, with their carriages burned. This probably was the Sand Battery. The only inhabitants found were five blacks who joined the officers when they returned to the *Galena*, but they had no useful information for the Northerners.[22]

USS *Galena*
U.S. Naval Historical Center

While the *Galena* was conducting its reconnaissance, the situation turned dramatically in the Union navy's favor. On May 9, the Confederates abandoned Norfolk, leaving the CSS *Virginia* without a port. Two days later the anticipated rematch with the *Monitor* became impossible. Unable to sail the James or to find safety, the *Virginia* was blown up by its own crew to avoid capture. The following day found the *Monitor* free to join the fleet now

USS *Monitor*
U.S. Naval Historical Center

that its armored counterpart was gone. The morning of May 12 was clear and pleasant as the *Monitor*, joined by the *Naugatuck*, ascended the James River. With the exception of brief fire they received at Day's Point, they advanced uncontested past abandoned batteries. At noon they reached Jamestown where the *Galena, Port Royal,* and *Aroostook* awaited them opposite the church tower. One of the *Monitor's* crew members also noted that, adjacent to the tower, there was "a deserted rebel earth work bringing in strong contrast the deep toned piety of the early settlers & the perjured villainy of their degenerate offspring."[23]

United at Jamestown under Commander John Rodgers, the five vessels continued up the James toward Richmond. They noted how the river's width was comparable to the sea until reaching Jamestown where, although still wide and deep, it narrowed somewhat. About seven miles below Richmond they encountered a high position, recently fortified, known as Drewry's Bluff. Among the Confederates awaiting them was the crew of the *Virginia*, this time prepared to challenge the Union navy from guns on land. With them was their lieutenant, Catesby Jones, who undoubtedly gained great satisfaction from the four-hour battle which sent the Unionists limping back to his former post at Jamestown.[24]

The USS *Port Royal* reached Jamestown first, arriving around 10 P.M. on May 16. Lieutenant George U. Morris, the gunboat's commander, sent a boat ashore and satisfied himself that the island was still deserted. Several cutters ventured toward land the following morning, bearing the bodies of thirteen men killed aboard the *Galena* during the fight at Drewry's Bluff. Crewmen from the *Naugatuck*, which came alongside the *Port Royal*, assisted with the burials on the shore. Morris was relieved to have the bodies interred, for they were "very much decomposed and offensive." He found a black man that morning and employed him to deliver a dispatch to Federals in Williamsburg. Lincoln was gone from the Peninsula, but his secretary of state, William H. Seward, had sailed to Jamestown and met the returning gunboats there. He, in turn, reported on events to Secretary of War Edwin M. Stanton who said that the Union fatalities buried at Jamestown totaled seventeen. William Faxon, chief clerk of the Navy Department, visited Jamestown that night to assess the situation, then returned to Washington. By May 20 word of the battle at Drewry's Bluff had reached civilians in Williamsburg, who had a completely different view of matters. Harriette Cary started her diary entry that day by writing, "Heard a little cheering news this morning." She then described the "two Yankee gunboats" which she heard had fifteen dead sailors who were buried at Jamestown.[25]

On May 20, Union gunboats started patrolling the James River to monitor Confederate activity. Meanwhile, McClellan's army moved closer to Richmond and fought the Battle of Seven Pines on May 31 and June 1. The Army of the Potomac now was well beyond its naval support. Jamestown, which was far behind Union battle lines, became the point where the army and navy safely communicated with each other. All vessels were asked to stop at Jamestown to exchange information with the army. While on their routine patrol of the river, crewmen aboard the *Monitor* did not get fresh vegetables, fruit, or meat, and they were prohibited from confiscating food from local citizens. Each time the vessel passed Jamestown the island received longing looks, for it was known that there was a large barn there filled with sweet potatoes that had been stockpiled during Confederate occupation.[26]

In June the navy decided to wreck abandoned Confederate fortifications and artillery. The USS *Aroostook* was given this assignment for Jamestown. Arriving on June 10, a party was sent ashore in the final daylight hours of 6–8 P.M. to begin destroying ordnance stores. The following day crewmen returned to shore. They dug up guns which the Confederates had buried and spiked those which had not already been disabled. Spare iron and brass work for gun carriages were destroyed, as were magazines and large trucks used to transport guns. On the twelfth several crews of cutters returned again, this time to finish burning carriages, quarters, and other buildings attached to the various batteries. One barracks was spared behind Fort Pocahontas because former slaves now occupied it. Although the navy's work appeared finished, the *Aroostook* sent a final party ashore two days later from 4–8 A.M. It was a futile trip, though, as they tried unsuccessfully

USS *Aroostook*

to burst guns by exploding 8-inch shells in them. Nonetheless, the nine 8-inch army Columbiads and four navy 32-pounders at Jamestown and vicinity were reported as useless.[27]

By mid-June the black population which the navy encountered at Jamestown was a concern to local white citizens. Jamestown became a rendezvous point for blacks, and they communicated with other runaway slaves who were upriver at Sandy Point. Whites became even more alarmed by the rumor that the blacks at Sandy Point had acquired arms.[28]

The Seven Days' battles which decided the fate of the Peninsula campaign began a short distance from Richmond on June 25. Throughout this week of heavy fighting the Union navy watched anxiously as the armies clashed. By June 28, McClellan's withdrawal and change of supply base were well under way. Still there was confidence that the transports, now at anchorage at Jamestown, could remain there rather than be rushed upriver for a major evacuation. Two days later, as the retreat continued, Commander Rodgers was less sanguine. Haunted by the memory of captured guns along the James that were not totally destroyed, he wished that they had been broken up and rendered worthless. To remedy the matter he urged that several steamers be sent with marines to finish this business. Fearful of a total Union withdrawal, he worried that if the Confederates re-established their batteries "we shall not hear the last of it."[29]

July 1 was the last of the Seven Days' battles, and McClellan's new base along the James at Harrison's Landing was quickly established. The navy responded by supporting the army there and at numerous other positions, including Jamestown. The island was guarded by the USS *Jacob Bell*, a side-wheel steamer that was among the oldest of the civilian ships converted to naval use. Meanwhile, Major General John A. Dix, the recently appointed commander at Fort Monroe, acted on Stanton's wish for better communications. Stanton was anxious about McClellan's situation and wanted more timely exchanges between the War Department and his field commander. McClellan, in turn, was enthusiastic about the U.S. Military Telegraph. Accordingly, Dix dispatched a party to run wires from Williamsburg to Jamestown, thereby extending telegraph service to the river. Messages then were transported between McClellan and Jamestown by boat. The lines were finished around July 5, thereby enabling McClellan to report to Washington three times daily instead of the former rate of one message per day.[30]

There was little activity for the remainder of the month as McClellan awaited replacements for his casualties. Union gunboats supported him by guarding the James. Late in July, Commodore Charles Wilkes of the USS *Wachusett* was informed about two vessels "affiliating with the enemy." When advised that the offenders were anchored by Chippokes Creek near Claremont, he decided to investigate. On the night of July 27 he sent three small boats which discovered and captured a schooner and a lighter; the Federals also saw three vessels that had been scuttled. Wilkes learned that the schooner, *J. W. Sturges*, belonged to the man who owned Claremont, William Allen, but the Confederate citizen-soldier's name meant nothing to him. Few, if any, Unionists would have recognized Allen's name. Wilkes was new to James River operations, having arrived as flotilla commander only a few weeks earlier. His first assignment of the war had been as commander of the USS *Merrimack* in Norfolk, but he did not reach Hampton Roads until the vessel had been scuttled and abandoned to the Confederates. He gained his greatest notoriety in the *Trent* affair when he captured Confederate agents bound for England. His Peninsula duties went smoother than these previous ones, and far better than later events in the war which ended in his court-martial.[31]

A later incident demonstrated the risk that the navy took whenever it investigated potential threats along the river. Early in August a Federal gunboat near Jamestown sent a cutter to investigate a white flag on the shore. As it drew near, the boat was blasted by gunmen hidden in the bushes. McClellan protested to Lee about this deceptive tactic, and the graycoat commander replied that it was not authorized by him, nor did he believe that men from his army were that far down river. He insinuated that the navy might have invited this reception from local citizens as a response to its meddlesome inquiries.[32]

Jamestown Island remained important to McClellan for, in addition to its telegraph office, the sizable transport fleet still was anchored offshore. Escaped slaves constantly brought news of activities by southern sympathizers in the area, including shipbuilding across the river at Cobham Creek. Signal lights could be seen flashing at night on both banks of the river, and there were reports that Confederates on the bluff opposite Jamestown were too numerous for assault by picket parties. Commander Maxwell Woodhull, who guarded the transport fleet with the USS *Cimarron*, was sent mortar boats to protect the vessels. The mortar boats were necessary compensation for the loss of the *Jacob Bell*, which was sent to the Chickahominy in mid-August.[33]

While McClellan remained idle on the Peninsula, Major General John Pope was assembling the Army of Virginia for a new offensive from Washington. On August 3, General-in-Chief Henry W. Halleck ordered McClellan to move his army to Aquia Creek in northeastern Virginia to reinforce Pope. When Halleck suggested that McClellan's withdrawal was too slow, "Little Mac" made an energetic effort to persuade him that his pace was justified. At 7 A.M. on August 13 he left Harrison's Landing by gunboat and traveled to Jamestown so that he could converse with Halleck by telegram. But upon arrival he found the telegraph out of order. This was not a total surprise to soldiers stationed there, for on the evening of the eleventh the telegraph operator counted 159 gray horsemen across the river at Cobham Creek with potential to cut the wires. Undaunted, McClellan continued to Fort Monroe which he reached at 8:30 P.M. only to find that the cable was broken there. In

Major General George B. McClellan

Massachusetts Commandery,
Military Order of the Loyal Legion,
U.S. Army Military History Institute

a final effort he proceeded by ship to Cherrystone Inlet on the Eastern Shore, arriving at 11 P.M. By that late hour Halleck was willing to send only one message to McClellan, and it was a reiteration that he abandon the Peninsula as quickly as possible.[34]

Despite his urgent business, McClellan, like countless others before him, had paused briefly while at Jamestown to ponder its history. In a letter written to his wife the following day, he reported finding nothing from the colonial period but the brick church tower and cemetery. In an effort to read the aging tombstones, the oldest legible one he could find was dated 1698. He also commented on "a poor young wife" aged sixteen years, eleven months. In a last, sentimental moment before continuing his trek, he had picked some flowers near the church and enclosed them with his letter.[35]

Upon McClellan's return to Harrison's Landing on August 14, the infantry started its march to Fort Monroe. The foot soldiers had been preceded by the artillery, cavalry, supplies, and the sick and wounded. Two days later the transport fleet at Jamestown Island was ordered to Fort Monroe to meet the army there and ferry it north. This relieved Woodhull of an awkward situation. While guarding the fleet, he found himself in the middle of disputes between the army and navy. When he had transmitted orders for vessels with food supplies to move upriver to McClellan, an army commissary officer refused to comply. The commissary officer felt that he had the authority to determine which vessels should proceed, and that he needed a convoy for protection. Wilkes advised Woodhull to let the army have its way by selecting the boats that would be sent with supplies, but in turn there was no assurance of a navy escort.[36]

Illness was another naval concern. The torrid heat and humidity caused sickness that reduced the size of crews. To make matters worse, a new regulation soon would abolish the navy's traditional liquor ration. There was a general consensus among the officers, including Woodhull, that whiskey was a useful ally against river fogs and damp nights. Even Woodhull's surgeon, who practiced total abstinence, was fearful of the consequences and favored alcohol's use by sailors who served in the South. The fleet's withdrawal would end this potential crisis for the time being.[37]

Woodhull's withdrawal from the waters off Jamestown was complicated by yet another matter—the growing number of "contrabands," or escaped slaves, who were congregating at Jamestown. Blacks crossed the river from the Surry County side almost daily and assembled on the island. Woodhull was under the impression that the army, which now was leaving, had provided the refugees with food. He wondered if

McClellan realized the size of what Woodhull termed a "large colony." Nonetheless, he had to comply with orders to secure the Federal withdrawal, and this required that he destroy all boats in the area. Their destruction was intended to further sever communications between Southern sympathizers on both banks of the James. This task was accomplished by August 17, but it intensified the anxiety of the more than 100 black men, women, and children who feared being abandoned for recapture. Woodhull made a plea to Wilkes on their behalf, and apparently an empty coal schooner was used to evacuate them to Fort Monroe.[38]

By August 20, McClellan's army had withdrawn and was embarking for Aquia Creek from ports at Fort Monroe, Newport News, and Yorktown. The navy continued to patrol the James River for another week. Typical duties included the USS *Currituck's* assignment to examine the shores from Jordan's Point to Jamestown for Confederate batteries and to fire upon any positions that had been reoccupied. Two days later the USS *Maratanza* received the same orders to cast a watchful eye toward Jamestown.[39]

As Woodhull was completing his duties at Jamestown there was a flurry of activity, some of which was puzzling to him. After McClellan's withdrawal, occupation posts were established to maintain the Union foothold on the middle Peninsula. Williamsburg, which was commanded by Colonel David Campbell, was one of the locations. For reasons unknown to Woodhull, Campbell ordered him to convey a white woman and child and a black female servant across the river on August 27. That night a pleasure sloop, the *Day Book*, was escorted to Woodhull. The vessel bore nine or ten blacks, so Woodhull had them spend the night at Jamestown since facilities already were available there. Campbell explained their mysterious arrival the next morning, saying that he had loaned the boat to one of the blacks named Mason who was taking the party to Fort Monroe. Satisfied that the movement was legitimate, Woodhull allowed them to continue.[40]

Wilkes started to withdraw his flotilla from its upper reaches along the James River on August 28. That day he fell back as far as Jamestown, then continued to Newport News which became the navy's most advanced position. Despite its failure to capture Richmond or destroy Lee's army, McClellan's campaign had gained a permanent, if tenuous, position as far as the middle Peninsula. Union army and naval forces were even stronger down river at Newport News and Hampton, as well as Norfolk. For a brief time, though, there would be a lull in military activities at Jamestown Island.[41]

Just prior to McClellan's withdrawal from the Peninsula, William Allen reassessed his personal finances and his future role in the war. After Jamestown's evacuation, his efforts had been recognized by General Magruder who praised him for his "self-sacrificing conduct." Magruder acknowledged Allen's monetary contributions at Jamestown which started with construction of the earthworks and continued through the Confederacy's final day there. Allen lost a considerable amount of property during the evacuation while saving the army's.[1]

Personal losses, which had no end in sight, concerned Allen. It was no exaggeration for Virginia's wealthiest citizen when he reflected upon the civil conflict's first year and assessed himself as "one of the largest losers by the war." By late summer of 1862 most of Allen's property was in Union possession or on the perimeter of the contested area. His financial contribution to the war effort, combined with property abandoned to the Federals, was enormous. Allen estimated the figure at $450,000 and mounting daily. Unable to concentrate longer on military operations, he submitted his letter of resignation to Secretary of War Randolph, citing his hardship as his reason. He justified his decision by pointing out that his ability to save a sizable amount of his property would benefit the government, which was true based on the generous support that characterized his devotion to the South both before and after his resignation.[2]

Like its owner, Jamestown experienced many changes after the Peninsula campaign. Briefly abandoned by both armies, former slaves ruled Allen's property. It apparently was during the late summer or early autumn that rebellious blacks burned the Ambler house. A court deposition substantiates that Allen's slaves committed the act, with no indication that Union forces were responsible for the conflagration. Indeed, all evidence of Union activity at Jamestown that summer shows a high regard for private property in compliance with McClellan's order that it should be protected. When Confederate property was destroyed by the Union navy in June, the sailors were careful to protect structures that provided shelter for black refugees. Prior to that, the Federals had been prohibited from so much as taking food from Jamestown. Warfare on the Peninsula in 1862 was not akin to the destructive acts against property that characterized actions two years later in Georgia and the Shenandoah Valley.[3]

With the Peninsula partially occupied by Union forces and unstable elsewhere, the Allens moved first to Petersburg during the summer of 1861, then to Richmond. At least one member of the household, Jacob Morton Shriver, remained at Claremont. Shriver, an uncle of Allen's wife, was a clerk in his early forties who retained his Canadian citizenship. On Monday morning, October 20, Shriver left Claremont by boat with his slave, Littleton, and Gilbert Wooten, a free black. They embarked on private business, one source saying that it was to acquire slaves while another states that they sought tools to repair a mill. The trio first went to Four Mile Tree, the residence of Joseph A. Graves, who was Surry County commonwealth attorney. Graves was not at home, so they waited there until about 4 P.M., at which time he returned. Graves and his nephew George Graves, who was a child, joined them, and they proceeded to Jamestown. Shriver and the elder Graves were armed with double barrel birding guns.[4]

An hour later the boat docked at Jamestown near the church tower. Everyone walked from the church to the Ambler house, which was about one-quarter mile away, except Wooten, who remained with the boat. While waiting, Wooten heard voices from the direction of the bridge which connected with the mainland at Neck of Land. Soon he spotted seven armed men whom he recognized as slaves from Allen's Neck of Land property. Too late to shout an alarm or escape, Wooten surrendered. He was greeted ominously by one member of the party, William Parsons, who pronounced, "Wooten is the very boy we have long time been wanting." The remark reflected their contempt for the free black who remained loyal to Allen.[5]

Parsons, joined by Henry Moore and three men known only as Jesse, Aleck, and Mike, walked toward the Ambler house in pursuit of Wooten's companions. The two other blacks, George Thomas and Norborne Baker, joined Wooten in the boat. Baker continued the sinister nature of the conversation, asking Wooten if he expected to return home to Surry County. When his captive answered in the affirmative, Baker stated that he thought otherwise. Wooten then was taken by boat around the western end of the island to the bridge. While en route he heard four shots from the vicinity of the Ambler house, to which

Baker commented that "they have either them or they have got them one; that was not a rifle." Upon reaching the bridge, Wooten was ordered out of the boat and to sit there and await the others. Soon Wooten's comrades arrived, disarmed and in the custody of their pursuers.[6]

Once united, the group from Surry was marched from the bridge to the overseer's house at Neck of Land. They were halted at the yard's entrance gate and left guarded by Mike and Aleck, who now had the guns brought by Shriver and Graves. The other five blacks went to the house and were met by a slave named Windsor, whom they referred to as "the judge." The conferees spoke in inaudible tones until Windsor inquired, "Is that Gilbert?" Wooten answered for himself, and Windsor, like the others, was hostile, saying that he had "no use for [him]" and that he had been "a long time wanting [him]." After a pause, Graves tried to change the charged atmosphere, asking who the group's captain was. He suggested that if their intention was to turn them over to Federal authorities in Williamsburg, then they should do so immediately; otherwise, they should be permitted to leave for home since it would be dark soon. There was no response, and after about five minutes Graves and his associates were escorted back to the bridge.[7]

While making the return walk, there were about fifteen or twenty blacks in the band, and all but one were recognized as Allen's slaves. Some of them were from the James City County side of the river, while others were escapees from Claremont. Graves broke the silence and attempted to assert himself, asking why the wheat was not threshed out. Moore would not tolerate him and said that it would be done when they were ready to do it. Boldly, Graves persevered and spoke of the houses burned at Jamestown. Again, it was Moore who rebuked him, testily asking what business it was of his. Graves expressed his disappointment in seeing the property destroyed, and there was no further conversation.[8]

It was about sunset when the party reached the bridge. The number of blacks who had gathered there raised the total to about 100, including men, women, and children. As the prisoners took a few steps onto the bridge, stopped, and clustered at its Neck of Land side, the assembly of onlookers fell back about ten paces. Sensing the gravity of the situation, Shriver spoke up this time, repeating Graves's earlier appeal to send them home or to turn them over to the Union troops at Williamsburg. "I don't think you will go home tonight, or to Williamsburg, either," Moore responded. About half a dozen men loaded their guns while others waited, their weapons ready. Graves then made a plea to spare his life and his comrades', offering bond and security for money. Desperate, the attorney resorted to the logic he might present to a jury, noting that his party obviously meant no harm; otherwise, they would not have brought a child with them. But his argument fell on deaf ears. Sympathetic toward Shriver's slave, Littleton, the blacks summoned him to join them. Despite the harsh welcome he had received, Wooten followed Littleton, perhaps hoping that his loyalty to Allen and his freedman status would be overlooked. Young George Graves panicked and joined Wooten.[9]

Shriver and Graves now stood alone. Six or seven blacks fired their guns simultaneously, and both men fell. Jim Diggs, one of Allen's slaves who joined the execution squad during the march to the bridge, tried to shoot Wooten. The freedman held him in check until Thomas broke his grip and pulled him back, at which time Diggs shot him in the stomach. Wooten fell and was shot again. Graves's young nephew George, who was surrounded by the crowd, begged in vain that his life be spared. The boy was picked up, thrown over the bridge into the marsh, and shot. Littleton then was ordered to take each victim's overcoat and search the pockets for money; immediately afterward, the bodies of Shriver and Graves were tossed into the water. Shriver, who was still alive, tried to swim to safety, but several men chased him by boat and beat him with oars, finishing him. Shriver's surprise effort diverted everyone's attention and enabled Wooten, who also was alive, to crawl undetected into the marsh about fifty yards; he reached a gut and then continued down the narrow passage for another twenty-five or thirty yards. Soon his absence was noticed. With only his face above water in order to breathe, Wooten watched his pursuers come closer. Darkness had come and hindered their search, and one man even stepped unknowingly on Wooten's hand. Confident that Wooten's wounds to the stomach, head, and neck were fatal, the hunt was abandoned until the next morning.[10]

After two hours in his watery hiding place, Wooten crawled back toward the bridge. He arrived just in time to see two of the men take Shriver's boat away, and with it went his means of escape. After resting, he crawled to Jamestown that night and searched without success for another boat. The following day he worked his way along a Neck of Land creek to its bridge, then followed the main road to the home of a man named Copeland, which he reached about 3 P.M. Copeland assisted him in reaching John Cassaday, a mulatto in his sixties, at Green Spring. After spending the remainder of that day at Green Spring, Cassaday took Wooten on October 22 to Graves's house where he was befriended by Graves's wife, Martha. She, in turn, arranged for Wooten's return home. Three days later, Wooten gave a deposition at Claremont about his terrifying experience.[11]

There are questions about these murders which are difficult to answer. Wooten, who was the lone source for the incident, portrays the slaves as having a hostile attitude toward him. Perhaps this was because he was a free black who, furthermore, remained loyal to Allen. One also wonders if he exaggerated this hostility for fear that whites might question why the only person to return was a black man, although his wounds showed that there was no favoritism toward him. Wooten obviously was known on both sides of the river and was familiar with Allen's business in Surry and James City counties—so much so that he knew the names of overseers and slaves alike. The escaped slaves' leader, Windsor, allegedly was from Claremont, which explains how he would have known Wooten. Wooten suggested no motive for the murders or the earlier destruction of Jamestown property, so one can only speculate that this was a rebellion against the institution of slavery and those who supported it. Local newspapers disingenuously reported that the affair was inspired by the Union army. When news of the deed reached Surry County, there was an immediate call for an election for commonwealth attorney to replace Graves, followed by the court's resolution of sympathy. Allen, who recently had resigned from the military to tend to personal affairs, found life further complicated as he administered Shriver's estate.[12]

Rear Admiral Samuel P. Lee
U.S. Naval Historical Center

During the week of the Jamestown murders, Acting Rear Admiral Samuel P. Lee sought to modify the navy's role with the army. Lee had been ordered to Norfolk early in September to replace Goldsborough as commander of the North Atlantic Blockading Squadron. A Virginian and career navy man who retained his national loyalty, Lee was a veteran of the Mexican War and had served the Union navy recently at New Orleans. Upon reaching his new assignment he found that, due to the navy's control of the Chesapeake Bay, the ports of Norfolk and Richmond had been closed to foreign trade since the war began, thereby verifying the effectiveness of the blockade. The navy now was entering a period where its objective for the Chesapeake region was to maintain the status quo. No immediate concerted army-navy effort was anticipated, so Lee recommended through Secretary of the Navy Gideon Welles that the army consolidate its scattered posts on the Peninsula. Otherwise, the navy was subordinate to the army, covering its flanks and keeping its communications open. Furthermore, by obligating the navy to protect weak army posts, ships were prevented from tightening the blockade.[13]

Contrary to Lee's wishes, the army's way prevailed. Garrisons were maintained from Fort Monroe to Williamsburg, and Union vessels continued to patrol the James River. In April 1863, Federals along both the James and York Rivers were alarmed by Lieutenant General James Longstreet's advance against Suffolk. To complicate matters, Brigadier General Henry A. Wise was sent from Richmond to launch a diversionary attack on the Peninsula. Wise's feint was successful. Major General Erasmus D. Keyes, whose Fourth Corps was assigned to the Department of Virginia after the Peninsula campaign, immediately requested aid from the navy. Gunboats were needed to reinforce Yorktown, and he wanted a reconnaissance to detect Confederate movement along the James as far north as Jamestown. When Wise attacked the garrison at Williamsburg on the morning of April 11, Keyes lost telegraph communications with the post. Fearful that the grayclads simultaneously might have crossed onto the Peninsula at Jamestown Island, Keyes wanted the navy to confirm or deny this and relieve pressure on Williamsburg, as well.[14]

Lee responded later that day from aboard the USS *Minnesota* at Newport News. He informed Keyes that he could provide only partial support for the James River and Williamsburg. Furthermore, he was unable to send additional vessels to Yorktown due to commitments his squadron had offshore North Carolina. On the positive side, Lee had consoling words to dispel fears that Southerners were landing at Jamestown. Two vessels from City Point had reached him that day, and there were no sightings of enemy activity. This report gave Lee second thoughts about sending several vessels upriver to Jamestown the following day. Finally, Lee demonstrated that he never was one to drop an argument by pointing out that during the previous summer he had encouraged the army to consolidate its position and destroy its captured posts along the Peninsula. This, he noted, would discourage the Confederates from returning to reoccupy them, as was happening now.[15]

By April 12, the situation had changed dramatically. Suffolk now was in the greatest danger, and Lee countermanded orders for a reconnaissance of the James River. He told Secretary Welles that he was embarrassed at being unable to respond to the army's simultaneous calls to cover the posts in the sounds of Carolina and along the Nansemond, James, and York Rivers. Again he attributed his predicament to the army's insistence upon maintaining scattered forts. The following day, as attention turned more toward Suffolk, Lee still was criticizing the army. Even in his orders to subordinates who were responding to Longstreet's actions at Suffolk, Lee could not resist hammering at what he deemed as the army's unsound strategy. He also belittled the navy's use of civilian vessels that had been converted to warships in order to implement this strategy. "The truth is the army should cease the impolicy of occupying so many detached and weak positions," he insisted, "and relying upon what are called ferryboats in New York and gunboats here to make such positions tenable."[16]

Longstreet was driven from Suffolk in early May, but conflicts between the Union army and navy continued on the Peninsula. Meanwhile, the Confederates concluded that the best way to stabilize their position on the James was to build ironclad vessels and a sturdy fortification. Fort Powhatan, located at a bend in the river between City Point and the mouth of the Chickahominy, became a symbol of hope. Dix was at such odds with naval officers that he decided to remain at Fort Monroe rather than cooperate with the navy in an attack made against Fort Powhatan before construction work was completed there. His inaction set the stage for yet another crisis.[17]

Flushed with a stunning victory at Chancellorsville and rejoined by Longstreet, General Robert E. Lee turned his thoughts toward an invasion of the North. Dix made several feeble efforts to create a diversion, but he never launched a concentrated move that threatened Richmond and required a response from Lee's army. After the Confederates started their march toward Pennsylvania, Jamestown became involved in one of Dix's hollow gestures. Much to Admiral Lee's disgust, the operation was undertaken with minimal communication between the two service branches, which reinforced his belief that the navy's potential was being wasted. On June 10, Keyes advised the navy of procedures that were to be followed that night. Keyes requested that three gunboats and two transports be sent up the James. The sailors were instructed to light lanterns on the starboard side to make themselves visible from Kingsmill Wharf, below Jamestown. At Kingsmill they would stop, pick up final orders from soldiers who awaited them, and resume their course upriver. Lanterns were to be extinguished at Kingsmill to conceal the vessels from Confederate observers who were posted on both sides of the river from about that point onward. The navy's next stop was Jamestown, where Keyes had

USS *Commodore Morris*

U.S. Naval Historical Center

infantry waiting to board the transports at midnight. The combined force then was to proceed to the Chickahominy River.[18]

Keyes sent these orders to Lieutenant Commander John P. Gillis, who was surprised to receive them. Gillis hastened from Yorktown to Newport News to confer with Lee, meanwhile assembling the vessels that Keyes requested. Lee, who was agitated by this "irregular and objectionable" manner of starting an expedition, overlooked the affront from Keyes and made haste to comply. The transports that were chosen, *Express* and *Thomas A. Morgan*, were accompanied by two gunboats, the USS *Commodore Jones* and the USS *Commodore Morris*. Both warships were typical of the converted ferryboats Lee despised. The *Commodore Jones* would be sunk by a torpedo the following year, but the *Commodore Morris* would serve seven more decades in New York City's ferryboat fleet with one more wartime interruption, that being the army's use of the boat in World War I. The navy started upriver at 9:30 P.M., but Keyes's plan quickly ran amuck. It was an extremely dark night, and navigation was impossible. The

Commodore Morris ran aground, and the *Commodore Jones* anchored in order to avoid the same fate. Concerned about Confederate ironclads as he drew closer to Richmond, Lee sent ironclads of his own to provide a buffer, but these vessels, too, were grounded in the blackness.[19]

Despite this nocturnal fiasco, Keyes was ready to try again the following night. He notified Gillis that 1,200 infantrymen with two days' rations would be waiting for him at Jamestown wharf at midnight. Meanwhile Lee, who considered the previous night's disaster a hopeless matter, was en route to Newport News when he learned of Keyes's intentions. During the return trip he noted that his vessels were observed by Confederate signal stations as far down river as Kingsmill. Shelling them was useless, for this did not prevent word of the Union activity from reaching Richmond within hours as couriers dashed to the nearest telegraph operator. Lee decided that the only way to handle the developing foray was to meet personally with Keyes. By afternoon all of his boats had returned upriver as far as Jamestown, and some were almost at the Chickahominy. Before meeting with Keyes, Lee's pilot on the Chickahominy reported that the river was stumpy and dangerous, even for vessels with a shallow draft. This reinforced Lee's inclination to return to Newport News. Armed with this new information, he docked at Jamestown and asked cavalrymen there to arrange a meeting with Keyes. At 3:30 in the afternoon Keyes learned of Lee's wishes and set out with his staff for Jamestown. The *Commodore Jones* hosted the conference offshore. Keyes was receptive to Lee's advice about the dangers of nighttime navigation, especially after Lee illustrated his point by cruising toward the Chickahominy with Keyes and then returning to Jamestown. With the element of surprise already gone, Keyes agreed to wait until the next morning before continuing his probe northward.[20]

Around 2 A.M. on June 12, a large fire was visible from Jamestown. The navy investigated and found that it was a nearby wharf, burned by the Confederates. Having established that it was no threat to the day's operations, infantry under Brigadier General George H. Gordon embarked on the transports at dawn. A small fleet took Gordon's men a mile or two up the Chickahominy where they landed and conducted a reconnaissance which caused little anxiety in the enemy's capital. These joint army-navy operations lasted two days and were monitored enthusiastically by Keyes and Dix. When their humble mission was accomplished, the troops were ferried back to Jamestown.[21]

For the remainder of the month Union troops on the Peninsula continued to play their minor role in the Gettysburg campaign. A cavalry raid late in June raised concern in Confederate minds about

Richmond's safety and scotched any notion to release additional troops
for Lee. But official Washington was not impressed. Keyes, who was
accused by Dix of withdrawing in the face of an inferior force, was
relieved of his command by the War Department, and Dix likewise
was transferred from Fort Monroe. Even though the month's latter
activities bore some favorable results, those of mid-June which involved Jamestown as the launching point were an abysmal failure.
Admiral Lee, the Peninsula's only high ranking survivor of these es-
capades, assessed them sarcastically in a confidential report to Welles.
"The movement seemed to have no important results," he wrote, "but,
as far as the navy was concerned, [it] afforded an opportunity to move
the ironclads and clean their bottoms in the fresh water."[22]

For the remainder of the year it was quiet at Jamestown. In the
autumn a lack of cooperation between the army and navy again
thwarted proposed action against Fort Powhatan. This reduced the
navy to its original role of patrolling the James. Simultaneously, the
Confederates enlarged the James River Squadron to include three
ironclads, making it a more formidable opponent. Obstructions at
Drewry's Bluff remained an imposing barrier between the two navies.[23]

Meanwhile, it was the Union army that dramatically transformed
Jamestown Island's status. Naval patrols which fulfilled the army's
reconnaissance needs were no substitute for twenty-four hour sur-
veillance on the fringe of enemy territory. Williamsburg, the Union's
most advanced position on the Peninsula toward Richmond, required
immediate knowledge of Confederate movements. The recent Suffolk
campaign, which caused confusion in Union officers' minds about the
positions of grayclad troops, emphasized this need. Accordingly,
Jamestown became an outpost for Williamsburg.[24]

In August of 1863 the 1st New York Mounted Rifles was assigned
to Williamsburg. Shortly thereafter, its picket line was established near
the College of William and Mary and extended on its left toward
Jamestown. Troops then were assigned to Jamestown itself to observe
activities along the river and to guard this outer most flank. A captain
in the regiment described the island as "one of the most important
salient points in the whole front line of the Union army."[25]

Jamestown continued as an observation post for the remainder
of the war. Usually a company of dismounted cavalry pickets was assigned there with a mounted reserve nearby on the mainland. It originally was intended to rotate these troopers on a weekly basis, but
their period of service frequently was longer. Other units from
Williamsburg shared this duty with the New Yorkers. When there was
news to report, fast horsemen acted as messengers to Williamsburg.[26]

Pickets were stationed at several locations at Jamestown for a more comprehensive assessment of Confederate activity. The western end of the island was the focal point but, unlike the period of Confederate occupation, this time eyes were turned upriver toward Richmond as the source of danger. With shipbuilding in progress at the Southern capital, there was constant vigilance for an approaching ironclad. Smoke or suspicious haze sent troopers scurrying to the top of the seventeenth-century church tower for a better view, while others watched from within Fort Pocahontas which likewise provided an elevated view. The opposite shore of Surry County also was scrutinized in daylight hours.[27]

Routine security and night duty were another matter. The mounted reserve on the mainland stayed near the bridge to prevent the island from being attacked from the rear. Concealed in a grove of trees near the lower side of the road, the Federals were poised to strike potential assailants with a deadly, short-range fire that was intended to surprise and scatter them. The loose plank bridge that connected Jamestown with the mainland offered some protection with its flimsiness, for it was believed that it would collapse under the pounding hoofs of a cavalry charge. At night additional precautions were taken. Several planks were removed from the bridge's girders, and in the darkness it appeared normal to the unsuspecting intruder. Furthermore, the gaps were too wide for a horse to leap even if they were

Site of the Jamestown Bridge

Photograph by author

detected. On the island itself, the pickets were doubled at some stations to watch for smuggling, for river crossings by boat, and for the landing of spies who circulated in the Williamsburg area. In the stillness of the night, the sound of splashing oars carried for a long distance.[28]

Assignments at Jamestown usually were quiet and uneventful. One cavalryman described the island as having "slumbrous air, bothersome mosquitoes, and monotonous scenery." To compensate for the lack of amenities, soldiers were permitted to pursue a wide variety of activities when off duty. Hunting and fishing were allowed, but use of firearms was forbidden in order to prevent disclosing their position. This proved to be no hindrance. Hunters found that the wildlife was tame, and they speculated that it was from years of being ignored by human predators. Turkeys, partridges, and ducks were trapped with ease, and oysters were easy prey in the water. To further supplement their diets, the men found nuts, berries, grapes, and persimmons when in season.[29]

Reading was another source of diversion. A soldier's reading material included such typical items as newspapers and letters from home, but there was an additional option available for Jamestown. Books were taken from the libraries of abandoned homes in Williamsburg, and many of them concerned Virginia history. Some of the Unionists had no interest in them, though, and the contrast in their appeal was quite obvious one day when a soldier who was enjoying his pilfered volume sat amid comrades who preferred to discuss horse races, circuses, and theater.

"George," a well-read sergeant asked one of his troopers, "didn't you ever hear of Powhatan?"

"Nope," was the disinterested response.

"George," the sergeant continued, this time mournful over the soldier's contentment with his ignorance, "didn't you ever hear of Pocahontas?"

This time he received a perky answer. "Yes, of course I've heard of her, but I never seen her trot. But I've seen Flora Temple go a mile in two forty."[30]

During the winter there was little military activity at Jamestown. The main excitement was generated by cavalry raids that involved some of the troops assigned to Williamsburg. In early February, Brigadier General Isaac J. Wistar led an abortive raid that was launched from the Peninsula against Richmond, the objective being to free Union prisoners in the capital, destroy public property, and capture Confederate officials. Members of the 1st New York Mounted Rifles participated in this attack, but it was checked before it reached the city. Weeks later a similar and more spectacular raid was directed at Richmond from the north. With separate columns commanded by Brigadier General Hugh Judson Kilpatrick and Colonel Ulric Dahlgren, both attackers were repulsed on the city's outskirts in March. Dahlgren, who was killed, bore papers which fell into Confederate hands and called for action comparable to Wistar's raid, plus specific instructions to kill Davis and his cabinet. Kilpatrick's men, who retreated in a different direction, took refuge behind Williamsburg's defenses.[31]

Soon after the Kilpatrick-Dahlgren raid, the war's complexion changed with the appointment of Ulysses S. Grant as general-in-chief. The new lieutenant general devised a spring campaign that called for a simultaneous offensive against the Confederate armies in all theaters of the war. In Virginia, Grant personally accompanied the Army of the Potomac in its thrust southward toward Lee's army and Richmond. There also were armies active in the Shenandoah Valley and on the Peninsula, the latter army commanded by General Butler. Butler's Army of the James was to threaten Richmond from the rear and wreck rail lines. As Grant's army marched into the Wilderness on May 4, Butler's troops sailed up the James, noting the Jamestown church as they passed it. Before the month ended, Butler was defeated and bottled up at Bermuda Hundred, thereby removed from Grant's strategic plan.[32]

Major General Benjamin F. Butler
Massachusetts Commandery,
Military Order of the Loyal Legion,
U.S. Army Military History Institute

When Grant launched his great offensive, Jamestown played a role in addition to the one it already had as an outpost. Still on the perimeter of territory under Northern control, its position along the river provided Butler an ideal communication link with Fort Monroe, which in turn had telegraph connections with Washington. When Butler's advance was checked, telegraph lines were run between Bermuda Hundred and his headquarters. Imitating McClellan's Peninsula operations, telegraph wires were strung from Jamestown to Fort Magruder in Williamsburg, and the navy carried messages between Butler's army and Jamestown to bridge the gap. Jamestown's telegraph station was tucked under a white tent in the angle of Fort Pocahontas's bastion, close to the church tower. Grant, who was an advocate of the U.S. Military Telegraph, wisely used telegraphic communications to link his armies. As he pushed southward he wasted no time in setting up telegraph lines between his own headquarters and corps and division commanders.[33]

When Grant learned of Butler's debacle, he sent Brigadier General Montgomery C. Meigs, Quartermaster General of the U.S. Army, and Brigadier General John G. Barnard, Chief Engineer of Washington Defenses, to investigate the situation. Their report was sent via telegraph from Jamestown on May 24. Shortly afterward, Barnard reported to Grant in person, and it was Barnard's words that were modified by Grant to describe Butler's position as comparable to being "in a bottle strongly corked."[34]

There were additional changes at Jamestown which coincided with the Bermuda Hundred campaign. Troops posted at the island reported to a new commander in Williamsburg, Colonel William H. P. Steere of the 4th Rhode Island Infantry. On May 1, soldiers from the 1st U.S. Colored Cavalry were assigned to Jamestown for two months. As was customary for black units, the officers were white. On May 2, Lieutenant Charles H. Libean and twenty men in squadron "B" were detailed briefly at Grove's Wharf, below Jamestown, to receive and guard a shipment of hay until it was safely removed; the remainder of the time was spent at Jamestown. It was relatively quiet during the first weeks of Grant's offensive, and guarding the telegraph was a new function of outpost duty on the island. Then on May 22 an escaped slave told Libean that some forty Confederates were across the river at Surry Court House. There also were numerous black refugees on the opposite shore, anxious to reach the Jamestown side. But Libean's force was inadequate and improperly outfitted to render assistance, so the blacks remained in Surry.[35]

Two weeks later Libean reported a twist of history, although the lieutenant himself failed to realize it. On June 4, a steam tug docked at the island to report a Confederate battery that fired upon it at the Point of Shoals, down river. An enemy gunboat also was sighted. A second vessel stopped at Jamestown later that day to confirm the incident, and it carried a message from Brigadier General Edward A. Wild that Jamestown's telegraph office forwarded to Fort Monroe, requesting that the navy shell out the offenders. The twist was that the steam tug that docked first with the news was named the *Mayflower* and that the officer who confirmed it, General Wild, was a native of Massachusetts. Virginians always had reminded their northern brethren that Jamestown was founded thirteen years before Plymouth, and now Jamestown had been visited by the *Mayflower*.[36]

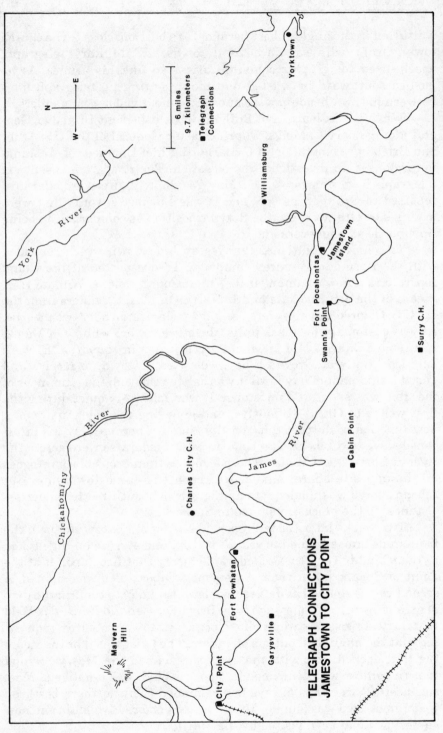

Map by Blake A. Magner

**TELEGRAPH CONNECTIONS
JAMESTOWN TO CITY POINT**

■ Telegraph
Connections

6 miles
9.7 kilometers

York River

Williamsburg ●

Yorktown ●

Jamestown Island

Fort Pocahontas

Swann's Point ■

Surry C.H. ■

Chickahominy River

Charles City C. H. ●

James River

Cabin Point ■

Fort Powhatan ■

Garysville ■

City Point ●

Malvern Hill

Swann's Point, on Horizon, Viewed from Jamestown

Photograph by author

During June, Jamestown's telegraph wires hummed with the news of battles fought by Grant and Butler. These assaults were indecisive, though, and led to the siege of Lee's army at Petersburg which began in mid-June and lasted almost ten months. On June 15, medical officers and equipment for Grant's army reached Jamestown. The physicians had been ordered to rendezvous at the island to await orders. That afternoon word came and, in order to support the long campaign that was just beginning, they were directed to City Point to establish a hospital depot there.[37]

During Grant's siege of Petersburg he established his headquarters at City Point. Jamestown's telegraph needed to be linked directly with the army, rather than by naval courier. As early as June 11 material was assembled to join Jamestown with Swann's Point on the opposite side of the river, and from thence to Cabin Point, Garysville, and City Point. The men assigned with construction duty recognized the urgency, but they requested protection for their building parties which would be operating in hostile territory. Butler and Major General George G. Meade, commander of the Army of the Potomac, quickly provided troops for the project. By June 19, many of the telegraph wires were strung, but their service was interrupted as soon as it began. The party sent to investigate the problem found the line cut in several places near Swann's Point and quickly repaired it. On June

23, the wires were cut again, this time by North Carolinians. Butler
sent cavalry who identified guerrillas as the culprits. The general
bluntly put the residents of Surry Court House on notice that there
should be no more meddling with the wires or "their houses will be
burned and some of them get hanged."[38]

Butler's threat worked, at least temporarily. The very next day
the telegraph became fully operational with Grant, Meade, and But-
ler in communication with one another and with the War Department.
Wires ran from Washington to Wilmington, the Eastern Shore, and
Cherrystone Point, where they were connected with cable to Fort
Monroe and ran up the Peninsula to Yorktown, Williamsburg, and
Jamestown. At Jamestown the wires ran under the James River to
Swann's Point, and from there to Surry Court House, Fort Powhatan
which now was in Union hands, and Grant's headquarters at City
Point. Although guerrillas remained a problem, the basic equipment
now was in place.[39]

Meanwhile, in one of the routine duty rotations at Jamestown,
the detachment from the 1st U.S. Colored Cavalry was replaced by
members of the 1st New York Mounted Rifles. Shortly thereafter, the
Federals suffered their only fatality on the island. Private Griffin
Oatman of Company C, who was a clerk before enlisting in the unit,
was twenty years of age and near-sighted. On the night of June 26 he
was patrolling the lower shore in the midst of a storm when last seen.
When the next rounds were made, Oatman was missing. The official
conclusion was that his poor vision and the rain caused him to walk
directly into the river or possibly slip down the bank into the water, at
which point he was swept away by the current and drowned. Other
sentinels would not accept this version and insisted that they heard
sounds of a struggle. They persistently noted the spot where he last
was seen and interpreted the beach's appearance as "evidence" of a
fight. Their theory was that Oatman was knifed by a stealthy scout
who wanted his rifle. Officers regarded this tale as bunk but decided
not to dispute it—some even encouraged its belief. Their ploy was that
sentries would be more alert if there was a greater sense of danger.[40]

There was no question about the peril that existed along the new
telegraph route. On the morning of July 5, Grant learned that two
and one-half miles of wire had been destroyed. Grant, in turn, ordered
Butler to continue the patrol between Fort Powhatan and Jamestown
Island to insure uninterrupted communications. Although this improved matters, it did not stop the wily guerrillas entirely. Determined
to win this contest, the Federals added an extension to their submarine cable at Jamestown and ran it twenty-two miles under the James

to Fort Powhatan, which was the point where adequate land protection began. The task was finished by late July, and the cable's efficiency exceeded expectations. Anchors dropped by friendly vessels or defects in the line caused only sporadic interruptions for the remainder of the war, and a repair boat quickly corrected the damage. Despite the cable's success, the army continued to maintain the line from Swann's Point to Fort Powhatan, although less energetically. This served both as a backup for the submarine cable and as a deception to keep the guerrillas' attention focused away from the water route.[41]

Colonel Gustavus S. Innis, commander of Fort Powhatan, was in a predicament after he repaired the wires around July 23. His aggressive action was akin to Butler's earlier threat against civilians. On this particular expedition he had four citizens taken as hostages. People who lived near the telegraph line were told that they would be held responsible for the wires' safety, and that the well being of the hostages depended upon the telegraph's continuous operation. Trapped by his tough proclamation, Innis did not really know what to do with his civilian prisoners. The hostage problem became embarrassing when he learned that one of them was a minister who had cared for a Union soldier. Six days later Innis gained reliable information about the hideout of the guerrillas who had cut the wires between Fort Powhatan and Swann's Point. He requested cavalry to attack them, but received only 150 infantrymen and a long list of complications that were cited as reasons for not sending horsemen. It was apparent that the submarine cable already had relegated the wires on land to a lower priority.[42]

Telegraph work became deadly on the night of August 5. Members of a U.S. Colored Cavalry unit were attacked while repairing wires, and two of them were killed while another was listed as missing. Five days later Lieutenant Colonel Christopher Kleinz was ordered to Fort Powhatan with the 5th Pennsylvania Cavalry, arriving that evening. The next day, August 11, the cavalry left the fort, divided into squadrons, and repaired wires cut between Cabin Point and Swann's Point. Upon their return on the twelfth, the Pennsylvanians learned that the wires already had been severed again, so they resumed their mission. When they returned on the morning of the fourteenth, the wires were in good order, but they had failed to capture the scoundrels responsible for the mischief. As a substitute they nabbed every white male they found in their path.[43]

Meanwhile, it was deceptively quiet on the opposite side of the river at Jamestown. The only notable event in August was that W. N. Embree, Jamestown's telegraph operator, was replaced by T. N. Loucks. There also were personnel changes at Williamsburg that summer, including the reassignment of Captain David E. Cronin, 1st New York Mounted Rifles, to the Petersburg front. For Jamestown, his transfer affected the historical record more than anything else. While serving as provost marshal, Cronin recorded numerous events in the town and surrounding counties, including those at Jamestown. However, he apparently confused the August 5 attack upon black cavalrymen on the Surry side of the river with an incident that occurred near Jamestown in early September, after his departure. The similarity of the attacks upon Union troops, the corresponding number of casualties, and the presence of U.S. Colored Cavalry on both sides of the river make it easy to understand how Cronin intertwined the events in his memoirs. The incident near Jamestown occurred as follows.[44]

On September 3, Federals at Jamestown telegraphed Fort Magruder and requested an ambulance for three soldiers who were ill. Colonel Joseph J. Morrison, who now commanded the entire Williamsburg garrison in addition to his own 16th New York Heavy Artillery, summoned an ambulance. He ordered Lieutenant John D. Lee of Company H, 20th New York Cavalry, to provide an escort. There was little manpower available, for Morrison's troops served guard and picket duty from Fort Monroe to Fort Magruder. Moreover, many of the men, like those at Jamestown, were sick, and the shortage of troops required that picket duty be assigned with greater frequency to the soldiers who were healthy. Consequently, Lee found only two privates and a corporal who had just been relieved from picket duty. The ambulance and trio of soldiers proceeded to Jamestown and, when within a mile of their destination, guerrillas unleashed lethal gunfire from their concealed positions in the woods. Responding quickly to the emergency, the ambulance driver changed direction and hurried his team of horses back to Williamsburg, but all of the cavalrymen fell victim to the ambush. The corporal was killed and the privates were captured, one of them being severely wounded. Two horses, one belonging to the corporal and one to the wounded private, returned to Fort Magruder bathed in the blood of their riders.[45]

When informed of the ambuscade, Morrison again contacted Lee. The lieutenant was ordered to assemble as many men as possible and pursue the guerrillas, whose number the ambulance driver estimated at fifteen. With no fresh troopers available, Lee gathered twenty-one soldiers, including those who had just finished twenty-four hours of picket duty and others who were on the sick list. The cavalrymen searched an area within ten miles of the attack, but without success. Curiously, when local citizens were interrogated, several of the male members were absent from home, their families unable to say where they were. This further inflamed suspicions that James City County residents were responsible for the deed. At the site of the ambush the Federals found the corporal's body, punctured by fourteen buckshot wounds. The attackers obviously fled in haste, leaving the corporal's Sharps carbine and saber with him. Upon its return to Fort Magruder, all the exhausted squad had to show for its effort was the corporal's body, his weapons, and the two horses that preceded them back to Williamsburg.[46]

This incident verified the constant danger of outpost duty on the middle Peninsula, even with Grant's army to the west and greater naval penetration of the James River. The latest naval concern was that the Confederates

Lieutenant General Ulysses S. Grant
Massachusetts Commandery,
Military Order of the Loyal Legion,
U.S. Army Military History Institute

were placing torpedoes in the river. On September 21, a gunboat on the Chickahominy was sent to patrol the James down to Jamestown, and another gunboat was instructed to search as far as Wilcox's Wharf. There was such apprehension about torpedoes at Jamestown that still another vessel, the *Hunchback*, was ordered to examine the island's swash channel on a daily basis. Soon after these measures were taken, the North Atlantic Blockading Squadron received a new commander when Rear Admiral David Dixon Porter replaced Lee in October. Porter, like Grant, came from the war's western theater and imparted the spirit of the offense into operations.[47]

In mid-October, Grant lost patience with the guerrillas who disrupted telegraph communications between Fort Powhatan and Jamestown. Wires were cut almost as quickly as the Federals repaired them, and Grant preferred not to rely exclusively upon the cable in the river. He instructed the 6th Ohio Cavalry to drive out the perpetrators, and to assure success he sent his personal escort under Captain Julius W. Mason who was familiar with the territory. On October 16–18 the blue horsemen penetrated deep in several directions, their reach extending to the shore opposite Jamestown. They captured wagons, blacks who were at large, and suspect whites.[48]

Meanwhile, Jamestown assumed a new role. Regarded as a relatively secure position behind the Petersburg lines, it became a place where veteran troops were assigned when their terms of enlistment were nearly expired. Two Pennsylvania infantry regiments occupied the island in this capacity in October. A Zouave unit, the 76th Pennsylvania, stayed into November and spent about six weeks there while awaiting transportation. Its only duty was to picket for its own protection; otherwise, the foraging was good and the atmosphere was "festive." In contrast, the 85th Pennsylvania took a dim view of the island. The steamer *Ironsides* reached Jamestown after dark around 9 P.M. on Saturday, October 15, and the regiment could see little besides the "old tumbledown dock" where it disembarked. Sunday's dawn enabled the new arrivals to view their new environment in full daylight, but their feelings were still negative. They concluded that "whatever its past renown had been, it seemed like a place of exile." To make matters worse, a rumor circulated that the regiment's new assignment was to guard Jamestown's telegraph station. Later that morning there was a collective sigh of relief when the steamer *Blackbird* arrived with orders to take the regiment to Portsmouth. The Keystone Staters departed with much jubilation, having stayed only about twelve hours.[49]

As winter approached, Porter ordered that precautions should be taken to keep the James River open if there were prolonged freezing conditions. It was imperative for Grant's army that river traffic continue without interruption. Porter instructed that the bows of vessels should be sheathed and, once ice began to form, they should constantly move up and down the river to maintain a route. His perspicacity was appreciated by Federal troops several weeks later when cold temperatures settled in.[50]

Two days later, on December 6, the Federals were reminded that Confederates, not weather, remained their constant adversary. Brigadier General Charles Graham was aboard a boat that ran aground at Jamestown that day. While at the island he telegraphed news that graycoats had burned a schooner and captured a boat down river the previous night in the vicinity of Pagan Creek. Shortly thereafter, Fort Monroe sent an expedition across the river to pursue a band of thirty men who assaulted government property at will. The Southerners ranged from the Nansemond River, below the Pagan Creek incident, to Hog Island, almost opposite Jamestown. In addition to property damage, the raiders posed a threat by gathering intelligence, so the bluecoats responded with another of their retaliatory raids.[51]

In December Jamestown again became a haven for retiring Federals whose terms of enlistment had expired. Senior members of

the 100th New York Infantry were sent to the island to await transportation north, leaving their comrades to finish the war. Their commander, Captain Frank C. Brunck, was a printer with the local newspaper when the war began. In all, Brunck had 174 men with him at
Jamestown through New Year's. Transportation to begin the trip to
Buffalo arrived early in January, and by the ninth the New Yorkers
were civilians once more. A few weeks after their departure, winter
weather comparable to that of the Empire State engulfed southeast-
ern Virginia. The wisdom of Porter's order to keep vessels moving in
the river became evident, for even with this plan in operation the navy
experienced some difficulties.[52]

During January 1865 the garrison for Fort Magruder and outposts such as Jamestown remained stable, although some of the cavalry lacked horses. In early February artillerymen, rather than cavalry, were stationed at Jamestown. Second Lieutenant David S. Murwin
commanded this contingent of thirty-five members of the 16th New
York Heavy Artillery until February 11 when he was ordered to Norfolk. Murwin's absence was brief, but in the interim Second Lieutenant Carlo Blomberg of the 16th's Company D was sent from Fort
Magruder as his replacement.[53]

A few days after Blomberg's arrival, he received significant news
and promptly notified Fort Magruder. The fort's security had been
compromised by a black man who frequently visited Williamsburg and
now was identified as a liaison with Confederate scouts. There also
was enemy activity in the area. On the previous night and that morning, February 17, Confederate cavalry was seen on the Richmond Road
at Burnt Ordinary. Also that night, four graycoats descended upon a
house above Jamestown Island, took two mules, and threatened to
shoot the owner. Blomberg was concerned by all this activity, especially since he had only three dozen men and was short on ammunition. His anxiety was manifested even more by houses "across [from]
the island" on the mainland which provided shelter for enemy scouts.
Taking his worry one step further to include all eventualities, he reported that these structures even could be dismantled easily and made
into rafts to cross over to the lower end of the island. Blomberg felt
that the houses should be burned.[54]

Major Julius C. Hicks, acting commander of Fort Magruder,
shared Blomberg's concern when he received his message. Hicks passed
the word to General Gordon, adding that his own garrison was so
undersized that he was unable to reinforce Jamestown if it were attacked. Recently he had asked for two more companies of cavalry, and
now he reiterated his request. Gordon supported Hicks and forwarded

his request to Major General Edward O. C. Ord, who had assumed command of the Army of the James. Ord consented on February 18, although one of the two companies of U.S. Colored Cavalry he sent was dismounted. Hicks meanwhile repeated his call for assistance, adding that Confederate deserters said there was a large grayclad force between Williamsburg and the Chickahominy, and black refugees and his own picket line sighted the enemy near Jamestown and along the York River. He suspected that the Confederates' objective was to gather horses for their cavalry. Unfortunately, there were no horsemen to conduct his own reconnaissance. Of the 115 men available for duty, thirty-three of them were on daily guard assignments. Nonetheless, he had such confidence in his infantry's strong picket line and reserve that he was willing to grant furloughs that he had issued recently, but he would approve no more.[55]

The guerrillas struck Jamestown and Fort Magruder on February 21 with their common tactic of cutting the telegraph wire between the two points. Hicks was unaware that his communications had been interrupted until after darkness fell, so he had to wait until the next day to repair the line. By now Federal tolerance was low for marauding on any scale. Hicks was so irritated that he wanted to implement Order No. 196, issued December 1 of the previous year, which permitted the army to burn all houses in the vicinity of disruptive acts, but there is no evidence that he did so.[56]

Fort Magruder was placed under Brevet Brigadier General Benjamin C. Ludlow on February 24. As the officer in charge of all posts between the James and York Rivers, Ludlow's tenure at the fort was brief, and in early March command of Fort Magruder reverted to Morrison with Ludlow remaining Morrison's superior as Peninsula commander. Ludlow's assignment was the futile task of eliminating guerrilla activity from the Chickahominy to the York River. He made a positive step in this direction when he was directed to requisition horses. This removed horses from potentially hostile citizens while simultaneously providing mounts for his own cavalrymen who needed them.[57]

As spring approached, Grant made final preparations for an assault against Lee's army at Petersburg. Two days into March, Major General Philip H. Sheridan crushed Lieutenant General Jubal A. Early's army at Waynesboro and rejoined the Army of the Potomac. To rid himself of another nuisance, Grant sent an expedition under Colonel Samuel H. Roberts to break up illicit trade between unscrupulous Northern and Southern businessmen. The entrepreneurs made their transactions along the Rappahannock River in the Fredericksburg area. Grant offered gunboats from as far south as Jamestown to the expedition's corps commander, Major General John Gibbon, so secure was the James by this time.[58]

In late March, Grant's plan for attacking Petersburg was in motion. On March 27, Ord began crossing his army to the south side of the James to join in. Ludlow remained in position along the Peninsula outposts. Having assessed his situation since taking command a few weeks earlier, Ludlow offered a solution to the never-ending communications problem which became even more critical with major combat imminent. Ludlow noted that the telegraph wires at Jamestown crossed the Back River to the mainland at the island's upper, or western, end. From there they ran in open territory to Williamsburg. To give the wires better protection, Ludlow suggested that they be strung down the island, cross the Back River at Jamestown's lower end, and follow the shore from there to the mouth of College Creek, which was guarded by a small outpost. Lines then could run the remaining distance to Fort Magruder under closer observation. Ludlow's plan apparently was never tested because of the rapid pace of the war's conclusion.[59]

Grant launched his final assault against Petersburg on April 2, and both Petersburg and Richmond were occupied by Union troops the following day. On April 4, Ludlow was ordered to leave Williamsburg and take his troops to Richmond as Grant's army continued to pursue Lee, who retreated westward. The war in Virginia ended when Lee surrendered on April 9 at Appomattox Court House. Two days later the main activity near Jamestown once again was naval. Porter promptly turned his attention toward regulating river traffic and assuring protection for the numerous boats using it. Vessels were stationed at strategic locations, one being Swann's Point across from Jamestown. In mid-April the mission was modified. President Lincoln died on April 15 from an assassin's bullet, and the next day the navy joined the hunt for his killer. Secretary of the Navy Welles proclaimed that no vessel should be permitted to go to sea until it was searched, lest the assassin escape. Ten days later the army ended the chase when the perpetrator was found and killed.[60]

By the end of April the army was reorganizing to meet the needs of peace and reconstruction. Ord was assigned to the Department of Virginia with Gordon under him in charge of the District of Eastern Virginia. Within the latter, Ludlow commanded the District of the Peninsula with headquarters at Williamsburg. Sundry military matters and the affairs of newly freed blacks occupied his attention. During May, Union troops continued to administer the Oath of Allegiance to the

Colonel David M. Evans
Massachusetts Commandery,
Military Order of the Loyal Legion,
U.S. Army Military History Institute

United States to former Confederate soldiers, and Jamestown was one
of the locations where members of the 20th New York Cavalry, commanded by Colonel David M. Evans, performed this duty. Then, on
May 10, Ludlow was ordered to remove troops from Williamsburg and
vicinity as part of a realignment of Union forces. The war was over at
Jamestown.[61]

Chapter 7

Postwar Change and Historic Preservation

William Allen's fortune collapsed with the Confederacy. When he resigned from the army in 1862 and declared himself "one of the largest losers by the war" it was only the beginning. Decades later, members of Surry County's Bohannan family wrote admiringly in books and articles about his devotion to duty. This viewpoint most assuredly originated through oral tradition conveyed by Aurelius Powhatan Bohannan.[1]

Born in Portsmouth, Virginia, in 1842, Bohannan became a merchant in Surry County. In the postwar years he also was postmaster at Claremont and, later, he also filled that post at Surry Court House. He concluded his career as county treasurer, a position he held until his death in 1905. He knew Allen as a neighbor and as commander of the 10th Battalion Virginia Heavy Artillery, in which Bohannan served as second lieutenant. Bohannan witnessed the extent of Allen's wartime devotion: Allen uniformed and equipped his unit at his own expense; his slaves assisted in the construction of Jamestown's earthworks; rails from his railroad were converted to form some of the iron plate for the CSS *Virginia*; he used and lost a schooner for the Confederacy; and large quantities of personal property were sold, rented, or donated, while still others were abandoned with the fall of the Peninsula or destroyed to prevent their use by the Federals.[2]

Allen also watched the fortunes of other wealthy property owners disappear along the James River. He shared the sense of loss with John A. Selden of Westover. Together they experienced a 100 percent profit in March 1862 through their separate $10,000 investments in Richmond's mercantile firm, Selden and Miller. A few months later, their financial status changed dramatically. Soon after Allen resigned from the army, McClellan withdrew from the Peninsula and Allen joined Selden to inspect his friend's home. Their visit was on September 17, the day when McClellan faced Lee on a new battlefield at Antietam. McClellan was gone from Virginia, but the ravages of war remained. Allen and

Selden found Westover ruined. Only a month later a party from Surry
County visited Allen's property at Jamestown, found comparable destruction, and had three of its members murdered by former slaves.[3]

During the war's latter years, the Allens were familiar figures in
the Richmond neighborhood they moved to, although some time was
spent on their Curles Neck property, too. Richmond citizens likewise
became accustomed to seeing Allen in his yacht, *The Breeze*, early in
the war. The Allens' lavish entertainment provided an occasional re-
spite from the worries of war. As late as 1864 the wealthy couple hosted
a party for 250 people that included an array of meats, ices, and champagne. But the Allens did not forget war's grim reality. The threat of
enemy armies, the reliance upon the city's defenses, and witnessing
such events as prisoner-of-war exchanges were constant reminders.[4]

Extravagant living and the Confederacy's defeat combined to spell
Allen's financial doom. In 1868 he lost his house in Richmond. By 1872
he was able to consolidate his debts in a mortgage on land in Surry
County, and in about 1874 he moved back to Claremont. The irony
was that his actions were limited by the conditions of his great-uncle's
will, which was the source of his wealth. Since the will stipulated that
the land Allen inherited must be transferred to his eldest son upon
Allen's death, Allen was forbidden to sell it. He could act without re-
striction only with property that was acquired after the date of his
inheritance. Jamestown was one of those later purchases that was
free of legal constraints.[5]

Allen lost no time in facing his massive debts. Only a month after
the Confederate surrender at Appomattox, Allen leased his Jamestown
and Neck of Land properties to enterprising New Yorkers on May 15,
1865. The lessees were granted tenancy until January 1, 1871, to use
the land for farming and timber. On December 1, 1866, Allen placed
both properties in a deed of trust. His need for money was so great,
however, that he soon sold Jamestown Island outright for $10,000 on
New Year's Eve in 1868.[6]

Property sales scarcely alleviated Allen's financial woes. His fortune was gone forever, replaced by debts. It was under these circum-
stances that death came suddenly to the former millionaire. On May
13, 1875, he made numerous purchases on credit at Meade & Baker,
an apothecary in Richmond. The receipt shows no indication of medical problems, and Richmonders believed Allen was in good health. A
few days later, on May 19, he was struck with a congestive chill while
boating, probably on the James River. Several servants nursed him,
but their efforts failed. He died that same day, apparently at Claremont.
Telegrams were sent immediately to family members and friends, with

arrangements to transport some of Allen's children to Claremont by rail and carriage. At the time of his death, Allen had no clothes with him other than what he was wearing, so Bohannan bought a suit, gloves, and other items for his friend's burial. Newspapers throughout the state carried the news of Allen's death. His Episcopalian funeral and interment were at 2 P.M. on May 21 at Claremont. Hundreds of persons attended, including upper class whites, laborers, and former slaves. The rosewood casket was silver mounted and bore a plate with the inscription, "William Allen, aged 46."[7]

William Allen was remembered fondly. One newspaper wrote that few men were more popular in Virginia, while another remembered him as a generous and hospitable man who would be missed by his many friends. One private citizen described Allen as weak and having a big heart, suggesting that his charitable and fun-loving nature complicated his own efforts to recover financially. Others praised Allen for his attempt during his last decade to restore order to the postwar havoc in Virginia. As the eulogies faded, all that remained for Allen's wife and four children was debt. Much of Allen's personal property was appraised a few weeks after his death and sold shortly thereafter, except for five French bronzes, four paintings, a clock, and two chairs. But the hope of retaining anything was merely a postponement of the inevitable, for even these items were auctioned in Richmond six years later. All semblance of the Allen fortune vanished.[8]

Jamestown was changing, too. Almost a quarter of a century after Allen sold the island, it became the property of Edward E. Barney and his wife, Louise, in 1892. In recognition of Jamestown's significance in the history of colonial America, the Barneys donated 22½ acres to the Association for the Preservation of Virginia Antiquities (APVA) the following year. The APVA property was at the western end of the island. It included the seventeenth-century church tower and the most important of the Confederate earthworks, Fort Pocahontas. The fort was regarded as a "relic of the 'Lost Cause,'" and the association considered it appropriate that this recent period of history should be represented alongside a symbol of the nation's birth, for both had great impact upon the state and upon the nation. There was a dilemma in the 1890s as to which flag should fly above the Confederate fort. One of the association's officers, Mary Jeffery Galt, suggested flying the American flag, but not over the fort itself. Lucy Parke Chamberlayne Bagby, who chaired the APVA's Jamestown Committee, felt that the association's own flag was preferable.[9]

More important than the flag issue was the physical integrity of the island itself. Erosion was taking its toll upon Jamestown, and it

Fort Pocahontas, ca. 1900

National Park Service,
Colonial National Historical Park

was measurable for scores of years as the church tower's shoreline
receded. By the mid-1890s, Fort Pocahontas was another measuring
stick as concerned observers reported that the James River had eroded
one of the earthwork's walls. In 1901 a seawall was completed under
the direction of Samuel H. Yonge that protected the western end of
Jamestown Island, including Fort Pocahontas.[10]

The Civil War was remembered a few years later when the three
hundredth anniversary of Jamestown's founding was observed at Norfolk, Virginia, in 1907. For seven months the event was celebrated at
the Jamestown Tercentennial Exposition. A combination of models and
art work, called a spectatorium, featured the naval battle at Hampton
Roads between the *Monitor* and *Virginia*, which was identified by its
former name, *Merrimack*, in the exhibit. It enjoyed such popularity
that it was declared the exposition's most successful amusement con-
cession. Cycloramas of the Battles of Manassas and Gettysburg, the
latter by Paul Philippoteaux, were located next to the *Monitor-Virginia*
exhibit. Former soldiers participated in the exposition, including a
regiment of Confederate veterans from Tennessee. Another kind of
contribution was made by an officer who actually served at Jamestown

Archeological Excavations at the Elay-Swann Tract

National Park Service,
Colonial National Historical Park

during the war. Emmett M. Morrison, the lieutenant who helped train new recruits at the island, wrote a history of his native Isle of Wight County for distribution at the exposition.[11]

Jamestown Island itself witnessed major changes several decades later. In 1930, Colonial National Monument, renamed Colonial National Historical Park six years later, was established as a park administered by the National Park Service. Jamestown was included in the park's boundaries, and the island formally was acquired in 1934, excluding the acreage owned by the APVA. That same year archeological excavations were started, and they continued until their interruption by World War II. One of the sites excavated by Carl Miller and J. C. Harrington during this period was the Elay-Swann tract, down river from the colonial town site. Numerous nineteenth-century artifacts were found there in 1937, as were the remains of structures from the same period. This discredited a theory that the oldest settlement site was located on this tract rather than the island's western end. Additionally, it provided more evidence of activity that occurred there during the days of Allen's ownership and the Civil War.[12]

Archeologists and historians also interviewed persons connected with the island's history. Yonge, who had constructed the seawall and had written his own book about Jamestown, shared his belief that Fort Pocahontas probably occupied the same ground as the 1607 settlers' fort. He reasoned that the Confederates, like the colonists, appreciated the site's strategic location. Yonge speculated that little would be found in excavating the fort and he questioned the wisdom in removing the landmark. It was a mystery to him as to where the Confederates obtained the dirt for the fort. Morrison was one of the people who remembered the answer to that question. He was about ninety years old when he was interviewed, a typical age for the Civil War veterans whose ranks were thin by the 1930s. Morrison assured his listeners that the soil was imported from property near Jamestown. His memory for dates, chronology, and some of the officers' ranks and units was faulty, but he remembered events from his Confederate days at Jamestown that were unknown to most people, including Lee's visit. He also gave a description of the island and the interior of the Ambler house.[13]

When archeology was conducted at Jamestown in the 1950s, the Civil War veterans were gone. The archeologists of that period turned to other sources for their interviews, including children of the Barneys who had purchased Jamestown in 1892. A memorandum attached to notes of this conversation wisely advised that the information should be used with caution because the interviewer had reservations about their memories. Furthermore, some of the events that were discussed, such as the Civil War, were secondhand information. Errors about the war years were abundant. Their account of the tests for the CSS *Virginia's* armor was erroneous. They did not regard Fort Pocahontas as the main fort, saying that that status belonged to an earthwork "halfway down the Island," perhaps referring to the Square Redoubt because of its size instead of its significance. They mistakenly stated that chains ran across The Thoroughfare from Black Point to the mainland, perhaps confusing this with an experiment down river that involved a chain and torpedoes, or with the obstructions upriver at Drewry's Bluff. Finally, McClellan's army was accused of vandalizing the Ambler house bricks for winter quarters, whereas his army actually had hurried past Jamestown in the spring while the Confederates who preceded them freely admitted using bricks from another old structure for fireplaces and tent chimneys.[14]

The archeological excavations proved to be more significant than the interviews. With the approach of Jamestown's 350th anniversary in 1957, the National Park Service (NPS) renewed its exploration of the island and associated sites. Excavations were conducted during the years 1954–1956 under the direction of John L. Cotter. A re-examination of the Elay-Swann tract reaffirmed the original conclusion that there was no seventeenth-century habitation there. Once again the structural remains and artifacts were primarily nineteenth century, and many of them coincided with the Civil War era.[15]

Joel Shiner, who conducted the work at Elay-Swann, also explored the area of the Confederates' Fort Pocahontas on APVA grounds. Referred to as Project 100, the objective was to locate the colonists' original fort. Project 100 was inconclusive because, while it did not positively locate the fort, it did not disprove that this was its location, either. Indeed, the abundance of early seventeenth-century artifacts found there reinforced the notion that the first English settlers resided in this area. Surprisingly, few Civil War artifacts were found. Shiner's test pits which were designated as numbers eleven and eighteen confirmed accounts that the earthen walls of Fort Pocahontas were formed by piling dirt from other locations. Test pit number twelve, which was inside the fort, showed why Confederates discovered armor. Soil from the colonial era had been disturbed here, and Shiner found colonial rubble scraped into the earthwork floor. Since the objective in 1861 was to raise walls and have an open field of fire, this probably was an atypical instance where the Confederates dug deeply into the soil. Shiner challenged the idea that the riverside wall of Fort Pocahontas had eroded. He believed that the missing dirt was scraped away, possibly as part of the effort to stop erosion, but reports, maps, and photography of the 1890s and early 1900s verify that erosion was the cause.[16]

Some three decades after Cotter and Shiner examined Jamestown, a new archeological study began in preparation for 2007, the 400th anniversary of the settlement's founding. In 1992, the National Park Service initiated an archeological assessment of the island, conducted in cooperation with the Colonial Williamsburg Foundation and the College of William and Mary. The assessment, which was intended to precede future NPS excavations, was a multidisciplinary approach that included analysis of the island's historical and archeological record, environmental reconstruction, and a comprehensive survey of historic and prehistoric sites. Two years later, the APVA started independent archeological excavations near the church tower and Fort Pocahontas to verify the site of the original Jamestown fort and settlement. These projects, like their predecessors, expanded the knowledge of all periods of occupation at Jamestown.[17]

New studies of Jamestown frequently shed light on its role in the Civil War. Some of the principal figures nearly were forgotten, including its wartime owner and first Confederate commander, William Allen.

Yet it was in the war's early months that the island was Richmond's key defensive point along the James River, continuing its military tradition under Allen and the leadership of Catesby ap Roger Jones. After Confederates abandoned it in the Peninsula campaign, Union forces recognized Jamestown's importance for guarding their perimeter and, later, as a vital link in their communications. As with the nation, the Civil War became another chapter in Jamestown's long history.

APPENDIX A

JAMESTOWN CIVIL WAR CHRONOLOGY

April 1861

Late in the month Captain William Allen occupied Jamestown Island with the Brandon Artillery, later called the Jamestown Heavy Artillery, for the state of Virginia.

May 2, 1861

Colonel Andrew Talcott, following orders by Major General Robert E. Lee to select the best defensive site on the James River for a gun battery, chose Jamestown Island.

May 3, 1861

Talcott laid out a battery for eighteen guns and departed. Lieutenant Catesby ap Roger Jones of the navy and Captain Edmund Trowbridge Dana Myers of the engineers, who had accompanied Talcott, remained at Jamestown. Jones was placed in charge of the battery. Construction started immediately on an earthwork, called Fort Pocahontas, at the western end of the island.

May 4, 1861

Seventeen members of the Williamsburg Junior Guard arrived in the evening and were ordered back to Williamsburg the following day.

May 5, 1861

Allen's artillery was ordered to remain at Jamestown.

More than 100 slaves from plantations owned by Allen and other Tidewater planters were engaged in constructing Fort Pocahontas.

Commander Matthew Fontaine Maury brought twenty members of the Greensville Guard, under Captain William H. Briggs, and four 32-pounders from Fort Powhatan to Jamestown.

May 6, 1861

The *Raney*, a tug, was assigned to Jamestown to serve as a lookout along the river but was recalled to Richmond in less than a week.

115

May 7, 1861

Major John M. Patton, Jr., was appointed to command and train infantrymen at Jamestown. Simultaneously, Second Lieutenant Emmett M. Morrison was ordered there to instruct the new infantry recruits.

May 8, 1861

By this date the remainder of the Greensville Guard reached Jamestown from Fort Powhatan.

May 10, 1861

The Charles City Southern Guards, under Captain George M. Waddill, were ordered from Fort Powhatan to Jamestown. They soon united with the Greensville Guard and became Waddill's Battalion.

Total garrison strength was about 250 men.

Eight guns had been mounted at Fort Pocahontas, two 9-inch Dahlgrens and six 32-pounders.

May 11, 1861

Talcott returned to Jamestown to inspect progress on the fort.

May 15, 1861

Talcott made his third visit and departed the next day. On this trip he selected another site for a river battery on the south central part of the island. Called the Sand Battery, it was intended to have five guns. Construction was well under way by the first week of June.

Talcott was accompanied on this visit by Lieutenant John M. Brooke, naval aide to Lee, and Captain Archibald Fairfax, ordnance officer at Norfolk Navy Yard. The trio filed a report recommending that Fort Powhatan be abandoned, but they praised the construction of Fort Pocahontas and the plan for additional earthworks at Jamestown. They also recommended that a battery be erected across the river at Swann's Point.

May 16, 1861

Total garrison strength was 214 men.

May 24, 1861

The Hanover Artillery, commanded by Captain William Nelson, arrived at Jamestown.

May 27, 1861

Two of the five Columbiads that had been sent recently were mounted at Fort Pocahontas.

May 29, 1861

The Bedford Light Artillery, commanded by Captain Tyler Calhoun Jordan, and the 14th Virginia Infantry, commanded by Colonel James Gregory Hodges, were sent to Jamestown.

The CSS *Teaser* was assigned to Jamestown and vicinity to assist in transporting troops and supplies between the island and the mainland.

Two more of the five Columbiads were mounted at Fort Pocahontas.

Bridge construction was about to begin, joining Jamestown with the mainland. Within a week, work was well under way.

May 30, 1861

Total garrison strength was 1,000 men.

June 5, 1861

Lee and Talcott visited Jamestown. Their inspection was part of a five-day trip to assure that batteries on the James and York Rivers were in satisfactory condition when transferred from Virginia forces to the Confederate States.

June 6, 1861

Virginia Governor John Letcher wrote a proclamation that transferred the state's land and naval forces to the Confederate States. It was published two days later, and the formal change took place on July 1.

June 11, 1861

Jones's rank was converted from lieutenant in the Virginia navy to lieutenant in the Confederate navy and he remained commander of the batteries. Patton's rank of major remained the same, as did that of other army officers at the island.

Jamestown's armament now included twenty guns: three 9-inch Dahlgrens, nine 8-inch Columbiads, six 32-pounders, and two 12-pounders.

June 12, 1861

Buoys were sent to mark the river channel.

June 17, 1861

On about this date the Cockade Mounted Battery, commanded by Captain Gilbert V. Rambaut, arrived at Jamestown.

June 18, 1861

The CSS *Teaser* was ordered to join in the defense of Jamestown.

At about this time Lieutenant Beverly Kennon started studying the island's topography. Twenty-two naval officers manned the guns and gave instruction to recruits. In addition, Jamestown continued to have an important wharf for supplies and troops destined for the mainland.

Jones was bedridden by illness, an affliction caused by the climate that started earlier in the month and lasted for about four weeks.

July 4, 1861

The eighty-fifth anniversary of Independence Day was celebrated with former President John Tyler as the featured speaker.

July 13, 1861

Brigadier General John B. Magruder inspected Jamestown. Fort Pocahontas and the Sand Battery were operational. Additional earthworks that were completed or under construction included the Square Redoubt which was inland on the south central part of the island, a redan that guarded the bridge and causeway at the north-western end of the island, and a lunette that served as a rifle pit near the bridge. Magruder wanted an additional battery with two guns at Black Point, the island's eastern tip, which became known as Point of Island Battery. He also wanted to move several guns, including two guns from the Square Redoubt to Point of Island Battery, the 8-inch Columbiad at the bridge earthwork to Spratley's farm with replacement by a 6-pounder, and a 32-pounder to Kingsmill.

July 15, 1861

Talcott visited Jamestown to assess Magruder's proposal to construct Point of Island Battery.

July 16, 1861

Lee approved Magruder's proposal to erect Point of Island Battery and to relocate several guns, but the guns were not to be moved until their new defensive positions were completed.

July 21, 1861

Talcott visited Jamestown to examine work on the defenses.

July 24, 1861

Lieutenant Colonel David J. Goodwin and Companies A, D, F, and I of the 14th Virginia Infantry were ordered to Spratley's farm. From mid-June until this time, Jamestown's garrison was at its maximum strength, although the exact figure cannot be ascertained.

Typhoid fever afflicted many troops in July–August.

Patton was promoted to lieutenant colonel, probably during July, left Jamestown, and joined his new regiment, the 21st Virginia Infantry, on July 30.

Jamestown continued its prominent role not only as a fortified point but also as a place of debarkation for troops and supplies for the Peninsula.

August 1, 1861

Waddill's Battalion was transferred from Jamestown to Mulberry Island.

August 2, 1861

Hodges and the remaining six companies of the 14th Virginia departed Jamestown. Later in the month the regiment was reunited at its new assignment, Mulberry Island.

August 11, 1861

Talcott examined Jamestown defenses.

August 16, 1861

Talcott made his final inspection visit at Jamestown and departed the following day.

August 22, 1861

Magruder ordered Jones to construct boats for the batteries at Jamestown and Mulberry Island.

August 26, 1861

Magruder ordered Jones to fill canal boats with granite and sand and to sink them in the channel of the James and Warwick Rivers to impede Union traffic. By early September, Jones had accomplished his mission for the swash channel between Mulberry Point and Harden's Bluff.

September 9, 1861

Jones finished constructing a target for ordnance experiments for the CSS *Merrimack*, later renamed *Virginia*. The tests were completed by September 16 using several different guns and powder charges.

Around mid-September, Jamestown was inspected by Colonel George Washington Custis Lee of President Jefferson Davis's staff.

By mid-September, Jones officially was commander of the entire island.

October 1861

During the first or second week of October, Jones and Lieutenant John M. Brooke tested the strength of iron plating for the CSS *Merrimack* by firing upon it with Jamestown's heavy ordnance. The plate was two inches thick, double the original proposed thickness, and double layered. The plate successfully resisted total penetration.

October 4, 1861

Lieutenant Junius A. de Lagnel was ordered from Jamestown to Mulberry Island to sink canal boats as obstructions in the Warwick River.

October 12, 1861

Jones conducted the second experiment at Jamestown to test the thickness of iron needed for the CSS *Merrimack*. In this test he used railroad T-iron which allowed greater penetration than did the two-inch plate tested earlier.

October 28, 1861

Construction began on small lumber houses which served as winter quarters.

The Hanover Artillery was transferred from Jamestown to Yorktown earlier in the month and took its place there by the end of October.

November 6, 1861

Jones was ordered to the Navy Department in Richmond, where he reported three days later. He was assigned to the CSS *Merrimack*.

November–December 1861

Major John Redman Coxe Lewis became the new commander at Jamestown. In December, he temporarily reorganized the artillery into Lewis's Battalion of three companies: Company A, the Bedford Light Artillery; Company B, the Jamestown Artillery; and Company C, the Cockade Mounted Battery.

December 12, 1861

The 52d Virginia Militia, commanded by Colonel Hill Carter and consisting of only two consolidated companies, reported to Jamestown.

With Carter's arrival, Jamestown resumed a dual command system: Carter commanded the infantry, and Lewis commanded the artillery.

December 1861

In mid-December, Lieutenant Charles T. Mason, an engineer officer, was assigned to Jamestown to improve the earthworks and repair the road. Work continued through the winter.

January 19, 1862

Carter protested Magruder's proposal to transfer guns from Jamestown to Mulberry Island.

January 31, 1862

Total garrison strength was 323 men with twenty pieces of heavy artillery.

February 15, 1862

Allen wrote to the secretary of war and requested permission to raise a battalion of heavy artillery. The request was granted.

February 20, 1862

Frustrated by the government's inability to furnish heavy guns for Yorktown and lower forts on the James River, Magruder proposed transferring artillery from Jamestown to Mulberry Island and Harden's Bluff.

February 23, 1862

Captain John R. Tucker, commander of the James River Squadron, endorsed Brigadier General Raleigh Colston's recommendation for obstructions in the James River, but he rejected the general's suggestion that Jamestown was a suitable location for them.

February 28, 1862

Total garrison strength was 169 men with fifteen pieces of heavy artillery and four pieces of field artillery. The latter guns were for the Bedford Light Artillery and their imminent transfer.

March 12, 1862

Following the duel at Hampton Roads between the ironclads USS *Monitor* and CSS *Virginia*, the Engineer Bureau sent President Davis an assessment of the James River and Richmond defenses. Magruder simultaneously was strengthening defenses on the Peninsula, including Jamestown, with slave labor gathered from neighboring plantations. Confederate engineers regarded the defenses as "rapidly improving" and "good protection against wooden fleets" but not against ironclads. They recommended that heavy guns be used in conjunction with obstructions in the river, possibly even torpedoes. Fear of the *Monitor* was such that Davis considered moving Jamestown's guns to Fort Huger in hopes of containing the ironclad farther from Richmond.

March 17, 1862

Major General George B. McClellan started transporting troops to the Virginia Peninsula for an advance toward Richmond.

March 18, 1862

Davis authorized Magruder to extend martial law to James City County, thereby solidifying military control of all activities near Jamestown.

Carter's 52d Virginia Militia, which had lost additional men by transfer to other units, merged again, this time from two companies to one. The company was called Charles Carter's Consolidated Company, with Hill Carter still colonel of the militia.

March 20, 1862

Magruder wrote Lee about his concern that the *Monitor* and Union troops would ascend the James, capture Jamestown, and make his flank vulnerable. He reiterated the proposal that the river be obstructed, this time advocating that it be blocked as far as Jamestown. From Jamestown upward the river needed to remain open for supply ships, with Jamestown Island as the receiving station.

March 28, 1862

Total garrison strength was 520 men: about 400 were heavy artillery, about 100 were field artillery, and about 20 were militia.

Magruder issued General Orders No. 168, which stated, "The enemy is at length advancing. We shall fight him on the line of Warwick River."

April 4, 1862

McClellan's army marched from Fort Monroe, beginning his advance up the Peninsula.

As a result of his winter recruiting efforts, Allen organized the 10th Battalion Virginia Heavy Artillery which consisted of five companies and increased the island's strength. The five companies were Company A, the Metropolitan Guard; Company B, Captain James O. Hensley's Company; Company C, the Allen Artillery; Company D, the Jamestown Heavy Artillery, formerly the Brandon Artillery; and Company E, Captain Thomas Ballard Blake's Company. Allen was elected major of the battalion.

Carter was alerted that Jamestown Island was one of two points designated to receive the Peninsula army's sick soldiers for transport by boat to Richmond.

April 5, 1862

McClellan encountered the Confederates' primary defense line, the Warwick Line, and elected to take the main position at Yorktown by siege.

April 6, 1862

Lewis reported supply shortages, including ammunition, which were commonplace at Jamestown.

April 7, 1862

The first units of General Joseph E. Johnston's army reached Yorktown, with the remainder following in subsequent days.

There was demoralization in the Cockade Mounted Battery caused by competitive recruiting between two of the unit's lieutenants who were attempting to raise new companies.

April 8, 1862

Lee wrote Magruder to clarify Carter's misunderstanding of orders that the 52d Virginia Militia should leave Jamestown. Lee repeated his intention to defend Williamsburg and batteries along the James and York Rivers.

April 11, 1862

Total garrison strength was 750 men.

April 16, 1862

The Bedford Light Artillery departed Jamestown for the Yorktown defenses.

April 28, 1862

Captain Thomas Jefferson Page, Jr., requested that the thirty-two surplus men in the Jamestown Heavy Artillery be transferred to the Magruder Light Artillery at Yorktown.

April 30, 1862

Total garrison strength was 530 men: 500 artillery, 30 militia.

May 2, 1862

Having decided to evacuate the middle Peninsula, Johnston ordered the James River Squadron to offer assistance to the Jamestown garrison in transporting its troops and artillery to Richmond. Johnston estimated the garrison strength as 500 to 600 men.

May 3, 1862

In conjunction with Johnston's withdrawal from Yorktown, the Confederates abandoned Jamestown by river during the night. The order to evacuate came suddenly, and there was inadequate transportation. Allen used his personal vessels to assist in the operation. Only nine guns were withdrawn in the haste and confusion, three 9-inch Dahlgrens and six 32-pounders. The garrison retreated to Richmond.

May 6, 1862

Following the previous day's battle at Williamsburg, Union cavalry made a hasty inspection of the abandoned Confederate position at Jamestown.

May 8, 1862

Union cavalry returned to Jamestown around noon and spent the day observing river traffic, including the passage of three Confederate vessels.

May 10, 1862

At 4 P.M. several Union vessels anchored off Jamestown. The USS *Galena* quickly checked the deserted batteries.

May 11, 1862

Around 6 A.M. a cutter from the *Galena* explored the island and discovered all five Confederate batteries.

May 12, 1862

The USS *Monitor*, accompanied by the *Naugatuck*, ascended the James River and joined the *Galena*, *Port Royal*, and *Aroostook* at noon near the Jamestown church tower. From here they continued to Drewry's Bluff, where they were defeated on May 15.

May 16, 1862

The USS *Port Royal* was the first Union vessel to return to Jamestown from Drewry's Bluff, arriving around 10 P.M.

May 17, 1862

Thirteen of the *Galena's* crew members who were killed at Drewry's Bluff were buried on the shore of Jamestown. Secretary of State William H. Seward sailed to Jamestown and conferred with naval officers there, as did William Faxon, chief clerk of the Navy Department.

May 20, 1862

Union gunboats started patrolling the James River to monitor Confederate activity. As McClellan's army advanced up the Peninsula, Jamestown became the point behind Federal lines where the army and navy communicated.

June 10–12, 14, 1862

The USS *Aroostook* destroyed guns, ordnance stores, quarters, and equipment abandoned at Jamestown by the Confederates.

Mid-June 1862

By this time Jamestown was a rendezvous point for blacks who escaped from slavery as the Union army occupied the Peninsula.

June 25–July 1, 1862

During the Seven Days' battles, the Union transports were anchored at Jamestown, where they remained for weeks. The USS *Jacob Bell* guarded the island.

July 5, 1862

On about this date, telegraph lines were completed between Jamestown and Williamsburg, which were linked with Fort Monroe and Washington. The navy carried messages between Jamestown and McClellan by boat, thereby enabling him to communicate with Washington three times daily instead of the former rate of once per day.

Mid-August 1862

With the Union transport fleet still anchored off Jamestown, Commander Maxwell Woodhull of the USS *Cimarron* was sent mortar boats to protect the fleet and to compensate for the *Jacob Bell's* reassignment to the Chickahominy.

August 13, 1862

McClellan visited Jamestown to communicate directly with General-in-Chief Henry W. Halleck about his withdrawal from the Peninsula, but the telegraph was out of order.

August 16, 1862

The Union transport fleet was ordered to depart Jamestown for Fort Monroe, where it was to meet McClellan's army and ferry it north.

August 28, 1862

After patrolling the James and assisting black refugees, the Union navy fell back as far as Jamestown, then continued to Newport News which became its most advanced position.

September–October 1862

After Union forces evacuated Jamestown, Allen's former slaves burned the Ambler house.

October 20, 1862

Three civilians from Surry County were murdered at Jamestown by Allen's former slaves and a fourth man was severely wounded. The fatalities were Jacob M. Shriver, who lived at Claremont and was an uncle of Allen's wife, Joseph A. Graves, owner of Four Mile Tree and Surry County commonwealth attorney, and George Graves, nephew of Joseph Graves. Gilbert Wooten, a free black, was wounded but escaped back to Surry County.

Autumn 1862–Spring 1863

Union vessels continued to patrol the James River.

April 11, 1863

Brigadier General Henry A. Wise launched a diversionary attack upon the Union garrison at Williamsburg as part of the Suffolk campaign. Major General Erasmus D. Keyes feared that the Confederates might have crossed onto the Peninsula at Jamestown and requested a naval reconnaissance. However, Acting Rear Admiral Samuel P. Lee received word from other vessels that Jamestown was not occupied.

June 10–14, 1863

Jamestown was the staging area for Union infantrymen under Brigadier General George H. Gordon. The navy transported them to the Chickahominy as a feint against Richmond during the Gettysburg campaign.

August 1863

The 1st New York Mounted Rifles, which was garrisoned at Williamsburg, assigned a company to Jamestown to serve as an outpost. Union troops, usually a company of cavalry, routinely were rotated at Jamestown with this duty for most of the war's remainder.

May 1864

To coincide with Major General Benjamin F. Butler's Bermuda Hundred campaign, a telegraph station was established in Fort

Pocahontas at Jamestown to link Butler with Fort Monroe and Washington. The navy carried messages between Jamestown and Butler's army. Lieutenant General Ulysses S. Grant, who simultaneously drove southward with the Army of the Potomac, quickly expanded telegraph communications between the armies in Virginia.

May 1, 1864

Members of the 1st U.S. Colored Cavalry were assigned to Jamestown for nearly two months under Lieutenant Charles H. Libean.

June 4, 1864

A Union steam tug that was fired upon by Confederates down river stopped at Jamestown to report the incident. The tug's name was the *Mayflower*.

June 15, 1864

Medical officers and equipment bound for Grant's army rendezvoused at Jamestown to await orders which arrived later that day. The physicians were ordered to City Point, which soon became Grant's headquarters for the Petersburg campaign.

June 24, 1864

After two weeks of Union construction and disruptive action by guerrillas, telegraph communications became fully operational that linked Grant, Meade, and Butler with Washington, D.C. The line at Jamestown was extended under the James River to Swann's Point. From there it continued to Fort Powhatan and City Point, where it was linked with Union armies in the field.

June 26, 1864

Private Griffin Oatman of Company C, 1st New York Mounted Rifles, became the only Union fatality at Jamestown when he accidentally drowned in the river while on duty during a storm that night.

July 5, 1864

Grant ordered patrols between Jamestown and Fort Powhatan to prevent interruptions in telegraph service by guerrillas who continued to menace the lines.

July 1864

When Union patrols proved unable to protect telegraph lines, the Federals ran twenty-two miles of cable under the James River from Jamestown to Fort Powhatan, thereby providing communications both by land and by water.

August 1864

T. N. Loucks replaced W. N. Embree as telegraph operator at Jamestown.

September 3, 1864

Three members of the 20th New York Cavalry escorted an ambulance that was sent from Williamsburg to Jamestown to pick up soldiers who were ill on the island. Guerrillas ambushed the party near Jamestown. One Union soldier, a corporal, was killed; two privates, one of whom was wounded, were captured. The ambulance escaped and returned to Williamsburg.

September 21, 1864

Concerned that the Confederates might be placing torpedoes in the river, a Union gunboat searched the James from the Chickahominy to Jamestown. In addition, the *Hunchback* was directed to examine the island's swash channel on a daily basis.

October 15–16, 1864

The 85th Pennsylvania Infantry spent the night of October 15–16 at Jamestown after being relieved of duty in the Petersburg lines because terms of enlistment had expired.

October 16–18, 1864

Annoyed by guerrillas who continued to cut telegraph wires between Fort Powhatan and Jamestown, Grant sent the 6th Ohio Cavalry to drive them out.

October–November 1864

Veterans of the 76th Pennsylvania Infantry, a Zouave unit, spent about six weeks at Jamestown after being relieved of duty at Petersburg when their terms of enlistment expired.

December 4, 1864

Rear Admiral David Dixon Porter issued instructions for keeping the James River open to river traffic whenever ice formed, an order which paid dividends a few weeks later when cold temperatures settled in.

December 6, 1864

Brigadier General Charles Graham was aboard a boat that ran aground at Jamestown. While there, he telegraphed word on guerrilla action down river, which resulted in an expedition from Fort Monroe.

December 1864–January 1865

Senior members of the 100th New York Infantry under Captain Frank C. Brunck were assigned to Jamestown. They were awaiting transportation north because their terms of enlistment had expired.

February 1865

A contingent of the 16th New York Heavy Artillery was assigned to Jamestown instead of the customary cavalry unit.

February 16–17, 1865

Second Lieutenant Carlo Blomberg, temporary commander of the 16th New York Heavy Artillerymen at Jamestown, reported enemy activity around the island. Shortly thereafter, two companies of U.S. Colored Cavalry were sent to assist at Fort Magruder and vicinity.

February 21, 1865

Confederates cut the telegraph wire between Jamestown and Fort Magruder. The fort's acting commander, Major Julius C. Hicks, requested authorization to exercise Order No. 196 which permitted the army to burn all houses in the vicinity of subversive acts.

March 27, 1865

Grant's headquarters received Brevet Brigadier General Benjamin C. Ludlow's recommendation for changing the route of the telegraph wires from Jamestown to Fort Magruder. Ludlow's route offered greater security but apparently was not adopted because the war in Virginia ended two weeks later.

April 11, 1865

Two days after Lee's surrender at Appomattox, the Union navy selected strategic points to regulate river traffic. One vessel was assigned to Swann's Point, directly across the river from Jamestown.

May 1865

Jamestown was a location where the Oath of Allegiance to the United States was administered to former Confederates by members of the 20th New York Cavalry.

APPENDIX B

CONFEDERATE COMMANDERS AT JAMESTOWN

Captain William Allen	April–May 2, 1861
Lieutenant Catesby ap Roger Jones	May 2–May 7, 1861
Lieutenant Catesby ap Roger Jones*	May 7–August 1861
Major John M. Patton, Jr.**	May 7–ca. June 20, 1861
Colonel James Gregory Hodges**	June 20–August 2, 1861
Lieutenant Catesby ap Roger Jones	August–November 6, 1861
Major John Redman Coxe Lewis	November–December 1861
Major John Redman Coxe Lewis*	December 12, 1861–May 3, 1862
Colonel Hill Carter**	December 12, 1861–May 3, 1862

* Commanded artillery batteries only
** Commanded infantry only

    Captain William Allen occupied Jamestown for the state of Virginia with his Brandon Artillery, later called the Jamestown Heavy Artillery, in April 1861. He thereby became the first commander of the island.

    On May 2, Lieutenant Catesby ap Roger Jones, a Virginia naval officer, arrived at Jamestown and succeeded Allen. Five days later Major John M. Patton, Jr. was ordered to the island to command and train infantry there. This established a dual command system whereby Jones had charge of artillerymen at the batteries while Patton commanded the infantry which consisted of Waddill's Battalion. The 14th Virginia Infantry, which arrived a few weeks later, was led by Colonel James Gregory Hodges who outranked Patton and operated independently. During his last six weeks at Jamestown, Hodges commanded all infantry. When Virginia forces were transferred from the commonwealth to the Confederate States, Jones retained the rank of lieutenant, effective June 11. Patton was promoted to lieutenant colonel of the 21st Virginia Infantry, left Jamestown, and joined his new unit on July 30. The remainder of Jamestown's infantrymen also left within a few more days, restoring Jones to command of the entire island, a fact which he noted was official by at least mid-September.

The final change in the command structure at Jamestown was started on November 6 when Jones was ordered to the Navy Department in Richmond. He reported there three days later. Major John Redman Coxe Lewis, who first arrived at Jamestown with the navy in June, was Jones's successor. The dual command system was reinstated upon the arrival of Colonel Hill Carter and his 52d Virginia Militia on December 12. From that time until the Confederates evacuated the island on May 3, 1862, Lewis commanded the artillery and Carter led the infantry.

Name:	**Brandon Artillery**
	(Jamestown Heavy Artillery)
	Company E, 1st Regiment Virginia Artillery
Commander:	Captain William Allen
Date Arrived:	Late April 1861
Date Departed:	Night of May 3, 1862
Location:	Fort Pocahontas
Guns:	9-inch Dahlgrens, 8-inch Columbiads, 32-pounders
Notes:	Organized in April 1861; enlisted May 10, 1861. Served briefly as Co. B of Major John Redman Coxe Lewis's Battalion of Artillery when the three companies at Jamestown were reorganized in December 1861. Reorganized March 25, 1862 under Captain Charles S. Harrison and subsequently assigned as Co. D to 10th Battalion Virginia Heavy Artillery on April 4, 1862. See "10th Battalion Virginia Heavy Artillery," p. 135.
Name:	**Williamsburg Junior Guard**
	Company C, 32d Virginia Infantry
Commander:	Captain John A. Henley
Date Arrived:	May 4, 1861
Date Departed:	May 5, 1861
Location:	Did not remain at Jamestown long enough to establish a position.
Arms:	Unknown; presumably muskets
Notes:	It is unknown whether or not Henley was at Jamestown since only seventeen members of the company reported for duty there.

131

Name: **Greensville Guard**
Commander: Captain William H. Briggs
Date Arrived: May 5–[8?], 1861
Date Departed: August 1, 1861
Location: Western end of island, including Fort Pocahontas
Arms: Enfield muskets and flintlock muskets upon arrival; possibly altered percussion muskets were added in mid-May.
Notes: The Greensville Guard transferred from Fort Powhatan in two contingents: the first reached Jamestown on the evening of May 5, and the remainder of the unit was present by May 8. Total strength upon arrival was eighty-five men. The company united with the Charles City Southern Guards to form Waddill's Battalion soon after its arrival at Jamestown; the Greensville Guard became Company B. When the battalion left Jamestown it reported to Mulberry Island. See "Waddill's Battalion," below.

Name: **Charles City Southern Guards**
Commander: Captain George M. Waddill
Date Arrived: May 10, 1861
Date Departed: August 1, 1861
Location: Western end of island, including Fort Pocahontas
Arms: Probably Enfield muskets, flintlock muskets, and altered percussion muskets
Notes: The Charles City Southern Guards transferred from Fort Powhatan. The company united with the Greensville Guard to form Waddill's Battalion soon after its arrival at Jamestown; the Charles City Southern Guards became Company A. When the battalion left Jamestown it reported to Mulberry Island. See "Waddill's Battalion," below.

Name: **Waddill's Battalion**
Commander: Captain George M. Waddill
Date Arrived: May 5–10, 1861
Date Departed: August 1, 1861
Location: Western end of island, including Fort Pocahontas
Arms: Enfield muskets, flintlock muskets, and probably altered percussion muskets

Notes: Formed by merger of two companies, the Greensville Guard (which became Company B) and the Charles City Southern Guards (which became Company A); both companies transferred from Fort Powhatan to Jamestown as separate units. When the battalion left Jamestown it reported to Mulberry Island. See "Greensville Guard" and "Charles City Southern Guards," p. 132.

Name: **Hanover Artillery**
Commander: Captain William Nelson
Date Arrived: May 24, 1861
Date Departed: Apparently early October 1861
Location: Camped on Neck of Land and drilled at Fort Pocahontas during their first week at Jamestown; quartered on the island thereafter. Later served at a water battery along the river front, probably the Sand Battery.
Guns: Probably four 8-inch Columbiads or four 32-pounders
Notes: The battery left Jamestown for reassignment in the Yorktown defenses.

Name: **Bedford Light Artillery**
Commander: Captain Tyler Calhoun Jordan
Date Arrived: May 29, 1861
Date Departed: April 15, 1862
Location: Initial training was at Fort Pocahontas. Another possible site for service was at Point of Island Battery. It also is possible that a contingent of this battery served the gun that guarded the bridge, especially since then Brigadier General John B. Magruder recommended replacing the 8-inch Columbiad there with a lighter gun. The bridge assignment would be appropriate for a battery like the Bedford unit which desired service in the field with light artillery.
Guns: Initially served heavy artillery. During February 1862 the battery received four pieces of field artillery and began training for action as a light artillery unit.
Notes: Served briefly as Company A of Major John Redman Coxe Lewis's Battalion of Artillery when the three companies at Jamestown were reorganized in December 1861. Transferred to the Yorktown defenses.

Name:	**14th Virginia Infantry Regiment**
Commander:	Colonel James Gregory Hodges
Date Arrived:	May 29, 1861
Date Departed:	Companies A, D, F, and I were ordered to Spratley's farm on July 24, 1861; the remainder of the regiment left for the lower Peninsula on August 2, 1861.
Location:	Camp Allen, near the Square Redoubt
Arms:	Unknown; presumably muskets
Notes:	After its piecemeal departure from Jamestown, the regiment was reunited at Mulberry Island in late August 1861.

Name:	**Cockade Mounted Battery** (Rambaut's Company Virginia Heavy Artillery)
Commander:	Captain Gilbert V. Rambaut
Date Arrived:	About June 17, 1861
Date Departed:	Night of May 3, 1862
Location:	Probably served at the Square Redoubt
Guns:	Apparently four guns of heavy artillery; at least two guns probably were 32-pounders
Notes:	Served briefly as Company C of Major John Redman Coxe Lewis's Battalion of Artillery when the three companies at Jamestown were reorganized in December 1861. Retreated to Richmond upon departure.

Name:	**52d Virginia Militia**
Commander:	Colonel Hill Carter
Date Arrived:	December 12, 1861
Date Departed:	May 3, 1862
Location:	Apparently on western end of island
Arms:	Muskets
Notes:	Due to reduction in size by the time the unit was assigned to Jamestown, the militia was consolidated from four companies to two, Companies A and B. Transfers from the militia during the winter depleted its numbers further, and on March 18, 1862, the two companies were consolidated into one and designated as Charles Carter's Consolidated Company, with Hill Carter remaining as commander and colonel. After the evacuation of Jamestown, the unit apparently disbanded.

Name: **10th Battalion Virginia Heavy Artillery**
(Allen's Battalion Virginia Heavy Artillery)
Commander: Major William Allen
Date Arrived: April 4, 1862
Date Departed: Night of May 3, 1862
Location: Fort Pocahontas; it is possible that some companies were assigned to other earthworks.
Guns: 9-inch Dahlgrens, 8-inch Columbiads, 32-pounders
Notes: The Brandon Artillery (above) was reorganized and became Company D of this battalion; the Brandon Artillery's commander, Captain William Allen, raised the 10th Battalion and was promoted to major as its commander. The five companies which composed the 10th Battalion were Company A (Metropolitan Guards), Company B (Captain James O. Hensley's Company), Company C (Allen Artillery), Company D (Jamestown Heavy Artillery), and Company E (Captain Thomas Ballard Blake's Company). Retreated to Richmond upon departure.

DATES CONFEDERATE UNITS SERVED AT JAMESTOWN

1861

April	BA/JHA						
May	BA/JHA	WJG	WB	HA	BLA	14VI	
June	BA/JHA		WB	HA	BLA	14VI	CMB
July	BA/JHA		WB	HA	BLA	14VI	CMB
August	BA/JHA		WB	HA	BLA	14VI	CMB
September	BA/JHA			HA	BLA		CMB
October	BA/JHA			HA	BLA		CMB
November	BA/JHA				BLA		CMB
December	BA/JHA				BLA		CMB	52VM

1862

January	BA/JHA	BLA	CMB	52VM
February	BA/JHA	BLA	CMB	52VM
March	BA/JHA	BLA	CMB	52VM
April	10BVHA	BLA	CMB	52VM
May	10BVHA		CMB	52VM

Key:

BA/JHA	Brandon Artillery, later Jamestown Heavy Artillery
10BVHA	10th Battalion Virginia Heavy Artillery
WJG	Williamsburg Junior Guard
WB	Waddill's Battalion
HA	Hanover Artillery
BLA	Bedford Light Artillery
14VI	14th Virginia Infantry
CMB	Cockade Mounted Battery
52VM	52d Virginia Militia

APPENDIX E

CONFEDERATE STRENGTH AT JAMESTOWN

May 10, 1861	250
May 16, 1861	214
May 30, 1861	1000
ca. June 17–July 24, 1861	[1200+]
January 31, 1862	323
February 28, 1862	169
March 28, 1862	520
April 11, 1862	750
April 30, 1862	520
May 2, 1862	500–600

Lieutenant Catesby ap Roger Jones reported the garrison's strength twice in early May 1861 when he had only one artillery battery and one infantry unit present. Most of the units that served at Jamestown were present by the time of his final reference to troop strength late in May. Jamestown was at its maximum strength from about June 17, when the Cockade Mounted Battery arrived, until July 24, when four companies of the 14th Virginia departed. No official compilations can be found for this period, so the total of 1,200 men is an estimate. This figure is conservative because Civil War military units usually were well below the optimum strength. One unreliable postwar account estimates Jamestown's garrison as being "at least 2,500 men" which far exceeds normal figures for units of the type and number at Jamestown, and official reports are never in this range.

Official reports for January and February 1862 reflect the transfer of two infantry units to Mulberry Island and one artillery battery to Yorktown. By late March and early April the totals had risen again because of Major William Allen's recruiting effort which transformed his artillery battery into an entire battalion. The report for March 28 specifies that, of 520 men, about 400 were heavy artillery, about 100 were field artillery, and about twenty were militia. The slight decline

137

at the end of April reflects the transfer of yet another artillery battery to Yorktown. Tabulations at that time for artillery and infantry are comparable to those in March with 500 artillery and thirty militia. The final figure in May is misleading since it was recorded immediately after the April tally. Reported on the eve of the evacuation, it is the estimate of General Joseph E. Johnston and is not an official count.

APPENDIX F

CONFEDERATE ARTILLERY AT JAMESTOWN

Artillery Totals and Types for the Entire Island

Date	Total	9-inch Dahlgren	8-inch Columbiad	32-pdr. Navy	12-pdr. Army
May 5, 1861	4	-	-	4	-
May 10, 1861	8	2	-	6	-
June 10, 1861	20	3	9	6	2
January 31, 1862	20	(no gun types cited)			
February 28, 1862	19	(15 heavy, 4 field)			

These statistics are based on official reports and correspondence. The earliest figure is for guns acquired by Lieutenant Catesby ap Roger Jones shortly after he assumed command. No official totals were reported during the final two months of Confederate occupation.

Adjustments for the Entire Island

Date	Adjustment
July 24, 1861	8-inch transferred from Jamestown
Post-July 1861	2 32-pounders transferred from Jamestown
March 12, 1862	2 8-inch en route to Jamestown

Brigadier General John B. Magruder recommended transfers after his inspection in July 1861. He also suggested that the 8-inch gun guarding the bridge should be replaced by a 6-pounder. However, there is no evidence that a gun of this latter size was assigned to Jamestown after the 8-inch was removed on July 24. Two 8-inch guns were reported en route to Jamestown in the Engineer Bureau's report to President Jefferson Davis, but there is no confirmation of their arrival.

Fort Pocahontas Totals

Date	Total	9-inch Dahlgren	8-inch Columbiad	32-pdr. Navy	12-pdr. Army
May 5, 1861	4	-	-	4	-
May 10, 1861	8	2	-	6	-
May 29, 1861	12	2	4	6	-
March 12, 1862	13	4	4	5	-

Statistics for May 1861 are based on Jones's correspondence. Fort Pocahontas was the main battery at Jamestown and probably received some of the additional guns which reached the island by early June. Totals for March 1862 are based on the Engineer Bureau's report to Davis and a visit to Jamestown by Corporal Randolph H. McKim.

Artillery Evacuated by the Confederates

Date	Total	9-inch Dahlgren	8-inch Columbiad	32-pdr. Navy	12-pdr. Army
May 3, 1862	9	3	-	6	-

Jamestown was evacuated with such short notice that these figures represent only part of the Confederate artillery. It is probable that these guns came mainly from Fort Pocahontas since the gun types closely match the March 1862 figures for that fort. Furthermore, Fort Pocahontas was the earthwork with easiest access to the wharf. Since the evacuation was a hasty, nighttime movement by boat, both the fort's prominence and its proximity to the wharf made it the likely choice for immediate attention. When the USS *Galena* examined the batteries on May 11, 1862, it reported one battery with four 8-inch Columbiads, all spiked. This perhaps was the Sand Battery, which was intended to have five guns of this type but apparently never exceeded a total of four.

Artillery Destroyed by the Union at Jamestown and Vicinity

Date	Total	9-inch Dahlgren	8-inch Columbiad	32-pdr. Navy	12-pdr. Army
June 10–14, 1862	13	-	9	4	-

These figures provided by the Union navy do not tell exactly what guns were at Jamestown in addition to those evacuated by the Confederates. Since this count includes guns in the vicinity of Jamestown as well as those at the island itself, one can only speculate.

Artillery for the Jamestown Forts

Fort	Proposed Number of Guns	Actual Known Number of Guns
Fort Pocahontas	18	13+?
Sand Battery	5	4?
Square Redoubt	4?	4, 2, 0?
Bridge Redan	1?	1, 0?
Point of Island Battery	2	2?

The proposed number of guns is known for three of Jamestown's forts: Fort Pocahontas (eighteen), the Sand Battery (five), and Point of Island Battery (two), for a total of twenty-five guns. Because Magruder proposed moving two of the four guns from the Square Redoubt, it is known that at least that number existed at one time. Likewise, his removal of one gun from the fort guarding the bridge documents its presence and brings the Confederate total number of proposed guns to a minimum of thirty.

In contrast, the known maximum number of guns at Jamestown was twenty. Fort Pocahontas had at least thirteen, as documented by the Engineer Bureau and McKim in March 1862. It is possible that it had even more guns in early June 1861 when it is documented that the island had twenty guns and it is questionable that the other batteries were operational. There had to be a redistribution of guns after Magruder's July 1861 changes, and still others after departures of the Hanover Artillery in October 1861 and the Bedford Light Artillery in April 1862. Note that Fort Pocahontas has four 8-inch Columbiads for the two latter dates in the table showing its artillery types, and that the table showing artillery totals lists nine 8-inch Columbiads on the entire island on June 10, 1861. Jones had five Columbiads by May 29, four of which were mounted at Fort Pocahontas. If the fifth gun went to the bridge redan which had at least one Columbiad by July, then that leaves four for the Sand Battery, which is the figure generally associated with that earthwork.

The Confederates constructed five earthworks which served as forts for artillery and a sixth work for infantry. Another earthwork was started in April 1861 by Captain William Allen, but it either was abandoned when engineers began work that May or it was converted into what became known as Fort Pocahontas.

Shapes and measurements for the earthworks were acquired from the forts themselves when sufficient physical evidence survived. Maps and drawings also provided data. At the time of this book's publication, only two earthworks were accessible to the public, Fort Pocahontas and the Square Redoubt.

Name: None
Location: Presumably western end of island
Type/Shape: No description
Construction Date: April 1861
Designed By: Presumably Captain William Allen
Requested By: Captain William Allen
Artillery: None; Allen's battery had not obtained its guns yet
Unit(s) Served There: Brandon Artillery, later called Jamestown Heavy Artillery
Notes: Allen already had started constructing an earthwork when Colonel Andrew Talcott arrived on May 2, 1861, to lay out a fort. There is no data for this structure.

Name: Fort Pocahontas
Location: Western end of island, west of and adjacent to the seventeenth-century church tower, and facing the James River
Type/Shape: Five-sided

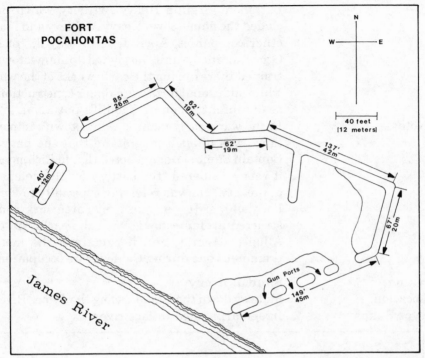

Map by Blake A. Magner

Construction Date:	May 1861 (starting date about May 3, 1861)
Designed By:	Colonel Andrew Talcott, May 3, 1861
Requested By:	Major General Robert E. Lee
Artillery:	Eighteen guns intended, but this total probably never was obtained. Lieutenant Catesby ap Roger Jones acquired four 32-pounders by May 5 and raised his total to eight by May 10 with two 9-inch Dahlgrens and six 32-pounders. By May 29 he had mounted four more guns, all 8-inch Columbiads. The Engineer Bureau reported thirteen guns at Fort Pocahontas on March 12, 1862, consisting of four 9-inch Dahlgrens, four 8-inch Columbiads, and five 32-pounders. The fort might have had its greatest number of guns in late May or early June 1861 when there were twenty guns at Jamestown and construction was not as advanced at other forts.
Unit(s) Served There:	Brandon Artillery, later called the Jamestown Heavy Artillery, April 1861–April 4, 1862; 10th

Battalion Virginia Heavy Artillery, which included the Jamestown Heavy Artillery and four other companies, April 4, 1862–May 3, 1862. Other artillery units assigned to Jamestown trained there during the early weeks of the war while additional forts were under construction, as did infantrymen in Waddill's Battalion.

Notes: In the war's early months, Jamestown's importance was of such magnitude that the navy's Captain Samuel Barron noted that in Richmond it was considered "the battery for the defense of the city." He was referring especially to Fort Pocahontas. It was the first earthwork constructed at Jamestown, with the exclusion of Allen's attempt, and it remained the most prominent one during Confederate occupation.

Name: **Sand Battery**
Location: Midway down the island, facing the James River
Type/Shape: Irregular; angled to face river

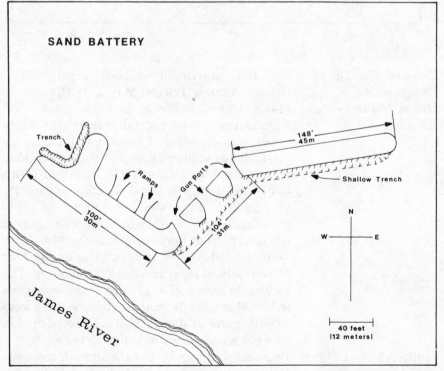

Map by Blake A. Magner

Construction Date: May–June 1861

Designed By: Colonel Andrew Talcott, May 15–16, 1861

Requested By: Unknown; possibly Major General Robert E. Lee

Artillery: Five 8-inch Columbiads were intended, but actual guns uncertain; it is probable that four Columbiads were used there.

Unit(s) Served There: It is possible that the Hanover Artillery occupied this fort prior to its transfer from Jamestown in October 1861. Private Henry R. Berkeley later wrote that the Hanoverians were along the waterfront with four 64-pounders. Perhaps he meant to say four 8-inch Columbiads, which fired 65-pound ammunition, or four 32-pounders, which fired 64-pound ammunition. After Jamestown was abandoned, it was examined on May 11, 1862, by crewmen of the USS *Galena*. They reported one battery as having four 8-inch Columbiads, all spiked. Since the Sand Battery was not near the wharf, it is probable that its guns were left behind in the hasty withdrawal. Furthermore, this gun total matches Berkeley's, so the *Galena's* crewmen probably were describing the Sand Battery.

Notes: In July 1861 Lee wrote that this, the second permanent fort constructed at Jamestown, initially was preferred over any site farther down river. This, he said, was to prevent spreading the Confederate position over so wide an area that it would be indefensible. The fort's name came from the nature of the terrain where it was located.

Name: **Square Redoubt**

Location: Inland, in the south central part of the island guarding the road and Passmore Creek

Type/Shape: Redoubt; slightly rectangular, despite its name. Except for its rectangular shape, it matches the design for a square redoubt as described in Mahan, *Treatise on Field Fortification*, 161–63.

Construction Date: June 1861

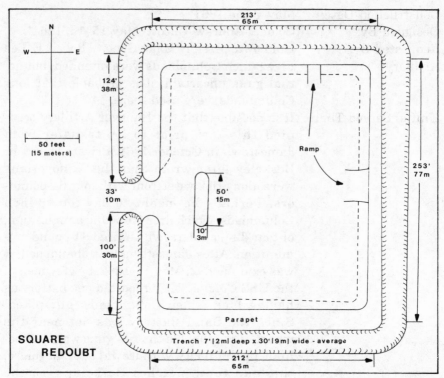

Map by Blake A. Magner

Designed By:	Probably Captain Edmund Trowbridge Dana Myers
Requested By:	Unknown
Artillery:	Four heavy guns by July 1861. At least two guns were 32-pounders and were transferred to Point of Island Battery after July 1861.
Unit(s) Served There:	Probably the Cockade Mounted Battery, which was quartered at nearby Camp Allen.
Notes:	Due to its interior location, it is possible that the Confederates placed less emphasis upon this site during periods when troop strength was reduced. General Magruder was among those who referred to this fort as the "square redoubt." A soldier in the 14th Virginia Infantry who helped construct the earthwork described it as a bank of dirt about six feet high surrounded by a ditch that was about fifteen feet wide and eight feet deep. He also said that there were four cannon on the walls facing in each direction.

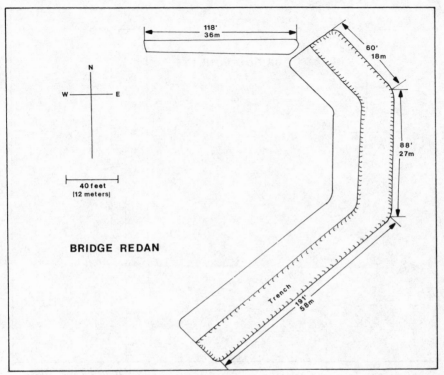

BRIDGE REDAN

Map by Blake A. Magner

Name:	**Unknown;** referred to as the bridge redan for identification purposes in this volume
Location:	Guarding bridge and causeway on Back River
Type/Shape:	Redan; apparently three-sided with each side approximately at ninety-degree angles to one another with the rear open. Archeological excavation located the third side.
Construction Date:	Probably June 1861; functional by July 1861
Designed By:	Probably Captain Edmund Trowbridge Dana Myers
Requested By:	Unknown
Artillery:	One 8-inch Columbiad which was transferred to Spratley's farm, July 1861. A 6-pounder was recommended as a replacement, but there is no evidence of a gun of this type being at Jamestown.
Unit(s) Served There:	This was a possible location for a contingent of the Bedford Light Artillery, which aspired to action in the field with light artillery.

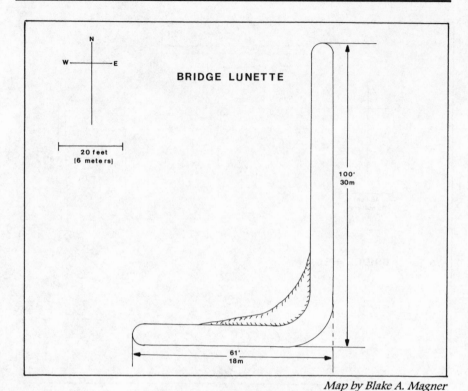

Map by Blake A. Magner

Notes:	It is possible that militia also was assigned there to oppose an attack by land as well as by water.
Name:	**Unknown;** referred to as the bridge lunette for identification purposes in this volume
Location:	Guarded bridge and causeway on Back River
Type/Shape:	Lunette; was rifle pit, not designed for artillery
Construction Date:	Probably June 1861; functional by July 1861
Designed By:	Probably Captain Edmund Trowbridge Dana Myers
Requested By:	Unknown
Artillery:	None; muskets only
Unit(s) Served There:	Probably members of Waddill's Battalion in June–July 1861; possibly artillerymen, August–December 1861; and the 52d Virginia Militia, December 1861–May 1862
Notes:	This apparently supported the bridge redan and bridge
Name:	**Point of Island Battery**
Location:	Black Point

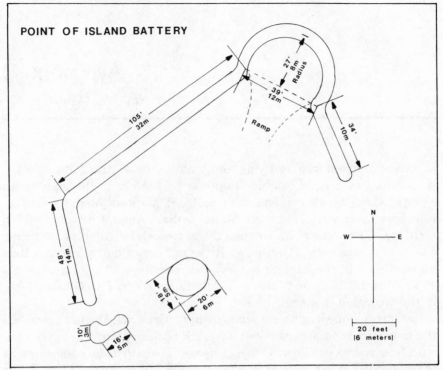

POINT OF ISLAND BATTERY

Map by Blake A. Magner

Type/Shape:	Redoubt
Construction Date:	Probably July–August 1861 and functional by August–September 1861
Designed By:	Probably Captain Edmund Trowbridge Dana Myers
Requested By:	Brigadier General John B. Magruder
Artillery:	Two heavy guns transferred from the Square Redoubt; one account indicates that they were 32-pounders.
Unit(s) Served There:	Possibly the Bedford Light Artillery in 1862 since it was indicated that this unit would move farther down the island upon acquisition of light artillery, and the Sand Battery apparently had Columbiads.
Notes:	Lee unenthusiastically approved Magruder's request to construct and arm this fort. He initially felt that the Sand Battery was sufficient to support Fort Pocahontas, and he commented that forts down river also assisted Jamestown.

APPENDIX H

THE AMBLER HOUSE

Known most frequently as "the Ambler house," the name dates to its original owner, the Ambler family, who built it in the eighteenth century. Confederate soldiers often called it "Captain Allen's house" in reference to its wartime owner, Major William Allen, who commanded artillery at Jamestown and owned the entire island. Allen's true home, Claremont, was across the James River in Surry County. He only took up residence in the Ambler house while serving at Jamestown, April 1861–May 1862. Prior to the war, Allen's overseer, J. C. Gibson, lived in the Georgian mansion.

One of Jamestown's previous owners, Goodrich Durfey, described the house in 1844 as a three-story brick building, forty by sixty feet, with four rooms per floor. These dimensions are virtually the same as the surviving ruins measured one and one-half centuries later. When interviewed in the 1930s, former Confederate Lieutenant Emmett M. Morrison remembered there being a wide hall lined with sofas, settees, divans, and a large buffet. "Magnificent" Venetian blinds adorned the windows. Morrison occupied one room and used it as an office; it was on the "left hand side," but he did not indicate whether he meant "left" from inside the house facing the river, or "left" from the outside, facing the house. Lacking furniture, his room was large and wainscoted for five feet. Captain Edward R. Young, who visited the house and recorded his account of it that day in his diary, perhaps is more accurate in his description of the wainscoting as seven or eight feet in height. Young also mentioned a mantle that was "beautifully carved and festooned." A Confederate engineer, Captain Edmund Trowbridge Dana Myers, was less complimentary of the brick structure decades later when he tersely described it as not in good repair but habitable.

During the period of Confederate occupation at Jamestown, the house had several functions in addition to Allen's residency and Morrison's office use. In 1862 Colonel Hill Carter boarded there with his servant and paid Allen rent. Allen also entertained brother officers at the house during evenings.

Located at the western end of the island, the house was a prominent feature on the otherwise flat landscape. It was situated on about an acre of grass, the only greenery in the area. There was a "beautiful grave opposite [the] house." Numerous outbuildings were nearby, listed in the 1840s as a kitchen, laundry, dairy, smokehouse, barns, stables, and an overseer's house. Numerous slave quarters also were present. In 1860 there were thirty blacks at Jamestown, which apparently was the average figure throughout Allen's first decade of farming there. Young also mentioned a large granary which accommodated guests for dancing during the Independence Day celebration in 1861.

Jamestown briefly was abandoned by both armies after the Peninsula campaign of 1862, the Federals departing in late August. Several weeks later, on October 20, several Surry County residents inspected the property and three of them were murdered by Allen's former slaves. These same blacks already had burned the Ambler house some time between the Union army's departure and the date of the murders.

Major General George B. McClellan's Army of the Potomac controlled Jamestown Island during most of the Peninsula campaign from early May into August 1862. However, no unit was given a lengthy assignment there. Cavalry quickly scouted the island after the Confederates evacuated it in May. The navy made a more thorough reconnaissance later that month with the USS *Galena*, and the USS *Aroostook* destroyed the abandoned fortifications in June. From late June until late August, the Federal transport fleet was anchored off Jamestown, guarded first by the USS *Jacob Bell* and subsequently by the USS *Cimarron*. A telegraph station operated on the island from about July 5 until mid-August to increase the frequency of McClellan's communications with the War Department. There is no reference to troops assigned to guard the telegraph, and it is possible that the navy's presence was considered adequate.

During the twelve months after McClellan's withdrawal, Jamestown merely was observed by Union naval patrols. In August 1863 the island was occupied by members of the 1st New York Mounted Rifles when horsemen were ordered to extend their picket line from Williamsburg. These troops were part of the Fort Magruder garrison in Williamsburg which served as a Union outpost. From August 1863 onward, Jamestown assumed the role of an outpost for Williamsburg. Soldiers from Fort Magruder, usually a company of cavalry, were rotated periodically at Jamestown. In May 1864 another Union telegraph station was established at Jamestown, and this time it remained operational for the remainder of the war. Lieutenant General Ulysses S. Grant used Jamestown as a communications link between Union armies in the field and Washington, D.C. The only two telegraph operators who have been identified are W. N. Embree, who was serving in August 1864, and T. N. Loucks, who replaced him at that time. Neither man's length of service is known. In the last three months of

152

1864, troops whose terms of enlistment had expired were sent from the Petersburg lines to Jamestown for brief periods while awaiting transportation north. Otherwise, Fort Magruder provided Jamestown's soldiers through the war's conclusion in 1865.

Not all periods of Jamestown's occupation are thoroughly documented. It can be ascertained that companies from the following units served as part of the Fort Magruder garrison during 1863–1865 and were potential sources for troops at Jamestown:

4th Massachusetts Cavalry
16th New York Heavy Artillery*
1st New York Mounted Rifles*
20th New York Cavalry*
100th New York Infantry*
76th Pennsylvania Infantry*
1st U.S. Colored Cavalry*
2d U.S. Colored Cavalry

* indicates that the unit's service at Jamestown is documented.

Using the *Official Records*, regimental histories, memoirs, and numerous sources from the National Archives, it is possible to verify that the following units had troops occupying Jamestown for the periods specified below:

August 1863–?	1st New York Mounted Rifles
May 1–late June 1864	1st U.S. Colored Cavalry
Late June 1864–?	1st New York Mounted Rifles
October 15–16, 1864	85th Pennsylvania Infantry
October–November 1864	76th Pennsylvania Infantry
December 1864–January 1865	100th New York Infantry
February 1865	16th New York Heavy Artillery
May 1865	20th New York Cavalry

APPENDIX J

ILLUSTRATIONS AT JAMESTOWN

During the Civil War, sites were documented visually by photographers, by artists, and by soldiers. To date there are no known photographic images of Jamestown during the Civil War, nor are there newspaper illustrations. Officers sometimes made sketches for official reports, and soldiers of all ranks occasionally made drawings in letters written to family and friends. It is this latter category, the officers and men in the field, who provided the only illustrations.

Lieutenant Catesby ap Roger Jones of the Confederate navy was the commander at Jamestown when he did his art work. He submitted a report on the railroad T-iron he tested on October 12, 1861, as a potential source of protective armor for the CSS *Merrimack*, later called the *Virginia*. The original document, including two illustrations, is entitled "Report of Ordnance Experiments at Jamestown" and is in the possession of the Virginia Historical Society. Both of his illustrations were published in October 1941 in *The Virginia Magazine of History and Biography* in T. Catesby Jones's article entitled "The Iron-Clad *Virginia*." The drawings show the target Jones used to conduct his tests. In one illustration, Jones provided six different views of the target, including before-and-after drawings to show the effects of shots fired into it. The second illustration shows only the target and the damage it received from the test firing. Unfortunately, these drawings show only the target and none of the surrounding terrain features.

A Union officer left a pictorial record that was more descriptive of the island itself. Throughout the nineteenth century, visitors to Jamestown frequently commented about the same landmarks, and these were the very same features that so impressed Captain David E. Cronin that he sketched them. Cronin visited numerous sites while he served with the 1st New York Mounted Rifles as provost marshal in Williamsburg in 1863–1864. After the war he wrote about his experiences, and one of his unpublished manuscripts is rich with illustrations. Entitled "The Vest Mansion: Its Historical and Romantic Associations as Confederate and Union Headquarters (1862–1865) in the American Civil War," the original manuscript is in his papers at the New-York Historical Society. Microfilm and typescript copies are in the possession of the Colonial Williamsburg Foundation. Jamestown illustrations appear on the first two pages of Chapter 24. One sketch depicts the church tower, which has been the subject of countless pictures. Cronin's is unique because there are two Union observers atop the tower. His second illustration shows a guard in the cemetery, which was adjacent to the church tower. For his third subject, Cronin drew a Union sentinel on the western shore of the island with a cypress tree in the background. The tree was a conversation piece because it stood offshore in the James River and was evidence of the island's erosion. More than a century later the cypress tree was toppled by a thunderstorm on the night of July 10, 1993.

NOTES

APVA	Association for the Preservation of Virginia Antiquities
CNHP	Colonial National Historical Park
CSR	Compiled Service Records
CWF	Colonial Williamsburg Foundation
CWM	College of William and Mary
FHS	Fluvanna Historical Society
FSNMP	Fredericksburg and Spotsylvania National Military Park
GCMF	George C. Marshall Foundation
HC	Hollywood Cemetery
LC	Library of Congress
LV	Library of Virginia
MC	Museum of the Confederacy
NA	National Archives
NYHS	New-York Historical Society
OR	U.S. War Department. *The War of the Rebellion: A Compilation of the Official Records of the Union and Confederate Armies*. 128 vols. Washington, D.C.: Government Printing Office, 1880–1901.
OR Atlas	U.S. War Department. *Atlas to Accompany the Official Records of the Union and Confederate Armies*. Washington, D.C.: Government Printing Office, 1891–1895.
ORN	U.S. Naval War Records Office. *Official Records of the Union and Confederate Navies in the War of the Rebellion*. 30 vols. Washington, D.C.: Government Printing Office, 1894–1922.
UNC	University of North Carolina
USAMHI	U.S. Army Military History Institute
UV	University of Virginia
VHS	Virginia Historical Society
VMI	Virginia Military Institute
WJCCC	Williamsburg-James City County Courthouse
YU	Yale University

CHAPTER 1
A MILITARY HERITAGE

1. Billings, Selby, and Tate, *Colonial Virginia*, 29; Billings, *Jamestown*, 19–20, 112; Yonge, *Site of Old "James Towne,"* 15; Tyler, *Cradle of the Republic*, 24–25; Shea, *Virginia Militia*, 7; Hatch, *Jamestown, Virginia*, 6.
2. Shea, *Virginia Militia*, 8; Billings, *Jamestown*, 33; Yonge, *Site of Old "James Towne,"* 31.

3. Shea, *Virginia Militia*, 9–11; Billings, *Jamestown*, 35; Hatch, *Jamestown, Virginia*, 9; Yonge, *Site of Old "James Towne,"* 34–35. For an analysis of the appearance of James Fort, see Mardis, "Visions of James Fort," 463–98.

4. Yonge, *Site of Old "James Towne,"* 98–101; Tyler, *Cradle of the Republic*, 112–14. Archeological work at Jamestown in 1993 confirmed the site of the turf fort (Horning, Edwards, and Brown, "1993 Archaeological Investigations in New Towne," 11).

5. Hatch, *Jamestown, Virginia*, 15; Shea, *Virginia Militia*, 14, 22–23, 25–27, 49, 56, 58–59, 61, 68; Rountree, *Pocahontas's People*, 81, 84–87; Billings, *Jamestown*, 45, 74.

6. Shea, *Virginia Militia*, 78, 86–95, 97–119, 124, 128; Billings, *Jamestown*, 79, 85–99; Hatch, *Jamestown, Virginia*, 30–31.

7. Yonge, *Site of Old "James Towne,"* 95–96; Billings, *Jamestown*, 99–100; Billings, Selby, and Tate, *Colonial Virginia*, 156.

8. *Executive Journals of the Council of Colonial Virginia*, 1:322, 339, 432–33, and 2:90, and 3:95, 97; "Council Papers 1698–1702," 155; Yonge, *Site of Old "James Towne,"* 50; *Journals of the House of Burgesses*, 4:200; "Papers from the Virginia State Auditor's Office," 383; Maury, *Memoirs of a Huguenot Family*, 271; Jones, *Present State of Virginia*, 66; Hatch, "Jamestown and the Revolution," 30.

9. Billings, *Jamestown*, 105–06; Hatch, *Jamestown, Virginia*, 33–34; Tyler, *Cradle of the Republic*, 82–89; Hendricks, "Land Ownership—Jamestown Island," 33–34.

10. *Virginia Gazette* (Purdie & Dixon), 2 Dec. 1773, 2; Tyler, *Cradle of the Republic*, 88; Hazard, "Journal of Ebenezer Hazard," 415.

11. Van Schreeven, Scribner, and Tarter, *Revolutionary Virginia*, 1:109, 2:178–79; Travis, *Travis (Travers) Family*, 68; Sanchez-Saavedra, *Guide to Virginia Military Organizations*, 17, 150.

12. *Virginia Gazette* (Purdie), 3 Nov. 1775, 2; *Virginia Gazette* (Dixon & Hunter), 4 Nov. 1775, 3; Van Schreeven, Scribner, and Tarter, *Revolutionary Virginia*, 4:9; Selby, *Revolution in Virginia*, 64; Peckham, *Toll of Independence*, 9–10; Sanchez-Saavedra, *Guide to Virginia Military Organizations*, 34.

13. *Virginia Gazette* (Purdie), 17 Nov. 1775, 2.

14. Ibid., and Supplement, 24 Nov. 1775, 1; Van Schreeven, Scribner, and Tarter, *Revolutionary Virginia*, 4:418; *Virginia Gazette* (Dixon & Hunter), 4 Nov. 1775, 3; Selby, *Revolution in Virginia*, 64. A more glorious account for the patriots appears in "James City County Petitions," 177–93, which is a recollection written in 1791; it apparently confuses the fighting of November 1775 with the capture of a British vessel in March 1776, mentioned later in this narrative. The *Virginia Gazette* (Purdie), 3 Nov. 1775, 2, and (Dixon & Hunter), 4 Nov. 1775, 3, indicate that there was an exchange of American-British fire earlier, including the shots which struck the ferry house.

15. *Virginia Gazette* (Dixon & Hunter), 23 March 1776, 3, and 13 April 1776, 3.

16. Van Schreeven, Scribner, and Tate, *Revolutionary Virginia*, 6:278, 514; *Calendar of Virginia State Papers*, 8:165–66, 183, 187, 215–16, 218; *Journals of the Council of the State of Virginia*, 1:25, 35, 37–38, 96; Sanchez-Saavedra, *Guide to Virginia Military Organizations*, 24.

17. Selby, *Revolution in Virginia*, 117; Van Schreeven, Scribner, and Tarter, *Revolutionary Virginia*, 7:12, 505.

18. *Virginia Gazette* (Purdie), 27 Sept. 1776, Supplement, 1; Hazard, "Journal of Ebenezer Hazard," 411; Hatch, "Jamestown and the Revolution," 33–34; Selby, *Revolution in Virginia*, 211; Johnston, *Yorktown Campaign*, 29 ff.; Idzerda et al., *Lafayette in the Age of the American Revolution*, 4:222, 270–71, 276, 502; Hatch, *Jamestown, Virginia*, 33.

19. Johnston, *Yorktown Campaign*, 60–61; Hatch, "'Affair Near James Island,'" 172, 180–83; Hatch, *Yorktown*, 6; Selby, *Revolution in Virginia*, 290.

20. Hatch, "'Affair Near James Island,'" 182–92; Johnston, *Yorktown Campaign*, 61–67; Hatch, *Yorktown*, 6; Selby, *Revolution in Virginia*, 290–91; Peckham, *Toll of Independence*, 87; Boatner, *Encyclopedia of the American Revolution*, 451–53.

21. Hatch, "'Affair Near James Island,'" 193; Johnston, *Yorktown Campaign*, 68; Idzerda et al., *Lafayette in the Age of the American Revolution*, 4:399, 506; Stille, *Major General*

Anthony Wayne, 280; Nelson, *Anthony Wayne*, 142; Gottschalk, *Lafayette and the Close of the American Revolution*, 299, 304.

22. Selby, *Revolution in Virginia*, 295, 301; Johnston, *Yorktown Campaign*, 98–102; *Calendar of Virginia State Papers*, 2:380–81, 385.

23. Tyler, *Cradle of the Republic*, 90–92; Butler, *Guide to Virginia Militia Units*, 24, 313; Ambler, "History of the Ambler Family," 66; *Calendar of Virginia State Papers*, 10:240, 326; Heitman, *Historical Register*, 1:991; Rogers, Faculty/Alumni Files, CWM.

CHAPTER 2
WILLIAM ALLEN PREPARES FOR WAR

1. Hendricks, "Land Ownership—Jamestown Island," 34; Tyler, *Cradle of the Republic*, 94; Will Book No. 6, Surry Co., 218–22, LV; Will Book 1, James City Co., 292–96, WJCCC.

2. French Papers, LV, is consistent with most sources in giving only Allen's year of birth; most sources say "1828" or "ca. 1828." Jesup, *Edward Jessup*, 265, gives the full date as 29 July 1829, but Gregory, *Claremont Manor*, 57, points out that Jesup might be in error on the year. Evidence to substantiate this is Allen's mother's petition, 21 Dec. 1842, Virginia Legislative Petitions, Surry Co., LV, which says Allen was between fourteen and fifteen years of age at that time. This is reinforced by the *Richmond Enquirer*, 23 May 1875, 4, which says that a plate on his casket read, "William Allen, aged 46" [Allen died 19 May 1875] and in 7th Census, 1850, Population Schedules, Surry Co., Va., 65, NA, and 8th Census, 1860, Population Schedules, Surry Co., Va., 950, NA: both years the census-taker visited Allen's home after July 29, and his age is listed as twenty-two in 1850 and thirty-two in 1860. Allen's place of birth is in *Petersburg Index and Appeal*, 21 May 1875, 3, and *Richmond Enquirer*, 20 May 1875, 4. For Orgain and Allen family information, see "Allen Family of Surry County," 112, 114–15; Tyler, *Encyclopedia of Virginia Biography*, 5:638; Gregory, *Claremont Manor*, 59, and the genealogical chart between pages 24 and 25; and Surry County records which show that Allen's father died in 1837, not 1830, as cited on his tombstone. For Richard Griffin Orgain's vocational information, see Gregory, *Claremont Manor*, 57–58, and Petersburg city records.

3. Will Book No. 6, Surry Co., 218–22, LV; Will Book 1, James City Co., 292–96, WJCCC; Gregory, *Claremont Manor*, 56. Evidence shows that William Allen should be cited by his first and last name only, not as "William Orgain Allen" or any other combination using his original name. His great-uncle's will specified that his name be changed to William Allen, and Allen's signature on his own will, deeds, military records, and correspondence always appears simply as "William Allen."

4. Fiduciary Accounts, Surry Co., 54, 56, 150, 164, 174, 278, 290, LV; Gregory, *Claremont Manor*, 61–63; Deed Book No. 13, Surry Co., 215, LV; *Fredericksburg News*, 24 May 1875, 3; *Richmond Daily Dispatch*, 21 May 1875, 2.

5. Frances M. (Whittle) Lewis Diary, 13 Nov. 1845, Whittle Papers, CWM; Wilkins, "Minge Family Register," 31–33; Warner, *Benjamin Harrison of Berkeley*, 50–51; "When Ex-President Tyler and Mrs. Tyler Visited Petersburg," 134; Wyatt, *Along Petersburg Streets*, 40; Tyler, *Encyclopedia of Virginia Biography*, 5:637–40; Hall, *Portraits*, 11–13; Hollywood Cemetery Burial Records, HC. The Allens' children were Fannie, b. 1853, d. Dec. 15, 1853 in infancy; William, b. Jan. 13, 1855, d. Mar. 2, 1917; John, b. Sept. 17, 1857, d. June 16, 1904; Mary, b. June 25, 1859, d. 1861; Frances Augusta, b. July 8, 1861, d. Sept. 9, 1899; and Jessup Lightfoot, b. Sept. 16, 1863, d. Jan. 15, 1912 (see Gregory, *Claremont Manor*, genealogical chart between pages 24 and 25; Jesup, *Edward Jessup*, 265–66; Hollywood Cemetery Burial Records, HC).

6. Goodwin, "'Kingsmill' Plantation," lxiii–lxv; 8th Census, 1860, Productions of Agriculture, James City Co., Va., 5–6, NA.

7. Meade, *Old Churches, Ministers and Families*, 1:114; Hatch, "Robert Sully at Jamestown," 347; 8th Census, 1860, Slave Schedule, James City Co., Va., 17, NA; Thompson, "Editor's Table," 397; Goodwin, "'Kingsmill' Plantation," lxiii; *Richmond Daily Dispatch*, 20 May

1875, 1; Stephenson, *Old Homes in Surry & Sussex*, 31; Kornwolf, *Guide to the Buildings of Surry*, 41; Hotchkiss Papers, Reel 59, Frame 306, LC.

8. 8th Census, 1860, Products of Industry, James City Co., Va., 206, NA; "Nathaniel Bacon's Land at Curles," 354–57; Hall, *Portraits*, 12; Deed Book No. 13, Surry Co., 708–09, LV; Deed Book No. 14, Surry Co., 134–36, 261, LV; Gregory, *Claremont Manor*, 67, 69; Crittenden, *The Comp'ny*, 1; Selden Diary, 28 Mar. 1862, VHS; Bassett and Fay, "Westover Journal," 261; Statement of William Allen, 23 Dec. 1851, Mason Family Papers, VHS; 8th Census, 1860, Population Schedules, Surry Co., Va., 950, NA. Allen's wealth would be about sixteen times as great in early 1990s money using the formula in McCusker, "How Much Is That in Real Money?" 312, 323–32. Allen's Surry County property and businesses are shown in Jedediah Hotchkiss's 1871 Map of Surry County in *Southern Planter and Farmer*, facing 321.

9. DeLeon, *Belles, Beaux and Brains*, 133; George H. Ritchie to Isabella Ritchie, 5 Jan. 1850, Ritchie-Harrison Papers, CWM; Hotchkiss Papers, Reel 59, Frame 306, LC; Gregory, *Claremont Manor*, 62; Selden Diary, 1 Dec. 1858, 18 June 1859, 8 May, 1 Sept. 1860, VHS; Kornwolf, *Guide to the Buildings of Surry*, 45; Richmond *Daily Dispatch*, 21 May 1875, 2; *Richmond Enquirer*, 20 May 1875, 4.

10. Lossing, *Pictorial Field-Book of the Revolution*, 2:240–41; Hatch, "Robert Sully at Jamestown," 343–52; Meade, *Old Churches, Ministers and Families*, 1:110; Isabella Ritchie to John Gittings, 20 Apr. 1859, Ritchie-Harrison Papers, CWM.

11. John Armistead to [Thomas Ritchie?], 11 Feb. 1854, Ritchie-Harrison Papers, CWM.

12. Jamestown Society, *Celebration of the Two Hundred and Fiftieth Anniversary*, 1; Rives, "Jamestown Celebration of 1857," 259; Hale, *True Stories of Jamestown*, 144; Couture, *To Preserve and Protect*, 12; "Letter in Dr. Tyler's Scrapbook," 10.

13. *19th Century*; Rives, "Jamestown Celebration of 1857," 262, 265–66, 269–70. Unlike the bicentennial event of 1807 and the 1822 Virginiad, there was a great military presence in 1857 as if foreshadowing events at Jamestown in the near future.

14. Jamestown Society, *Celebration of the Two Hundred and Fiftieth Anniversary*, 1, 28–31; Thompson, "Celebration at Jamestown," 465.

15. Hale, *True Stories of Jamestown*, 140; Isabella Ritchie to [John] Gittings, 20 Apr. 1859, Ritchie-Harrison Papers, CWM; Thompson, "Editor's Table," 395–97; John Tyler to Robert Tyler, 25 Apr. 1859, Tyler Family Papers, CWM; Militia Records, Surry Co., 1840–1861, LV; Military Affairs Papers, Box 12, 10th Battalion Virginia Heavy Artillery, LV; 10th Battalion Virginia Heavy Artillery, Confederate Rosters, LV; CSR, Virginia, 1st Artillery, NA; Wallace, *Guide to Virginia Military Organizations*, 3; Krick, *Lee's Colonels*, 28; *ORN* I 6:699.

16. Catesby ap Roger Jones to Harrison Henry Cocke, 3 May 1861, Cocke Family Papers, VHS; *ORN* I 6:699; Wallace, *Guide to Virginia Military Organizations*, 3.

17. Freeman, *Lee's Lieutenants*, 1:694–95; Clary, *Fortress America*, 99.

18. *OR Atlas*, Plate 17, Map 1; Tyler, *Cradle of the Republic*, 22–23; Yonge, *Site of Old "James Towne,"* 21–23, 25; Hendricks, "Land Ownership—Jamestown Island," 35; Meade, *Old Churches, Ministers and Families*, 1:115; *Calendar of Virginia State Papers*, 10:142; Ripley, *Artillery and Ammunition of the Civil War*, 368–71 (these pages provide range tables for the guns used at Jamestown).

19. Map of Western End of Jamestown Island, CNHP; Map of Jamestown Island, James City Co., CNHP; Map, Jamestown Island, Part of the Master Plan, CNHP; Map, Archeological Excavations, Unit B & APVA, Jamestown, CNHP.

20. "Jamestown Island in 1861," 39; Goodwin, "'Kingsmill' Plantation," lxiii–lxv; 8th Census, 1860, Productions of Agriculture, James City Co., Va., 5–6, NA.

21. Lossing, *Pictorial Field-Book of the Revolution*, 240–41; "Island of Jamestown," 303; Meade, *Old Churches, Ministers and Families*, 1:110–11, 114; Hatch, "Robert Sully at Jamestown," 348–51; Clayton, "Jamestown Island," 142; Interview with Emmett M. Morrison, 3, Jamestown Historical Records, CNHP; Tyler, *Cradle of the Republic*, 97; Preliminary Historical Study, Unit A, Northwestern End of Jamestown Island, 55–57, Jamestown Archeology Records, CNHP; Map, Historical Base Map, West Half of

Jamestown Island & Mainland, CNHP; Elay-Swann Tract, Jamestown Island, Jamestown Archeology Records, CNHP; Report on 1955 Excavations in the Elay-Swann Tract, Jamestown Archeology Records, CNHP. The cypress tree stood in the river until the night of July 10, 1993, when it was knocked over by a thunderstorm.

22. Goodrich Durfey, "Old James Town For Sale," 26 Nov. 1844, VHS; Interview with Emmett M. Morrison, 3, Jamestown Historical Records, CNHP; Young Diary, 11 June 1861, Private Collection. Young said that the musket was twelve or fourteen feet long.

23. "Jamestown Island in 1861," 39.

CHAPTER 3
VIRGINIANS IN DEFENSE OF RICHMOND

1. Wallace, *Guide to Virginia Military Organizations*, [i, iii].
2. *Dictionary of American Biography*, 18:281; *National Cyclopaedia*, 13:405.
3. Freeman, *Lee*, 1:103, 480; Nichols, *Confederate Engineers*, 17; *National Cyclopaedia*, 13:405; Andrew Talcott 1863 Diary, 27 Mar., 6 Aug. 1863, Talcott Family Papers, VHS. Talcott was imprisoned March 27–August 6 at Fort Lafayette, New York, and Fort Warren, Massachusetts.
4. *OR* I 2:788–89; Freeman, *Lee*, 1:480–81.
5. Andrew Talcott 1861 Diary, 3 May 1861, Talcott Family Papers, VHS; *ORN* I 6:699; Jones to Cocke, 3 May 1861, Cocke Family Papers, VHS; Freeman, *Lee*, 1:481. Myers's rank sometimes is given as major, but he did not attain this level until after his Jamestown assignment. While in the service of the state of Virginia he was a captain (*Journals and Papers of the Virginia State Convention* 3 Doct. 24:6), and he remained a captain after Virginia's forces were transferred to the Confederate States in June 1861 (*OR* I 2:978).
6. Freeman, *Lee*, 1:480; Faust, *Encyclopedia of the Civil War*, 401; Davis, *Duel Between the First Ironclads*, 30; *National Cyclopaedia*, 5:12; *OR* I 2:771; Scharf, *Confederate States Navy*, 130–33; Interview with Emmett M. Morrison, 2, Jamestown Historical Records, CNHP; Brooke, *John M. Brooke*, 227. Jones's rank is given as captain in *OR* I 2:771, and army officers sometimes referred to him as captain. But naval officers always addressed him as lieutenant, and it is documented that this was his rank in the Virginia navy in *Register of Officers of the Confederate States Navy*, 102 (which says the appointment was on May 2 to rank from April 23), *Proceedings of the Advisory Council*, 40, 42, *Journals and Papers of the Virginia State Convention* 3 Doct. 35:91, and *ORN* correspondence cited below. Jones remained a lieutenant when Virginia forces were transferred to the Confederate States in June 1861 as cited in *Register of Officers of the Confederate States Navy*, 102 (which says the appointment was on June 11), Dudley, *Going South*, 38, and *ORN* correspondence cited below. Moebs, *Confederate States Navy Research Guide*, 228, reprinted the *Register* and gives the same ranks for Jones.
7. Interview with Emmett M. Morrison, 4, Jamestown Historical Records, CNHP.
8. *ORN* I 6:699; Jones to Cocke, 3 May 1861, Cocke Family Papers, VHS.
9. Thomas, *Confederate Nation*, 98–100; Dabney, *Richmond*, 164.
10. Jones to Cocke, 3 May 1861, Cocke Family Papers, VHS; *ORN* I 6:699.
11. Long, *Civil War Day By Day*, 69; Jones to Cocke, 3 May 1861, Cocke Family Papers, VHS; *ORN* I 6:700.
12. Krick, *Lee's Colonels*, 120; Jensen, *32nd Virginia Infantry*, 1, 5.
13. *ORN* I 6:698; "Reminiscences of John Bankhead Magruder and the War," 8, Ewell Papers, CWM; "Reminiscences about General John Bankhead Magruder and Events around Williamsburg near the Beginning of the Civil War," 4, Ewell, Faculty/Alumni File, CWM.
14. Jensen, *32nd Virginia Infantry*, 6–7; Wallace, *Guide to Virginia Military Organizations*, 115–16; *ORN* I 6:698–99.
15. *ORN* I 6:698, 701; Wallace, *Guide to Virginia Military Organizations*, 3.
16. *ORN* I 6:701; Boatner, *Civil War Dictionary*, 520; Faust, *Encyclopedia of the Civil War*, 481; Williams, *Matthew Fontaine Maury*, 365–66.

17. *ORN* I 6:698, 700–02. Jones was not bashful in his second request of Ewell. Having just been denied a mere seventeen men of one company, this time he asked for two entire companies.
18. Wallace, *Guide to Virginia Military Organizations*, 89; *ORN* I 6:700.
19. *ORN* I 6:702.
20. *OR* I 51(2):70; Wallace, *Guide to Virginia Military Organizations*, 133; Military Affairs Papers, Box 58, 53d Virginia Infantry, LV; Krick, *Lee's Colonels*, 356.
21. *OR* I 51(2):70.
22. French Papers, LV; Cottrell, "John Mercer Patton, Jr.," 106–09; Krick, *Lee's Colonels*, 275; *V.M.I. Register*, 11; Worsham, *One of Jackson's Foot Cavalry*, 32; Chamberlayne, *Ham Chamberlayne*, 60; Riggs, *21st Virginia Infantry*, 3, 85; CSR, Virginia, 21st Infantry (John Mercer Patton, Jr.), NA; Commission, 16 Dec. 1862, Patton Family Papers, VHS.
23. Jones to Cocke, 3 May 1861, Cocke Family Papers, VHS; Andrew Talcott 1861 Diary, 3 May 1861, Talcott Family Papers, VHS; *ORN* I 6:699. In the excitement of those first days at Jamestown Jones gave different figures for the artillery. When writing to Cocke on May 3, the day of Talcott's departure, he used the same figure as Talcott (eighteen guns). Two days later, he wrote to Captain Samuel Barron and provided two different figures (ten and sixteen guns).
24. *ORN* I 6:699; Bohannan, "Jamestown Island and 'The Surry Side,'" 135; Interview with Samuel H. Yonge, 2, Jamestown Historical Records, CNHP; Interview with Emmett M. Morrison, 2, Jamestown Historical Records, CNHP; "Jamestown Island in 1861," 39.
25. *Yearbook APVA*, 3; Archives Accession Book, 221, VHS; Wynne, "Jamestown, Virginia," 53; Hankins to Johnston, 15 June 1955, VHS; Notes on Jamestown Island, APVA. The latter two sources are almost identical, both being Cyrus Hankins's recollections of an account from his uncle, Southey Savage Hankins. Thomas Hicks Wynne, who served as corresponding secretary for the Virginia Historical Society, stated in 1868 that he had two pieces of armor, two sword hilts, a caltrop, and several coins found by Confederates who dug the earthworks at Jamestown. (A caltrop was a small iron object with four points positioned at angles that assured that one point always projected upward, no matter how it rested on the ground. It was used against cavalry.) After his death in 1875, Wynne's widow presented the Society with "several pieces of rusted iron Armor dug up at the ruins of Jamestown" (VHS Accession Book, 221), and the VHS Minute Book, 1853–1882, notes that on July 2, 1875, the Society accepted "relics" of Jamestown. The Society presently has one object which presumably was among the Wynne items, that being accession number 875.3, listed as a "rusted iron elbow piece dug up at Jamestown" which has been preserved in the museum collection. For a discussion of this armor fragment, identified as a vambrace, see Kelso, Luccketti, and Straube, "A Re-Evaluation of the Archaeological Evidence Produced by Project 100," 34.
26. Morrison, Alumni Biographical File, VMI; *Smithfield Times*, 9 June 1932; *Suffolk News-Herald*, 8 June 1932; Interview with Emmett M. Morrison, 1, Jamestown Historical Records, CNHP; Krick, *Lee's Colonels*, 258; *OR* I 51(2):70.
27. Interview with Emmett M. Morrison, 2–3, Jamestown Historical Records, CNHP.
28. Andrew Talcott 1861 Diary, 11 May 1861, Talcott Family Papers, VHS; *ORN* I 6:702–03.
29. *ORN* I 6:702–03.
30. Ibid., 703.
31. Robert Saunders to Robert Page Saunders, 13 May 1861, Page-Saunders Papers, CWM; *National Cyclopaedia*, 3:236; *OR* I 51(2):89. Jones rounded the garrison's strength to 250 on May 10 (*ORN* I 6:703) and provided a more precise count of 214 on May 16 (Jones to Barron, 16 May 1861, Cocke Family Papers, VHS).
32. Andrew Talcott 1861 Diary, 15–16 May 1861, Talcott Family Papers, VHS; Report on Defenses of James River, 17 May 1861, Brooke Papers, GCMF; Brooke, *John M. Brooke*, 229; Jones to Barron, 16 May 1861, Cocke Family Papers, VHS.
33. Report on Defenses of James River, 17 May 1861, Brooke Papers, GCMF; Brooke, *John M. Brooke*, 229.

34. Jones to Barron, 16 May 1861, Cocke Family Papers, VHS; Bohannon, *Surry County at War*, 14.

35. Long, *Civil War Day By Day*, 75; Warner, *Generals in Blue*, 61; *OR* I 9:39; Boatner, *Civil War Dictionary*, 501; Warner, *Generals in Gray*, 207.

36. *OR* I 9:39; *OR Atlas*, Plate 18:2. For details on Mulberry Island's role in the war, refer to Davis, "Mulberry Island and the Civil War."

37. *ORN* I 6:704–05; *OR* I 2:979; Graves, *Bedford Light Artillery*, 13.

38. *ORN* I 6:704–05. Marks on the 9-inch guns were W.P. 110 and I.F. 276. All 32-pounders were marked I.F. and bore the numbers 392, 394, 401, 403, 406, and 408; their weight was 57 hundredweight. Ammunition requested for the 9-inch guns consisted of 130 10-pound cartridges, 130 shell, twenty-two stand of grape, and twelve canister. For the 32-pounders Jones wanted 204 9-pound cartridges, 102 shot, forty-five shell, seventy stand of grape, and thirty-six canister. He also needed 200 spare fuses, 500 primers, and two fuse wrenches. Supplies needed included spare lock strings, two vent drills, two spare beds and quoins, two spare trucks, spare double blocks, spare rope, spun yarn, one ladle for 9-inch gun, one worm, twelve lanterns, black lead, red lead, two pair of India rubber shoes for the magazine, one set of weights and scales, one set of copper measures, one funnel for filling shell, copper tools for opening powder barrels, two water buckets, and a copper dustpan.

39. Henry Robinson Berkeley Diary, 24 May 1861, Berkeley Papers, VHS; Berkeley, *Four Years in the Confederate Artillery*, 6; Wallace, *Guide to Virginia Military Organizations*, 27; Krick, *Lee's Colonels*, 265; Wise, *Long Arm of Lee*, 2:878. There is some confusion concerning the date of the Hanover Artillery's arrival. The unit's official record (CSR, Virginia, George W. Nelson's Company, Virginia Light Artillery, NA) says that the company reached Jamestown between May 21 and June 30; other records indicate that it was May. Wallace, loc. cit., says that the unit enrolled at Richmond on May 21. Berkeley, loc. cit., pinpointed the arrival date as Friday, May 23; however, May 23 was a Thursday. Two days later, Berkeley wrote about Sunday services on May 25. Berkeley's diary (covering the period 16 May 1861–24 June 1865) and his student notebook (covering the period Dec. 1859–20 Mar. 1861, with notes about the war) are actually recollections rather than a true diary for the early part of the war because Berkeley lost his original book. Apparently he failed to match the dates with the proper week days for this period. Each date cited herein from Berkeley's "diary" is one day later than that given by Berkeley, using the assumption that events actually correspond with the week day rather than the calendar date. This dating method was selected because he used Sunday services as a reference point. A realignment by this method requires that Friday, May 23, become Friday, May 24, in order that his Jamestown Sunday service be dated correctly, i.e., as May 26, not May 25. (The Hanover Artillery later was commanded by George W. Nelson, who succeeded William Nelson on April 30, 1862, and is listed under the former's name in most records.)

40. Berkeley Diary, 24–25 May 1861, Berkeley Papers, VHS; Berkeley, *Four Years in the Confederate Artillery*, 6–7.

41. Berkeley Diary, 26 May 1861, Berkeley Papers, VHS; Berkeley, *Four Years in the Confederate Artillery*, 7.

42. Berkeley Diary, 27 May 1861, Berkeley Papers, VHS; Berkeley, *Four Years in the Confederate Artillery*, 7.

43. *ORN* I 6:704–05; Jones to Barron, 30 May 1861, Barron Papers, UV.

44. Long, *Civil War Day By Day*, 79; Freeman, *Lee*, 1:511–12; Weinert and Arthur, *Defender of the Chesapeake*, 101; Cocke to Barron, 29 May 1861, Cocke Family Papers, VHS; *ORN* I 6:706.

45. *ORN* I 6:706–07; Scharf, *Confederate States Navy*, 139. Barron's reference to one of the *Teaser's* duties as ferrying troops and supplies between Jamestown and the mainland reinforces Jones's statement, noted later in the narrative, that bridge construction was about to begin; therefore, boat transportation still was necessary at this time.

46. *OR* I 51(2):119; CSR, Virginia, John D. Smith's Company Virginia Light Artillery, NA; Crocker, "Colonel James Gregory Hodges," 188; Crocker, *Colonel James Gregory Hodges*,

9; Barron to Cocke, 30 May 1861, Cocke Family Papers, VHS; Graves, *Bedford Light Artillery*, 12; Koleszar, *Ashland, Bedford, and Taylor Virginia Light Artillery*, 2. Graves's book must be used with caution as it contains a host of errors and elevates the unit's role at Jamestown, erroneously asserting that Captain Jordan was placed in charge of the fortifications. Koleszar modestly summarizes the Bedford Light Artillery's Peninsula service in one paragraph. Crocker's article overstates Hodges's command by extending it beyond the 14th Virginia to all infantry and artillery on the island but, as explained in Chapter 4, Hodges's authority never extended beyond the infantry.

47. Wallace, *Guide to Virginia Military Organizations*, 32, 97; Krick, *Lee's Colonels*, 177, 200; Crocker, "Colonel James Gregory Hodges," 184–85, 193. The Bedford Light Artillery generally is listed under John Donnell Smith's Company Virginia Light Artillery; Smith succeeded Jordan.

48. Jones to Barron, 29 May 1861, Barron, Waring, and Baylor Family Papers, UV; Jones to Barron, 30 May 1861, Barron Papers, UV.

49. Ibid.

50. G. A. Magruder, Jr., to Ewell, 8 June 1861, Ewell Papers, CWM; "Reminiscences about General John Bankhead Magruder and Events around Williamsburg near the Beginning of the Civil War," 4, Ewell Faculty/Alumni File, CWM.

51. William Jerdone Diary, 9, 28–31 May 1861, Jerdone Family Papers, CWM; CSR, Virginia, 53d Infantry (Andrew N. Gill), NA.

52. Berkeley, Diary [late May–early June 1861], Berkeley Papers, VHS; Berkeley, *Four Years in the Confederate Artillery*, 7; Jones to Barron, 29 May 1861, Barron, Waring, and Baylor Family Papers, UV; *ORN* I 6:703, 707–08.

53. Wallace, *Guide to Virginia Military Organizations*, [iii]; Freeman, *Lee*, 1:520.

54. Andrew Talcott 1861 Diary, 3–7 June 1861, Talcott Family Papers, VHS; Interview with Emmett M. Morrison, 2–3, Jamestown Historical Records, CNHP; Lee to Mary Custis Lee, 9 June 1861, Lee Family Papers, VHS; *OR* I 2:910, 916–18. There is a discrepancy about the date of the inspection trip, but Talcott's diary resolves this and several other details, as well. Morrison's recollections were recorded about seventy years after the event and contain several errors, including the date of the Lee-Talcott visit which he said occurred in August. Furthermore, Morrison believed the inspectors immediately returned by boat to Richmond (Talcott provides the correct itinerary). Morrison also said that two of Lee's daughters, Agnes and Mildred, were with their father (Talcott makes no mention of this); the Young Diary, 20 July 1861, Private Collection, clarifies this matter with its statement that two of Lee's daughters were present at evening dress parade more than a month after Lee and Talcott. Even Lee's biographer, Douglas Southall Freeman, erred on the inspection date, saying that it was June 6–8 (Freeman, *Lee*, 1:520). His sources include the June 9 letter to Mrs. Lee, cited above, which is written in such a manner that it sounds as if Lee had just returned, Lee in fact saying "I have just returned from a visit to the batteries...." However, in addition to the dates in Talcott's diary, the June 7 date which Talcott cites for the return to Richmond is verified by Lee himself who corresponded from Richmond on that same date (see *OR* I 2:910). Morrison wrote that Jamestown's commander accompanied Lee on the inspection of Jamestown; presumably this was in reference to Jones, the battery commander. Jones was ill for at least a month, June 6–July 5 (Thomas Jefferson Page to Cocke, 6 June, 5 July 1861, Cocke Family Papers, VHS).

55. Jones to Barron, 5 June 1861, Barron Papers, UV.

56. Young Diary, 6 June 1861, Private Collection; Interview with Emmett M. Morrison, 2, Jamestown Historical Records, CNHP.

57. *OR* I 2:911–12; Wallace, *Guide to Virginia Military Organizations*, [iii]; Confederate Rosters, Confederate Navy, Officers, LV; *Register of Officers of the Confederate States Navy*, 102.

58. The Confederates apparently started construction work on Fort Boykin at Day's Point in June (*ORN* I 7:390) and it became at least partially operational by July (*OR* I 2:975, 979). Construction at Mulberry Island started about August in conjunction with the 14th Virginia's departure from Jamestown, as discussed in Chapter 4.

CHAPTER 4

THE LEGACY OF CATESBY AP ROGER JONES

1. Weinert and Arthur, *Defender of the Chesapeake*, 103–06; Boatner, *Civil War Dictionary*, 63; Long, *Civil War Day By Day*, 84; Young Diary, 10 June 1861, Private Collection. Weinert and Arthur provide a detailed description of early clashes in Chapter 5 of their book.

2. Freeman, *Lee*, 1:528; *Calendar of Virginia State Papers*, 11:167; *Journals and Papers of the Virginia State Convention* 3 Doct. 35:91; Cocke to Barron, 10 June 1861, and Cocke to Beverley Randolph, 12 June 1861, Cocke Family Papers, VHS. Randolph responded to Cocke on June 13 with a large list of supplies needed at Jamestown.

3. Berkeley Diary, [June–July 1861], Berkeley Papers, VHS; Berkeley, *Four Years in the Confederate Artillery*, 7–8.

4. Interview with Emmett M. Morrison, 3, Jamestown Historical Records, CNHP; "Jamestown Island in 1861," 39; Young Diary, 11 June 1861, Private Collection; Receipt, Charles Carter from J. C. Gibson, 1 May 1862, Shirley Plantation Collection, CWF.

5. William H. Phillips to Marie F. Crowder, 15 June 1861, Phillips Papers, CWM; Ross Brothers Letters, n.d., FHS; Young Diary, 30 June 1861, Private Collection. Sergeant Phillips, a planter before the war, was about twenty-five years of age at the time (CSR, Virginia, 14th Infantry [William H. Phillips], NA). Two Ross brothers, Nathaniel Wheeler Ross and William Daniel Ross (who was known as Daniel), were with the 14th Virginia at Jamestown; Nathaniel died of disease April 2, 1863, and William Daniel was killed two months later at Gettysburg on July 3, 1863. A third brother, James Eastin Ross, enlisted in 1862 and was killed at Gettysburg (Crews and Parrish, *14th Virginia Infantry*, 136). The Young diary contains numerous references to the boat which visited the island almost daily and brought food and clothing. These goods often came via visitors or men returning from furlough.

6. Young Diary, 22, 27 June, 14 July 1861, Private Collection; CSR, Virginia, 14th Infantry (Henry S. Morton), NA.

7. Young Diary, 8–9 June, 2, 17 July 1861, Private Collection; Ross Brothers Letters, n.d., FHS; CSR, 18th Battalion Virginia Heavy Artillery (Record of Events and Gilbert V. Rambaut), NA; William H. Phillips to Marie F. Crowder, 15 June 1861, Phillips Papers, CWM. The latter three sources confirm the name "Camp Allen," with Phillips even writing it with the date at the top of his letter as "Camp Allen, Jamestown." There were questions about the 14th Virginia's location, but several members of the regiment resolve this. The Ross brothers provided figures for the fort which virtually match those of the Square Redoubt, in addition to describing their location as the center of the island. Another indication that the camp was some distance from the western end of the island was Young's reference to Jones and Fort Pocahontas as "the upper battery" (Young Diary, 12 July 1861, Private Collection). In 1995 an archeological survey of Jamestown Island by the College of William and Mary further verified the camp's site.

8. Young Diary, 11–12, 15, 18 June 1861, Private Collection; Ross Brothers Letters, n.d., FHS; Crews and Parrish, *14th Virginia Infantry*, 155. Family members soon became concerned about the health of soldiers at Jamestown (see Bettie McDermed to Charles Lewis Anthony McDermed, 12 July 1861, McDermed Papers, CWM).

9. CSR, 18th Battalion Virginia Heavy Artillery (Record of Events and Gilbert V. Rambaut), NA; Wallace, *Guide to Virginia Military Organizations*, 7; Chernault and Weaver, *18th and 20th Battalions of Heavy Artillery*, 7, 12; Lee to Barron, 16 June 1861, Cocke Family Papers, VHS; CSR, Virginia, 10th Battalion, Heavy Artillery, NA; Ross Brothers Letters, n.d., FHS. The Cockade Mounted Artillery became part of the 18th Battalion Virginia Heavy Artillery on June 21, 1862. Records indicate that Rambaut's unit had two temporary attachments, one in December 1861 as Company C, John R. C. Lewis's Battalion Artillery, and one in May 1862 with the 10th Battalion Virginia Heavy Artillery. The exact date of the company's arrival at Jamestown cannot be determined. However, in his letter

of June 16 Lee stated that the unit had been ordered to Jamestown, and Rambaut's CSR includes receipts for supplies received at Jamestown on June 18. An additional indication that the Cockade Mounted Artillery was located close to the 14th Virginia was the note in Captain Young's diary saying that he supped with Captain Rambaut and officers of his battery (Young Diary, 15 July 1861, Private Collection); Young had no association with other artillerymen except for occasional dinners at the Ambler house.

10. Lee, *Wartime Papers*, 50–52; *Journals and Papers of the Virginia State Convention*, 3 Doct. 35:73; Scharf, *Confederate States Navy*, 141.

11. *OR* I 2:935; Scharf, *Confederate States Navy*, 139–40; Carter to Barron, 20 June 1861, Barron Papers, UV.

12. *ORN* II 1(1):268; Silverstone, *Warships of the Civil War Navies*, 106, 242.

13. Werlich, *Admiral of the Amazon*, 25; Scharf, *Confederate States Navy*, 141–42; *ORN* II 1(1):257, 262; Silverstone, *Warships of the Civil War Navies*, 242. Progress with work on *Jamestown* and *Patrick Henry* was monitored closely by Jones, who noted that *Patrick Henry* made its trial trip on August 18 (Jones to Barron, 19 Aug. 1861, Barron Papers, UV). *Patrick Henry* arrived at Jamestown Island about August 7 to cooperate with Magruder, although Tucker did not regard it as ready for sea duty (Tucker to Barron, 7 Aug. 1861, Barron Papers, UV). In late August work on *Jamestown* was progressing slowly, and it was feared that another month's work would be required (Joseph N. Barney to Barron, 22 Aug. 1861, Barron Papers, UV).

14. List of Officers & Men of the Virginia Navy at Jamestown Batteries, William H. Face, comp., [June 1861], Cocke to Jones, 28 June 1861, Thomas Jefferson Page to Cocke, 6 June, 5 July 1861, and Beverley Randolph to Cocke, 13 June 1861, Cocke Family Papers, VHS; John Minson Galt II 7 June 1861–31 Mar. 1862 Diary, 19 June 1861, Galt Family Papers, CWM; *ORN* I 6:716; Barron to Lawrence Rousseau, 23 Aug. 1861, Samuel Barron Letterbook, Barron Papers, CWM.

15. Young Diary, 19, 21–22 June 1861, Private Collection. Young also noted severe storms on July 1, 13, and 22.

16. CSR, Virginia, George W. Nelson's Company Virginia Light Artillery, NA; CSR, Virginia, John D. Smith's Company Virginia Light Artillery, NA; 18th Battalion Virginia Heavy Artillery, NA; General Orders No. 25, 20 June 1861, Army of the Peninsula, NA; Riedel, "John Bankhead Magruder," 34; Long, *Civil War Day By Day*, 89; Perry, *Infernal Machines*, 6. Riedel makes no reference to the navy's presence in June and gives the impression that Hodges commanded the entire island. In his order announcing Hodges's assignment, Magruder continued by saying that he wanted him to make a special report on the mounted guns, ammunition, and state of the defenses at Jamestown. Jones routinely sent this information to his superiors in the navy, and Magruder perhaps felt that he needed a direct report from an army officer in order better to assess the overall situation on the Peninsula.

17. Silverstone, *Warships of the Civil War Navies*, 132–33, 242; John Minson Galt II 7 June 1861–31 Mar. 1862 Diary, 4, 6 July 1861, Galt Family Papers, CWM. By July Ewell had been promoted to colonel, as noted in Chapman, "Benjamin Stoddert Ewell," 127, and Krick, *Lee's Colonels*, 120.

18. Young Diary, 17 June, 4 July 1861, Private Collection.

19. Ibid., 3–4 July 1861.

20. John Minson Galt II 7 June 1861–31 Mar. 1862 Diary, 4, 6 July 1861, Galt Family Papers, CWM.

21. Young Diary, 8–9 July 1861, Private Collection.

22. Thomas Jefferson Page to Cocke, 6 June, 5 July 1861, Cocke to Barron, 6, 11 July 1861, Cocke to Letcher, 19 July 1861, Cocke Family Papers, VHS; Perry, *Infernal Machines*, 6–8; U.S. Naval War Records Office, *Register of Officers of the Confederate States Navy*, 107; *OR* I 2:972; *ORN* I 6:710; Mallory to Barron, 20 July 1861, Samuel Barron Letterbook, Barron Papers, CWM; Scharf, *Confederate States Navy*, 141. The order for Barron's new assignment was dated July 20, 1861.

23. *OR* I 2:977–78; Young Diary, 12 July 1861, Private Collection; "Jamestown Island in 1861," 38; Map of Western End of Jamestown Island, CNHP. Names for the three water batteries are cited in Graves, *Bedford Light Artillery*, 13; Magruder used the term "square redoubt" for the interior earthwork. The number of earthworks at Jamestown was listed erroneously in such postwar accounts as *Washington Post*, 4 Apr. 1904.

24. *OR* I 2:978.

25. Andrew Talcott 1861 Diary, 15 July 1861, Talcott Family Papers, VHS; *OR* I 2:979. Magruder was solidifying his position on the Peninsula and obviously had kept Talcott busy. Writing from Williamsburg on July 13, just prior to his Jamestown visit, Talcott commented that Magruder's presence for the past few days had taken his entire time while working on Williamsburg's defenses (*OR* I 51[2]:174). There was a severe storm on the night of July 13 which lowered the temperature and caused several cool mornings; this was in sharp contrast with Magruder's visit and the days that preceded it (Young Diary, 13–14, 16 July 1861, Private Collection).

26. John Minson Galt II 7 June 1861–31 Mar. 1862 Diary, 18 July 1861, Galt Family Papers, CWM.

27. Young Diary, 21 July 1861, Private Collection.

28. Andrew Talcott 1861 Diary, 21 July 1861, Talcott Family Papers, VHS; Young Diary, 22 July 1861, Private Collection; Berkeley Diary, [July 1861], Berkeley Papers, VHS; Berkeley, *Four Years in the Confederate Artillery*, 8.

29. Randolph Journal, 30 July 1861, Randolph Papers, MC; Riggs, *21st Virginia Infantry*, 3, 85; William H. Phillips to Mollie F. Crowder, 20 Aug. 1861, Phillips Papers, CWM. The exact date of Patton's departure from Jamestown is unknown; only the date when he reached the 21st Virginia is verified. Huntersville was in Virginia in 1861 and became part of West Virginia in 1863.

30. Young Diary, 26, 28–29, 31 July 1861, Private Collection.

31. CSR, Virginia, 14th Infantry, NA; Krick, *Lee's Colonels*, 143; *ORN* I 6:712; Crocker, "Colonel James Gregory Hodges," 188; Crocker, *Colonel James Gregory Hodges*, 9–11; Weinert and Arthur, *Defender of the Chesapeake*, 111; Long, *Civil War Day By Day*, 106; Young Diary, 2 Aug. 1861, Private Collection. Magruder's order to move the gun to Spratley's farm was dated July 23. Some visitors to the 14th Virginia left the island on July 30, possibly as part of the regiment's imminent departure, as evidenced by the pass issued to John C. Holland and his son in the John Clay Holland Papers, 1861, CNHP.

32. CSR, Virginia, 53d Infantry, NA; Andrew N. Gill to William Jerdone, 30 July 1861, and William Jerdone Diary, 3, 9 Aug. 1861, Jerdone Family Papers, CWM. Waddill's Battalion became Company K of the 53d Virginia Infantry on Nov. 9, 1861 (Wallace, *Guide to Virginia Military Organizations*, 133, 145).

33. CSR, Virginia, 53d Infantry, NA; *OR* I 51(2):89; William H. Phillips to Mollie F. Crowder, 20 Aug. 1861, Phillips Papers, CWM; Berkeley Diary, [Sept.–Oct. 1861], Berkeley Papers, VHS; Berkeley, *Four Years in the Confederate Artillery*, 8; Blanton, *Medicine in Virginia*, 416; *ORN* I 6:716; Barron to Lawrence Rousseau, 23 Aug. 1861, Samuel Barron Letterbook, Barron Papers, CWM; Jones to Barron, 19 Aug. 1861, Barron Papers, UV. A Williamsburg coffin maker recorded deaths of men in the 14th Virginia from August to December 1861 in the Richard Bucktrout Daybook, on deposit at Swem Library, CWM. Barron's recommendation that Jones be transferred was dated August 23. The new batteries under construction down river were Fort Boykin at Day's Point and Mulberry Island.

34. Andrew Talcott 1861 Diary, 11, 16–17 Aug. 1861, Talcott Family Papers, VHS; Lafayette McLaws to Emily McLaws, 18 Aug. 1861, McLaws Papers, UNC; Jones, *Lee's Tigers*, 31; John Minson Galt II 7 June 1861–31 Mar. 1862 Diary, 19 Aug. 1861, Galt Family Papers, CWM.

35. Warner, *Generals in Blue*, 573–74; Faust, *Encyclopedia of the Civil War*, 842; Weinert and Arthur, *Defender of the Chesapeake*, 112, 116; *ORN* I 6:715, 717, 720; *OR* I 51(2):256.

36. *ORN* I 6:722–23, 727–28; William Jerdone Diary, 1 Sept. 1861, Jerdone Family Papers, CWM; Jones to Robert D. Minor, 9 Sept. 1861, Minor Family Papers, VHS. Jerdone

was among plantation owners who constantly had his slaves taken by the military to work on various fortifications on the Peninsula, including Jamestown.

37. Jones to Robert D. Minor, 9 Sept. 1861, Minor Family Papers, VHS; Still, *Confederate Shipbuilding*, 34; Davis, *Duel Between the First Ironclads*, 29.

38. *ORN* I 6:728, 731; Jones to Minor, 9, 16, 22 Sept. 1861, Minor Family Papers, VHS; John A. Williams to Mollie R. Williams, 31 Aug., 7 Sept. 1861, John A. Williams Papers, VHS.

39. Jones to Minor, 16, 22 Sept. 1861, Minor Family Papers, VHS. Jones had always commanded the artillery and proclaimed that he would have it no other way since he was responsible for its efficiency. Allen was absent from Jamestown at the end of September, visiting with the Seldens at their Westover home and in Richmond. It is not indicated whether Allen was tending to his personal business ventures or if this furlough was spent entirely on social visits (Selden Diary, 28, 30 Sept. 1861, VHS).

40. Henry H. Wills to Mary F. Wills, 2, 12 Oct. 1861, Lindsey T. Wills to Mary F. Wills, 2 Oct. 1861, Wills Papers, FSNMP. CSR, Virginia, John D. Smith's Company Virginia Light Artillery (Lindsey T. Wills), NA, indicates that Lindsey Wills's middle initial was "T" rather than "J" as it appears in the typed transcript of his correspondence.

41. Henry H. Wills to Mary F. Wills, 12 Oct. 1861, Wills Papers, FSNMP; Yonge, *Site of Old "James Towne,"* 69.

42. Henry Martin Stringfellow to Elizabeth S. Ewell, n.d., Ewell Papers, CWM. This letter is signed only with the initials "HMS." In Henry H. Wills to Mary F. Wills, 12 Oct. 1861, Wills Papers, FSNMP, Wills stated that "I and a young preecher [sic] by the name of Stringfiller" visited the cemetery adjacent to the Jamestown church tower and prayed there together. In Berkeley Diary, 24, 26 May 1861, Berkeley Papers, VHS, and in Berkeley, *Four Years in the Confederate Artillery*, 6–7, Berkeley identified his messmates as including Henry Martin Stringfellow and stated that Martin Stringfellow officiated at his company's first Sunday services at Jamestown. Hence the identification of "HMS." Stringfellow's CSR (CSR, Virginia, George W. Nelson's Company Virginia Light Artillery [Henry Martin Stringfellow], NA) lists his prewar vocation as student in keeping with his identification as a theology student. *Confederate Veteran* 20:484 and Stringfellow File, CWM, state that he was born in 1839 in Winchester, graduated from the College of William and Mary in 1858, attended Virginia Theological Seminary 1859–1861, and married Alice Johnston in 1863. He became a prominent horticulturalist after the war and died in 1912. His middle name is spelled "Martyn" in his CSR, although this is not in his own handwriting. The "Martyn" spelling also appears in Watkins, *Life of Horace Stringfellow*, 73. However, "Martin" is used most frequently, including his obituary in *Confederate Veteran*, 20:484. The date of the "HMS" letter remains in question, although Stringfellow indicated that he had been at Jamestown continuously for three months. Judging by the number of men he says were at Jamestown at that time, the letter must have been written after the departure of Waddill's Battalion and the 14th Virginia. Stringfellow's length of time at Jamestown and the troop strength mean that the letter could have been written no earlier than late August 1861.

43. Berkeley Diary, [Oct. 1861], Berkeley Papers, VHS; Berkeley, *Four Years in the Confederate Artillery*, 8.

44. *OR* I 4:666; *ORN* I 6:737; Jones to Minor, 3 Oct. 1861, Minor Family Papers, VHS.

45. *OR* I 4:670; Davis, "Mulberry Island and the Civil War," 116. De Lagnel was a native of New Jersey who served as an artilleryman in the U.S. Army before the war. He spent a considerable amount of time during the Civil War as an ordnance officer in Richmond, and he declined promotion to brigadier general on July 31, 1862, following his appointment on April 18, to rank from April 15 (see Evans, *Confederate Military History*, 4:835; Warner, *Generals in Gray*, 71; Wright, *General Officers of the Confederate Army*, 80). The published article and unpublished study by Davis concerning Mulberry Island are similar. Page numbers given in these notes are from the article rather than the study because it is the more recent work, and because it is more readily available to researchers who wish to consult it.

46. Brooke, *John M. Brooke*, 238–40; Dew, *Ironmaker to the Confederacy*, 116; Davis, *Duel Between the First Ironclads*, 9–10, 29–30; Still, *Confederate Shipbuilding*, 34; Jones, "The Iron-Clad *Virginia*," 301.

47. *ORN* II 1:548, 785–86; John M. Brooke's Journal, 2 Nov. 1861, Brooke Papers, GCMF; Brooke, *John M. Brooke*, 240–41; Werlich, *Admiral of the Amazon*, 26; Dew, *Ironmaker to the Confederacy*, 116; Jones, "The Iron-Clad *Virginia*," 301–02; Jones, Report of Ordnance Experiments at Jamestown, VHS; Davis, *Duel Between the First Ironclads*, 30–31; Still, *Iron Afloat*, 20; Luraghi, *History of the Confederate Navy*, 97.

48. Jones, Report of Ordnance Experiments at Jamestown, VHS; Jones, "The Iron-Clad *Virginia*," 298–302; Davis, *Duel Between the First Ironclads*, 30–31; Still, *Iron Afloat*, 97–98; *ORN* II 1:578. Jones's test and his report, which was filed independently of Brooke, indicates that the test with railroad iron was conducted after Brooke's departure from Jamestown.

49. Interview with Mrs. H. L. Munger and Colonel J. P. Barney, 1–2, Jamestown Historical Records, CNHP; Bohannan, *Old Surry*, 29; Stephenson, *Old Homes in Surry & Sussex*, 31; Davis, *Duel Between the First Ironclads*, 31. When interviewed on 24 Apr. 1955, Colonel James P. Barney indicated his awareness of ordnance experiments at Jamestown. He said that iron sheathing was tested with cannon from the Confederate fort, and references to "the Confederate fort" generally mean Fort Pocahontas; when this is not the case, another fort usually is specified by name or location. He also said that "the few pieces of this sheathing still remained at Black Point" and that he "used to hang coon skins on them." Since the fort at Black Point did not have the same open area for firing that can be found at Fort Pocahontas, it is likely that the experiments were at the western end of the island. Furthermore, Fort Pocahontas was the main fort and is the only one known to have had a variety of guns. Jones's reference to different distances from the different gun types to the target also suggests that the shots were fired from heavy guns in a fixed position, as was the case at Fort Pocahontas.

50. *ORN* I 6:740; *OR* I 4:691; Davis, "Mulberry Island and the Civil War," 118; Henry H. Wills to Molly Wills and Frank Wills, 28 Oct. 1861, Wills Papers, FSNMP; Graves, *Bedford Light Artillery*, 15; Berkeley Diary, 14 Mar. 1862, Berkeley Papers, VHS; Berkeley, *Four Years in the Confederate Artillery*, 12; CSR, Virginia, George W. Nelson's Company Virginia Light Artillery, NA. Berkeley did not indicate exactly where his unit was assigned, saying merely that the Hanover Artillery had four 64-pounder guns in a water battery along the riverfront. It is probable that the Hanoverians occupied the Sand Battery. This fort was intended to have five 8-inch Columbiads which fired 65-pound ammunition. Another possibility is that the Hanover men had 32-pounders, which used 64-pound ammunition. Since Berkeley lost his original notes and wrote this information years later, perhaps he had an inaccurate recollection of the guns his unit served in 1861. He was mistaken about the date when the Hanover Artillery left Jamestown, saying that it was November. However, he was absent from his unit on sick furlough, beginning with October. The CSR and Wallace, *Guide to Virginia Military Organizations*, 27, state that the unit disbanded October 4, 1861, and that the men were distributed among other units. Captain Nelson's CSR indicates that the men were at Yorktown by at least October 29.

51. *ORN* I 6:742–43; Faust, *Encyclopedia of the Civil War*, 401–02; Melton, "The Selma Naval Ordnance Works," 18–25, 28–31; Melton, "Major Military Industries of the Confederate Government," 167–68, 178, 501–02, 509–10; Mabry, *Catesby ap R. Jones*, 10. Lieutenant Morrison's account of Jones's departure sounds whimsical. Seventy years later he recalled Jones as saying, "I shall be absent a few days; carry on the routine of the office..." (Interview with Emmett M. Morrison, 2, Jamestown Historical Records, CNHP). Melton's dissertation indicates that while at Selma Jones worked with the same fervor that he displayed at Jamestown, that he complained continuously in his correspondence just as he did at Jamestown, and that he achieved a great deal, also as he did at Jamestown. Jones's Selma operation is credited by Melton with producing "what appears to have been the most advanced, accurate and highest quality heavy ordnance made by either side." Jones also was praised highly in Luraghi, *History of the Confederate Navy*, 348, where

the author included him in his list of Confederates who "formed an elite rarely found in naval history."

52. CSR, Virginia, 53d Infantry (Thompson F. Waddill), NA; Interview with Emmett M. Morrison, 3, Jamestown Historical Records, CNHP.

53. Wallace, *Guide to Virginia Military Organizations*, 3, 7, 32; Krick, *Lee's Colonels*, 218; Norris, *Lower Shenandoah Valley*, 717; Scribner, "With Perry in Japan," 5; List of Officers & Men of the Virginia Navy at Jamestown Batteries, William H. Face, comp., [June 1861], Cocke Family Papers, VHS.

54. CSR, Virginia, 52d Militia, NA; Military Affairs Papers, Box 78, 52d Virginia Militia, LV; *OR* I 4:714. The militia first was summoned for duty in July 1861 (Wallace, *Guide to Virginia Military Organizations*, 258; Coski, "'All Confusion on the Plantations,'" 71). Members of the 52d Militia who had exemptions were proud of their offer to serve, as shown in S. P. Christian to William B. Taliaferro, 30 Dec. 1885, William Booth Taliaferro Papers, CWM.

55. Krick, *Lee's Colonels*, 74–75; Richmond *Daily Dispatch*, 21 May 1875, 2; *Fredericksburg News*, 24 May 1875, 3; Swem and Williams, *Register of the General Assembly*, 155, 157; Carter to John Tyler, 22 Feb. 1842, John Tyler Scrapbook, 107, CWM. Carter served in the Senate in 1842–43 and 1843–44. It was on February 22, 1842, that Carter wrote to President Tyler expressing his belief that one day there would be civil war and that he desired a naval appointment for his son. "Has it never occurred to our southern president," he stated, "& our southern secretary of the navy, too, that the more southern men we have in the army & navy the better for our country." The dual command system that took effect in December is reflected by numerous documents, one being Lewis to Magruder, 24 Mar. 1862, in Letters Received by the Confederate Secretary of War, NA, where Lewis signed as "Major Com[man]d[in]g Batteries."

56. Isaac Munroe St. John to Mason, 19 Dec. 1861, James O. Hensley to Mason, 21 Dec. 1861, and Alfred T. Rives to Mason, 23 Jan. 1862, Charles Tayloe Mason Papers, VHS; William Jerdone Diary, 14, 23, 31 Dec. 1861, 3 Jan., 13 Mar. 1862, Jerdone Family Papers, CWM. During December 13–18 there were thirty-two slaves at Jamestown who worked on the fortifications. They were owned by six different individuals, including Allen who owned eight of them and Carter who owned six. Hensley's letter to Mason specifies the number of slaves per owner and a list of quartermaster's supplies that was furnished for the blacks.

57. CSR, Virginia, 52d Militia, NA; *OR* I 9:39; *ORN* I 6:753–54; Long, *Civil War Day By Day*, 159. One of Jamestown's problems disappeared with the passing of the holidays. An artilleryman wrote that fifty men were drunk on Christmas (John A. Williams to Mollie R. Williams, 27 Dec. 1861, John A. Williams Papers, VHS).

58. *OR* I 51(2):445–46; Hill Carter to Robert R. Carter, 28 Jan. 1862, Shirley Plantation Collection, CWF; *ORN* I 6:759; *OR* I 9:36. On January 31 the Jamestown garrison also included seventy-seven men who were absent at the time.

59. Robert R. Carter to Hill Carter, 6 Feb. 1862, Shirley Plantation Collection, CWF; William Allen to Judah P. Benjamin, 15 Feb. 1862, Letters Received by the Confederate Secretary of War, NA. Numerous requests for permission to raise a company in Allen's proposed battalion can be found in Letters Received by the Confederate Secretary of War, NA, including correspondence from E. P. O. Lewis, 2 Feb. 1862, Miles Selden, 22 Feb. 1862, and George B. Swift, 9 Mar. 1862.

60. *ORN* I 6:767; *OR* I 9:41. Lieutenant Mason, the engineering officer at Jamestown during the winter of 1861–1862, was perceived as having a "gloomy view" of the war after the fall of Roanoke Island. Powhatan Bolling Starke, who wrote to him from Jamestown shortly after Roanoke Island's capture, shared sentiments expressed by Mason that the war should be brief in order to end the misery, and Starke believed that European intervention was imminent.

61. *ORN* I 6:774–76.

62. *OR* I 9:49, 62, I 51(2):507; Graves, *Bedford Light Artillery*, 15. Graves said that light artillery arrived in December but, as is frequently the case, his recollection does not match other official and unofficial records.

63. William Jerdone Diary, 6 Mar. 1862, and William Jerdone Memorandum Book, 1855–1863, 13 Mar. 1862, Jerdone Family Papers, CWM; Selden Diary, 13, 15 Mar., 13 Apr. 1862, VHS.

64. Long, *Civil War Day By Day*, 181–82; Symonds, *Joseph E. Johnston*, 145–46; Sears, *To the Gates of Richmond*, 14–15; Davis, *Duel Between the First Ironclads*, 103, 136–37.

65. "William H. Ware," 388; CSR, Virginia, 53d Infantry (William H. Ware), NA; *ORN* I 7:48, 58; Davis, *Duel Between the First Ironclads*, 103.

66. *OR* I 9:61–62, I 51(2):507; *ORN* II 2:170; Clifford I. Millard to Samuel H. Yonge, 19 Feb. 1934, Yonge Papers, CWM; McKim, *A Soldier's Recollections*, 70–71. The Engineer Bureau sent its report to Davis on March 12, 1862. McKim visited Charles Shirley Harrison at Jamestown on March 4 and counted the same number of artillery as did the engineers. He found Harrison "living like a lord" and hunted ducks with him.

67. *OR* I 51(2):503, 505. Magruder made his appeal through General Samuel Cooper, Adjutant and Inspector General, on March 15 and was authorized to extend martial law to James City County on March 18.

68. Sears, *To the Gates of Richmond*, 18–20.

CHAPTER 5

THE PENINSULA CAMPAIGN

1. Cullen, *Richmond National Battlefield Park*, 4; Sears, *To the Gates of Richmond*, 22–25; Boatner, *Civil War Dictionary*, 633; Faust, *Encyclopedia of the Civil War*, 571; CSR, Virginia, 52d Militia, NA.

2. *OR* I 11(3):387, 390, 433. Magruder sent his opinion to Lee on March 20 and 21. Obstructions are discussed at greater length in Bearss, *River of Lost Opportunities*, 23.

3. Lewis to Magruder, 24 Mar. 1862, Letters Received by the Confederate Secretary of War, NA; *OR* I 11(3):410. Carter's report on Jamestown's strength was dated March 28.

4. Sears, *To the Gates of Richmond*, 25–26, 60; Boatner, *Civil War Dictionary*, 632–33; Long, *Civil War Day By Day*, 189, 193; Hassler, *Commanders of the Army of the Potomac*, 42; Symonds, *Joseph E. Johnston*, 150; *OR* I 11(3):410, 433.

5. Long, *Civil War Day By Day*, 193; Sears, *To the Gates of Richmond*, 35–37; *OR* I 11(3):421; John A. Williams to Mollie R. Williams, 22 Apr. 1862, John A. Williams Papers, VHS.

6. Williams, *Lincoln and His Generals*, 88–89; Hassler, *George B. McClellan*, 85, 88, 90; Sears, *To the Gates of Richmond*, 37–38, 43, 46, 48.

7. Hassler, *Commanders of the Army of the Potomac*, 41; Sears, *To the Gates of Richmond*, 36; Hassler, *George B. McClellan*, 90–91; McClellan, *Papers of George B. McClellan*, 234; Hunter, "Four Years," VHS; H. M. Talley to his mother, 27 Apr. 1862, Talley Papers, VHS.

8. Isaac G. Bell to Mollie Jordan Bell, 26 Apr. 1862, Jordan-Bell Family Letters, VHS; James Thomas Petty Diaries, 24 Apr. 1862, MC.

9. *OR* I 11(3):424, 433; Sears, *To the Gates of Richmond*, 45; Rambaut to Randolph, 7 Apr. 1862, Letters Received by the Confederate Secretary of War, NA.

10. Freeman, *Lee's Lieutenants*, 1:146–47; Symonds, *Joseph E. Johnston*, 148–50.

11. *OR* I 11(3):436–37; Graves, *Bedford Light Artillery*, 18; Long, *Civil War Day By Day*, 200.

12. Long, *Civil War Day By Day*, 200; CSR, Virginia, 10th Battalion Heavy Artillery, NA; Wallace, *Guide to Virginia Military Organizations*, 5; Statement, William Allen elected major, 1862, Adjutant Inspector General and Quartermaster General, NA; *OR* I 11(3):481; Thomas Jefferson Page, Jr., to Randolph, 28 Apr. 1862, Letters Received by the Confederate Secretary of War, NA.

13. Johnston to Lee, 30 Apr. 1862, Dispatch Book of Joseph E. Johnston, 13 June 1861–3 Aug. 1862, Joseph E. Johnston Papers, CWM; Symonds, *Joseph E. Johnston*, 152–53; Receipt, Charles Carter from J. C. Gibson, 1 May 1862, Shirley Plantation Collection, CWF. Captain Carter made the payment on behalf of the colonel and was issued a receipt for $33.75.

14. *OR* I 11(3):489.

15. Selden Diary, 2–3 May 1862, VHS; CSR, Virginia, 10th Battalion Heavy Artillery, NA; Werlich, *Admiral of the Amazon*, 34; Lewis to Randolph, 22 Aug. 1862, Letters Received by the Confederate Secretary of War, NA; CSR, Virginia, 18th Battalion Virginia Heavy Artillery, NA; *OR* I 11(3):504; Discharge, 9 May 1862, James R. Rowland Papers, LV. Tucker's activities following the evacuation of Yorktown were credited with saving numerous vessels that were important for Richmond's defense (Werlich, loc. cit.) in addition to covering Magruder's retreat (Clayton, *Narrative of the Confederate States Navy*, 36). The Jamestown Heavy Artillery escaped from Jamestown on one of Allen's personal schooners, the *E. Miller* (CSR, Virginia, 10th Battalion Heavy Artillery, NA; John A. Williams to Mollie R. Williams, 13 May 1862, John A. Williams Papers, VHS). As for Allen's Claremont home, one source indicates that the Allen family relocated in Petersburg after the Battle of Big Bethel in June 1861, then moved to Richmond (Jesup, *Edward Jessup*, 265). However, as described in the next chapter, Claremont was occupied well into 1862 by at least one member of the Allen family.
16. *OR* I 51(1):596.
17. Selden Diary, 5 May 1862, VHS; Sears, *To the Gates of Richmond*, 69; *OR* I 11(1):463; Kettenburg, "Battle of Williamsburg," 68–69.
18. *OR* I 11(3):495; Keeler, *Aboard the USS* Monitor, 103–04.
19. *OR* I 11(3):146, 500.
20. Ibid., 146–47, 151; *ORN* I 7:326; Lincoln, *Collected Works of Abraham Lincoln*, 5:207.
21. Phisterer, *New York in the War of the Rebellion*, 3:2215; Floyd, *History of the Fortieth (Mozart) Regiment*, 150, 362; Jenkins to Benjamin, 17 May 1862, CWM; *OR Atlas*, Plate 92; "Amblers on the James," David Spencer Cowles Papers, CNHP; Cowles, *Genealogy of the Cowles Family*, 2:1106; Map of Eastern and Central Virginia, VHS; Map of New Kent, Charles City, James City, and York Counties, VHS.
22. *ORN* I 7:706, 722; Silverstone, *Warships of the Civil War Navies*, 16. See the appendixes concerning Confederate artillery and earthworks for an explanation as to why the battery explored in detail probably was the Sand Battery.
23. Long, *Civil War Day By Day*, 209–10; Davis, *Duel Between the First Ironclads*, 154; Keeler, *Aboard the USS* Monitor, 122.
24. Faust, *Encyclopedia of the Civil War*, 227; Keeler, *Aboard the USS* Monitor, 122; Robinson, "Drewry's Bluff," 171; Davis, *Duel Between the First Ironclads*, 155. Another Jamestown connection with the battle at Drewry's Bluff was the vessel CSS *Jamestown*, which was sunk as part of the obstructions in the river there.
25. *ORN* I 7:364, 723; Hackemer, "The Other Union Ironclad: The USS *Galena* and the Critical Summer of 1862," 237; *OR* I 11(3):177–79; Cary, "Diary of Miss Harriette Cary," 111.
26. *ORN* I 7:404, 452; Browning, *From Cape Charles to Cape Fear*, 55; Keeler, *Aboard the USS* Monitor, 138. Perhaps this was the building near the wharf which was identified by archeologists as a barn when the Elay-Swann tract was excavated.
27. *ORN* I 7:473–74, 566, 699.
28. "Confederate Letters," 187–88.
29. *ORN* I 7:522, 529.
30. U.S. Naval History Division, *Civil War Naval Chronology*, 2:79; Silverstone, *Warships of the Civil War Navies*, 85; *OR* I 11(3): 289; Scheips, "Union Signal Communications," 405; *ORN* I 7:650.
31. *ORN* I 7:597; *Dictionary of American Biography*, 20:217. In Sellers, *Civil War Manuscripts*, 5, there is reference to a Union hospital at Jamestown, with the Samuel E. Allen Letters, LC, given as the source. However, both the author and staff members of the Library of Congress examined this collection of two items dated July 19 and 29, 1862, and, although there is reference to several hospitals, none of them were located at Jamestown.
32. *ORN* I 7:646–47.
33. Ibid., 639–40, 642.
34. Sears, *To the Gates of Richmond*, 350; Hassler, *George B. McClellan*, 191, 199–200; *OR* I 11(1):88; McClellan, *McClellan's Own Story*, 467; *ORN* I 7:467.
35. McClellan, *McClellan's Own Story*, 468.

36. Hassler, *George B. McClellan*, 200; *ORN* I 7:633–34, 644, 654.
37. *ORN* I 7:649, 651–52.
38. Ibid., 651, 654, 658.
39. Hassler, *George B. McClellan*, 203; *ORN* I 7:668, 673.
40. *ORN* I 7:687.
41. Ibid., 686; Browning, *From Cape Charles to Cape Fear*, 63.

CHAPTER 6
UNION OUTPOST AND COMMUNICATIONS LINK

1. *OR* I 11(1):410.
2. Allen to Randolph, 15 Aug. 1862, CSR, 10th Battalion Virginia Heavy Artillery (William Allen), NA.
3. Wynne, "Jamestown, Virginia," 3:53; *Calendar of Virginia State Papers*, 11:235; Grimsley, *Hard Hand of War*, 72; *ORN* I 7:473; Keeler, *Aboard the USS* Monitor, 138. A study found that during the Peninsula campaign some Union soldiers rustled livestock and looted abandoned houses but usually left occupied structures alone (Grimsley, *Hard Hand of War*, 72), and it appears that structures at Jamestown were used by refugee slaves that summer.
4. Gregory, *Claremont Manor*, 66, 68; Jesup, *Edward Jessup*, 263, 265; 8th Census, 1860, Population Schedules, Surry Co., Va., 950, NA; Register of Deaths, Surry Co., 15, LV; Will Book No. 11, Surry Co., 138–43, LV; *Richmond Daily Whig*, 24 Oct. 1862, 1; *Daily Richmond Examiner*, 24 Oct. 1862, 1; *Daily Lynchburg Virginian*, 27 Oct. 1862, 2; Jordan, *Black Confederates and Afro-Yankees*, 178; *Calendar of Virginia State Papers*, 11:233–34; Order Book, Surry Co., 20, LV. There is a discrepancy in Shriver's age: the 1860 census says he was forty while the death register, recorded less than two years later, says he was fifty-one. Census information for other members of the Allen family at Claremont is correct, so that source is used for the narrative. A deposition of Gilbert Wooten is printed in the *Calendar* and is the main source for this visit to Jamestown, supplemented by newspaper accounts. The deposition contains numerous discrepancies, especially in names and spellings, which are clarified by other sources. Joseph Algernon Graves is incorrectly identified in the *Calendar* as James A. Graves. His name appears correctly in the 8th Census, 1860, Population Schedules, Surry Co., Va., 950, NA; Order Book, Surry Co., 20, LV; Will Book No. 10, Surry Co., 579–81, LV; and "The Sheild Family," 59. Graves was commonwealth attorney, as stated in the *Daily Lynchburg Virginian* and the Order Book which called for an election to replace him after his death; the two Richmond newspapers incorrectly described him as a former commonwealth attorney. There also is conflicting information about young George Graves, who is cited in the *Calendar*, the *Richmond Daily Whig*, and the *Daily Lynchburg Virginian* as Graves's nephew and in Bohannan, *Surry County at War*, 44, as his son. However, George was Graves's nephew as noted in the 8th Census, 1860, Population Schedules, Surry Co., Va., 950–51, and Graves's will in Will Book No. 10, Surry Co., 580, LV, in which Graves referred to the two children of his late brother, as well as in the *Richmond Daily Whig* and the *Daily Lynchburg Virginian*. The *Calendar* spells Wooten's name as "Wooton," and the 8th Census, 1860, Population Schedules, Surry Co., Va., 950, NA, uses the spelling "Wooten." "Wooten" has been chosen for the narrative due to greater accuracy in the census spellings. Shriver's name, which is consistently spelled "Shriver" everywhere except in the deposition, appears both correctly as "Shriver" and incorrectly as "Schriver" in the *Calendar*. Four Mile Tree is cited as Graves's home in *Calendar*, 11:236, and Bohannan, *Old Surry*, 24–25. The purpose of the visit to Jamestown varies with each newspaper account; the *Richmond Daily Whig* says that it was to obtain tools to repair a mill, the *Daily Richmond Examiner* says simply that it was to transact private business, and the *Daily Lynchburg Virginian* says that it was to get blacks for Allen, which perhaps means to retrieve

some of his runaway slaves. The discrepancies for the date of the visit are discussed in note 11, page 173.

5. *Calendar of Virginia State Papers*, 11:233. William Parsons also is called "Joe Parsons," but appears more frequently as "William."

6. Ibid., 233–34. Aleck also is spelled in the *Calendar* as "Alick."

7. 8th Census, 1860, Productions of Agriculture, James City County, Va., 5–6, NA; *Calendar of Virginia State Papers*, 11:234, 236. Wooten referred to the overseer's house at both Jamestown and Neck of Land as "the Great House." However, it is easy to distinguish between the two both by their locations and by his reference to the Neck of Land house as the one "where Mr. [William R.] Emory used to live"; J. C. Gibson was overseer at Jamestown and lived in the Ambler house. In contrast with Wooten's account which says that Windsor was called "the judge," the *Daily Richmond Examiner*, 24 Oct. 1862, 1, says that the blacks' leader was called "the colonel," in keeping with the paper's claim that the blacks identified themselves as a New York regiment. The paper further stated that the Union troops in Williamsburg encouraged the rebellious action. The *Richmond Daily Whig*, 24 Oct. 1862, 1, likewise said that the blacks called themselves Union soldiers. With less certainty, the *Daily Lynchburg Virginian*, 27 Oct. 1862, 2, felt that the blacks "probably" were ordered by Federals. Although Virginia newspapers used this incident at Jamestown to depict the Federals as sinister manipulators of former slaves, even Union soldiers were killed and robbed by blacks on the Peninsula, as described in Jordan, *Black Confederates and Afro-Yankees*, 178. A soldier in Allen's former battalion suggested a different motive for the murders, saying "I think that is a very bold move that is the effect of Old Abe's emancipation proclamation." He wrote that the black leader was called "the President" and that Confederate cavalry was sent in vain to capture the perpetrators (John A. Williams to Mollie R. Williams, 1 Nov. 1862, John A. Williams Papers, VHS).

8. *Calendar of Virginia State Papers*, 11:234–35.

9. Ibid.

10. Ibid., 235–36; *Richmond Daily Whig*, 24 Oct. 1862, 1; *Daily Richmond Examiner*, 24 Oct. 1862, 1; *Daily Lynchburg Virginian*, 27 Oct. 1862, 2. Wooten gave conflicting testimony here, saying that the bodies of Shriver, Graves, and Graves's nephew were thrown over the bridge after the shooting, even though he stated earlier that Graves's nephew was thrown over the bridge first and then shot. The newspaper accounts also have discrepancies. The body of young George Graves apparently was found a few weeks later. In the Richard Bucktrout Daybook, on deposit at Swem Library, CWM, there is an entry on November 12, 1862, by the coffin maker for "the little boy that was murdered by the negroes at Neck of Land." Graves was buried "to the East of the spring on the river shore at the farm called St. Georgie's [George's]" about 125 yards from the spring.

11. Ibid., 236. The deposition was dated October 25, and the Register of Deaths, Surry Co., 15, LV, states that Shriver was killed on October 24. The October 24 date is impossible based on the number of days that Wooten said transpired before he returned to Surry County, and two newspaper accounts of the event are dated October 24 (see below). Furthermore, Wooten's reference to the murders as occurring on Monday matches the 1862 calendar perfectly, which shows that Monday was October 20 and thereby allows for the proper number of days for Wooten's narrative. Probate papers for Shriver's will cite his death, and hence the date of the incident, as on or about October 20 (Will Book No. 11, Surry Co., 138, LV). Newspaper accounts in *Richmond Daily Whig*, 24 Oct. 1862, 1, *Daily Richmond Examiner*, 24 Oct. 1862, 1, and *Daily Lynchburg Virginian*, 27 Oct. 1862, 2, give the date as October 21. Most of the people Wooten encountered on his flight from Jamestown can be identified. "Mr. Copeland" was not matched with anyone in the 1860 census. Wooten's deposition refers to "John Cassidy" as "a free man of color." There is no free black near Jamestown with that spelling; however, the 8th Census, 1860, Population Schedules, James City Co., Va., 724, NA, lists John Cassaday, who at that time was a sixty-three-year-old mulatto

and farmer. Mrs. Graves was Martha Sheild Graves, as noted in 8th Census, 1860, Population Schedules, Surry Co., Va., 950, NA, and "The Sheild Family," 59.

12. Order Book, Surry Co., 20, 22, 25, 30, 120, LV; *Richmond Daily Whig*, 24 Oct. 1862, 1; *Daily Richmond Examiner*, 24 Oct. 1862, 1; *Daily Lynchburg Virginian*, 27 Oct. 1862, 2; Jordan, *Black Confederates and Afro-Yankees*, 178–79.

13. *ORN* I 7:695, 8:144–45; Browning, *From Cape Charles to Cape Fear*, 10, 60–61, 63.

14. Browning, *From Cape Charles to Cape Fear*, 71; Cormier, *Siege of Suffolk*, 124; Boatner, *Civil War Dictionary*, 458, 817; Warner, *Generals in Blue*, 264; *ORN* I 8:709–11.

15. *ORN* I 8:709, 711–12.

16. Ibid., 714–15, 717.

17. Browning, *From Cape Charles to Cape Fear*, 69.

18. Coddington, *Gettysburg Campaign*, 100–01; *ORN* I 9:68, 70; *OR* I 51(1):1049.

19. *ORN* I 9:70–71; Silverstone, *Warships of the Civil War Navies*, 100.

20. *OR* I 51(1):1050–51; *ORN* I 9:69, 71–73.

21. *ORN* I 9:71–72; *OR* I 51(1):1052, 1056.

22. Coddington, *Gettysburg Campaign*, 102; Faust, *Encyclopedia of the Civil War*, 222, 416; Warner, *Generals in Blue*, 264; *ORN* I 9:71.

23. Browning, *From Cape Charles to Cape Fear*, 69–71; Current, *Encyclopedia of the Confederacy*, 2:840; Beers, *The Confederacy*, 354.

24. Cronin, "Vest Mansion," 20, 62, 64, 171, CWF. This manuscript is a copy of the original in the Cronin Papers, NYHS.

25. Record of Events, New York, 1st Mounted Rifles, NA; Eyland [Cronin], *Evolution of a Life*, 186; Cronin, "Vest Mansion," 171, CWF.

26. Cronin, "Vest Mansion," 171, 173, CWF. An example of other units serving at Jamestown is in CSR, U.S. Colored Troops, 1st Cavalry, NA.

27. Cronin, "Vest Mansion," 171, CWF.

28. Ibid., 20, 172–73; Eyland [Cronin], *Evolution of a Life*, 186.

29. Cronin, "Vest Mansion," 173, CWF.

30. Ibid., 173–74.

31. Tidwell, Hall, and Gaddy, *Come Retribution*, 242–47; Eyland [Cronin], *Evolution of a Life*, 194–96; Jones, *Eight Hours Before Richmond*, 21–24, 77, 95–97, 100, 143–48.

32. Hassler, *Commanders of the Army of the Potomac*, 204, 206, 208, 216; Robertson, *Back Door to Richmond*, 59.

33. *OR* I 51(1):199; Cronin, "Vest Mansion," 176–77, CWF; Scheips, "Union Signal Communications," 411; Munden and Beers, *The Union*, 316; Grant, *Personal Memoirs*, 2:205.

34. Schiller, *Bermuda Hundred Campaign*, 311, 313–16; Robertson, *Back Door to Richmond*, 232; *OR* I 36(3):177–78.

35. *OR* I 36(3):112–13, 51(1):1162; CSR, U.S. Colored Troops, 1st Cavalry (Charles H. Libean), NA; 1st U.S. Colored Cavalry, Regimental Orders, Letters, and Endorsements Book, Special Orders No. 99, 2 May 1864, NA.

36. *OR* I 36(3):597; Silverstone, *Warships of the Civil War Navies*, 112.

37. *OR* I 40(1):22, 269; U.S. Surgeon General's Office, *Medical and Surgical History of the War*, I:1 Medical History Appendix, 192.

38. *OR* I 36(3):756, 40(2):210, 362; Grant, *Papers*, 11:83, 113.

39. *OR* I 51(1):200, 262.

40. CSR, New York, 1st Mounted Rifles (Griffin Oatman), NA; Cronin, "Vest Mansion," 176, CWF.

41. *OR* I 40(3):19, 51(1):262; Plum, *Military Telegraph During the Civil War*, 261.

42. *OR* I 40(3):421, 635.

43. *OR* I 42(1):831–32, 42(2):72, 140; Map, Military Map of South-Eastern Virginia, LC. The U.S. Colored Cavalry unit was not identified.

44. Plum, *Military Telegraph During the Civil War*, 260–61; *OR* I 42(2):72; Cronin, "Vest Mansion," 248–50. In Cronin's narrative, a company of U.S. Colored Cavalry was sent from Williamsburg to relieve a company of white soldiers at Jamestown. The relief company was ambushed near the Jamestown bridge and stampeded back to Williamsburg

with severe losses. Then the cavalrymen reformed at the college and returned to Jamestown to fulfill their duty. According to Cronin, the black troops were commanded by Captain Baryon Ives, "fresh from Yale College," who later attained higher rank. An examination of soldiers' compiled service records at the National Archives found only one person with black cavalrymen whose name was similar, that being Silliman B. Ives. Ives formerly was a captain with the 12th Connecticut Volunteers and then served as captain, Company C, 2d U.S. Colored Cavalry, from December 14, 1863 until December 29, 1864 when he was dismissed for desertion (CSR, U.S. Colored Troops, 2d Cavalry [Silliman B. Ives], NA). Upon consulting the Yale University archives for Silliman B. Ives, Baryon Ives, Silliman Baryon Ives, and Ives in general, no match was found. Eliot, *Yale in the Civil War*, lists three alumni with the Ives name who served during the war, but none with that name or comparable service records. The closest match is Brayton Ives, Class of 1861, who served with the 5th Connecticut Volunteers, rose to the rank of lieutenant colonel, and resigned for health reasons on August 5, 1863; he joined the 1st Connecticut Cavalry in May 1864 and remained with them, rising to colonel with a brigadier general's brevet (*Yale Obituary Record*, Ives, Alumni Files, YU).

45.　*OR* I 42(2):623, 696; 16th New York Heavy Artillery, Letter, Order, and Miscellaneous Book, 4 Sept. 1864, NA; Record of Events, New York, 20th Cavalry, NA; Phisterer, *New York in the War of the Rebellion*, 2:1040.

46.　*OR* I 42(2):696–97; 16th New York Heavy Artillery, Letter, Order, and Miscellaneous Book, 4 Sept. 1864, NA. The 20th New York Cavalry's losses officially were listed as one killed, one wounded for September 3. These were significant figures since the regiment had six men killed, and a total of forty-eight casualties, for the entire war (Phisterer, *New York in the War of the Rebellion*, 2:1040).

47.　Grant, *Papers*, 12:110; *OR* I 42(2):627, 952; Browning, *From Cape Charles to Cape Fear*, 78–79.

48.　*OR* I 42(1):98, 959–60, 42(3):195, 233, 241–42; Grant, *Papers*, 12:315–16.

49.　John A. Porter Papers, USAMHI; Porter, *76th Regiment Pennsylvania Volunteer Infantry*, 74; Dickey, *Eighty-fifth Regiment Pennsylvania Volunteer Infantry*, 409. The 76th Pennsylvania also had a detachment at Fort Magruder; see *OR* I 42(3):469.

50.　*ORN* I 11:135.

51.　*OR* I 42(1):1028–29, 42(3):840–41.

52.　Stowits, *One Hundredth Regiment of New York State Volunteers*, 319, 372–73; *ORN* I 11:135; Gibbon, *Personal Recollections*, 283.

53.　*OR* I 42(3):1129, 46(2):340, 590; 16th New York Heavy Artillery, Morning Reports Book, 5 Feb. 1865, NA; 16th New York Heavy Artillery, Order Book, Special Order No. 32, 11 Feb. 1865, NA. Blomberg's first name is listed as Carlo in contemporary records at the National Archives, above, which also give his rank as second lieutenant; the *OR's* also use "Carlo." However, Phisterer, *New York in the War of the Rebellion*, 2:1529, gives his first name as Charles and his rank as first lieutenant, 4 Feb. 1865, with rank from 11 Jan. 1865.

54.　*OR* I 46(2):582–83.

55.　Ibid., 582–83, 589–90.

56.　Ibid., 618–19. Hicks wanted to burn all houses within a mile's radius of the downed wires.

57.　Ibid., 682, 753, 792.

58.　Long, *Civil War Day By Day*, 645; Grant, *Papers*, 14:92, 100–101, 121; *OR* I 46(2):813. Grant made his offer to Gibbon on March 3, just before Roberts's departure. The Rappahannock expedition received little notice. Gibbon's biographers discussed only the Petersburg campaign for spring 1865 and made no reference to the operations at Fredericksburg and vicinity (Lavery and Jordan, *Iron Brigade General*, 124), nor did the military summary of Gibbon's promotions and campaigns in Cullum, *Biographical Register*, 2:193. Even Gibbon himself ignored them in his memoirs (Gibbon, *Personal Recollections*, 287).

59. Grant, *Papers*, 14:xxiv, 476; *OR* I 46(3):209. Ludlow's recommendation was forwarded to Grant's headquarters on March 27.
60. *OR* I 46(3):570; *ORN* I 12:112, 119.
61. *OR* I 46(3):985–86, 1035, 1130; CSR, Virginia, 13th Infantry (Charles H. Wood), NA; Riggs, *13th Virginia Infantry*, 149.

CHAPTER 7
POSTWAR CHANGE AND HISTORIC PRESERVATION

1. William Allen to George Wythe Randolph, 15 Aug. 1862, CSR, 10th Battalion Virginia Heavy Artillery (William Allen), NA. See the bibliography for publications by the Bohannans.
2. *Hardesty's Historical and Geographical Encyclopedia*, 425–26; Bruce, *Virginia: Rebirth of the Old Dominion*, 4:220; CSR, 10th Battalion Virginia Heavy Artillery (Aurelius P. Bohannan), NA; Bohannan, "Jamestown Island and 'The Surry Side,'" 135; Bohannan, *Surry County at War*, 21; Boddie, *Southside Virginia Families*, 1:4; Crittenden, *The Comp'ny*, 2; Hotchkiss Papers, Reel 59, Frame 306, LC; CSR, 10th Battalion Virginia Heavy Artillery (William Allen), NA. The latter contains a sizable list of supplies Allen furnished the Confederacy, and it also cites some of the supplies' uses, e.g., wood for a battery; wood for a wharf; 16,115 feet of inch boards; mules; oxen; bacon; corn; and hay in quantities of 60,000 pounds and 76,935 pounds. This incomplete list covers only from 1861 to mid-1863. Allen's contribution to the iron plate for the CSS *Virginia* was minor; most of the iron came from rails from the captured Baltimore & Ohio Railroad, indefensible rail lines, and iron materials from the Norfolk Navy Yard (Luraghi, *History of the Confederate Navy*, 97; Coski, *Capital Navy*, 25).
3. Selden Diary, 28 Mar., 17 Sept. 1862, VHS; *Calendar of Virginia State Papers*, 11:233–36.
4. Gregory, *Claremont Manor*, 68; DeLeon, *Belles, Beaux and Brains*, 133–34; "Letters from a Tyler Collection," 99; Chesnut, *Mary Chesnut's Civil War*, 599; Kay, "Drewry's Bluff or Fort Darling?", 194.
5. Gregory, *Claremont Manor*, 69; Deposition of Frances A. Allen, 29 May 1877, Box 27, Folder 7, Dunlop Papers, VHS; Will Book No. 6, Surry Co., 218–22, LV. In Frances Allen's deposition, she stated that at the time of her husband's death in 1875 his only real estate, excluding his inheritance, was property in Richmond, about 104½ acres in James City County, 24½ acres in Surry County, and a mill and mill site in Surry County. In addition to real estate, he sold numerous personal items to alleviate his debt, including most of his paintings and statuary. The dwindling of his personal real estate, as opposed to that which he inherited, was dramatic. His wife's deposition indicates that 129 acres remained in 1875; in comparison, Allen already had accumulated 3,724 acres of his own by 1850, as noted in Gregory, *Claremont Manor*, 63. Allen's property in Richmond at the time of his death was on 7th Street, fronting on the north side of Leigh Street between 7th and 8th Streets, as described in Bill of Complaint and Petition, 1876, 1882, Box 27, Folder 1, Decrees, 1876–1886, Box 27, Folder 2, Commissioners Reports, 1877–1886, Box 27, Folder 3, and Mills' Garden Lots, Seventh St., Richmond, Deed of Trust, Box 28, Folder 7, Dunlop Papers, VHS.
6. Deed Book 2, James City County, 110–12, 198–200, 204, WJCCC.
7. Accounts of William Allen 1875, Box 28, Folders 1, 2, and 3, and Miscellaneous Proceedings, Statement of Frances A. Allen, 25 May 1878, Box 27, Folder 7, Dunlop Papers, VHS; *Petersburg Index and Appeal*, 21 May 1875, 3, and 25 May 1875, 3; Richmond *Daily Dispatch*, 20 May 1875, 1–2, and 21 May 1875, 2; *Richmond Enquirer*, 20 May 1875, 4, and 21 May 1875, 4, and 23 May 1875, 4; *Fredericksburg News*, 24 May 1875, 3. Details of William Allen's death are contradictory. His wife's statements in the Dunlop Papers appear to be most reliable and are similar to some other accounts, such as the *Petersburg Index and Appeal*. The *Fredericksburg News* says he died at his farm of apoplexy. The *Richmond Enquirer* says he died at Waverly Station, which

probably was caused by Waverly Station serving as the source of telegrams that announced Allen's death, as stated in the Richmond *Daily Dispatch*. DeLeon, *Belles, Beaux and Brains*, 134, says Allen was alone in his boat on the James River when he died, and the Hotchkiss Papers, Reel 59, Frame 306, LC, says he was seized with a congestive chill while traveling by boat from Williamsburg to Kingsmill and that he died at the latter place; there is no corroboration for these stories.

8. *Fredericksburg News*, 24 May 1875, 3; Richmond *Daily Dispatch*, 20 May 1875, 1; James Alfred Jones to Edward C. Turner, 21 May 1875, Turner Family Papers, VHS; Miscellaneous Proceedings, Statement of Frances A. Allen, 25 May 1878, Box 27, Folder 7, Appraisal, 14 June 1875, Box 28, Folder 2, Deposition of Frances A. Allen, 29 May 1877, Box 27, Folder 7, and Accounts, Box 28, Folder 1, Dunlop Papers, VHS. With Claremont gone, Allen's wife and children were unable to be interred near him. Upon their deaths, Frances Allen and children William, Frances, John, and Jessup were buried at Hollywood Cemetery in Richmond, as was Mary, the wife of Allen's son, William (Hollywood Cemetery Burial Records, 2, 9, 12, 67, 212, 216, 222, 312).

9. Deed Book 5, James City County, 503–505, 536–42, WJCCC; Lindgren, *Preserving the Old Dominion*, 180–81.

10. Henry Donald Whitcomb to Wilfred Emory Cutshaw, 22 Apr. 1897, VHS; Yonge, *Site of Old "James Towne,"* 11, 25. See also note 16, page 177, for additional sources that document the erosion of Fort Pocahontas.

11. *Official Blue Book of the Jamestown Ter-Centennial Exposition*, 682–83; Kelton, "Armed Confederates at Jamestown," 389; *Suffolk News-Herald*, 8 June 1932; *Smithfield Times*, 9 June 1932; Morrison, Alumni Biographical File, VMI.

12. Hatch, *Jamestown, Virginia*, 36–37; Elay-Swann Tract, Jamestown Island: Preliminary Historical Study and Archeological Report, 52–53, Jamestown Archeology Records, CNHP; Elay-Swann, Accession 7, Jamestown Museum Collection, CNHP. During World War II military activity returned to Jamestown when Colonial National Historical Park was used for training exercises. For comments on an artillery unit at Jamestown in 1943, see Superintendent's Narrative Report for November 1943, Superintendent's Monthly Reports, 4, CNHP, and the Bagby Family Papers, VHS.

13. Interview with Samuel H. Yonge, 1–2, Jamestown Historical Records, CNHP; Interview with Emmett M. Morrison, 2–3, Jamestown Historical Records, CNHP.

14. Interview with Mrs. H. L. Munger and Colonel J. P. Barney, 1–2, Jamestown Historical Records, CNHP; Werlich, *Admiral of the Amazon*, 27–28, 34; Clayton, "Jamestown Island," 142. The Confederates said they used bricks from a structure in the river about seventy–five yards east of the church tower. For clarification of the contradictory account of the *Virginia's* armor tests, see Chapter 4, note 49.

15. Report on 1955 Excavations in the Elay-Swann Tract, 3, Jamestown Archeology Records, CNHP; Elay-Swann, Project 235, Accession 83, Jamestown Museum Collection, CNHP.

16. Final Report: Archeological Explorations in the Confederate Fort Area, 4–5, 8, 16–18, 20, Jamestown Archeology Records, CNHP; Project 100: The Confederate Fort, 2–4, Jamestown Archeology Records, CNHP; Fort Pocahontas/Confederate Fort, Project 100, Accession 81, Jamestown Museum Collection, CNHP/APVA; Plat of Land Situated on Jamestown Island in James River, Va., CNHP, NA, and Deed Book 5:539 and Plat Book 2:6, WJCCC; Map, Western End of Jamestown Island Showing Property of the APVA, CNHP; Map, Trenches Dug for Water & Sewer Lines, CNHP; Hobbs, Blanton, Gammisch, and Broadwater, "A Marine Archaeological Reconnaissance," Map, 357. Throughout the twentieth century a new wall took shape on the side of the fort which faced the river, thereby reducing the evidence of erosion. Nearly three decades after Shiner's archeological work, surviving earthworks at Jamestown and vicinity were recognized in their historical context in Robertson, *Civil War Sites in Virginia*, 65–66.

17. Brown, "National Park Service Archaeological Assessment of Jamestown, Virginia," 1–5; Bentley Boyd, "Jamestown: 1607–2007," Newport News *Daily Press*, 10 Nov. 1992, A1, A12; Bentley Boyd, "Archaeologists Near 1st Jamestown Fort," Newport News *Daily Press*, 23 Apr. 1994, C1–C2.

BIBLIOGRAPHY

ARCHIVES AND MANUSCRIPTS

Association for the Preservation of Virginia Antiquities. Richmond, Virginia.
Memorandum: Some Notes on Jamestown Island as Recalled by Cyrus
Hankins (Cyrus Hankins to Parke Rouse, Jr., 7 September 1969).
College of William and Mary. Williamsburg, Virginia.
Department of Manuscripts and Rare Books.
Barron, Samuel. Papers, I.
Bucktrout, Richard. Daybook. (On Deposit.)
Ewell Papers.
Galt Family Papers.
Hoar, Henry C. Memorial Collection.
Jenkins, John H. B. Letter to Mary A. Benjamin, 17 May 1862.
Jerdone Family Papers.
Johnston, Joseph E. Papers.
McDermed Papers.
Page-Saunders Papers.
Phillips, William H. Papers.
Ritchie-Harrison Papers.
Taliaferro, William Booth. Papers.
Tyler Family Papers, Group A.
Tyler, John. Scrapbook.
Whittle, Conway. Papers.
Yonge Papers.
University Archives.
Faculty/Alumni Files.
Ewell, Benjamin Stoddert.
Rogers, William Barton.
Stringfellow, Henry Martin.

Colonial National Historical Park. Jamestown and Yorktown, Virginia.
  Cowles, David Spencer. Papers, ca. 1850–1987.
  Holland, John Clay. Papers, 1861.
  Jamestown Archeology Records.
      Elay-Swann Tract, Jamestown Island: Preliminary Historical Study
          and Archeological Report on the 1937 Exploratory Excavations
          (J. C. Harrington, 15 May 1941).
      Final Report: Archeological Explorations in the Confederate Fort
          Area in the APVA Grounds (Jamestown National Historic Site)
          at Jamestown, Park Research Project No. 100 (Joel L. Shiner,
          24 June 1955).
      Project 100: The Confederate Fort.
      Report on 1955 Excavations in the Elay-Swann Tract on Jamestown
          Island (Joel L. Shiner, 23 June 1955).
  Jamestown Civil War Earthworks Records, 1989.
  Jamestown Historical Records.
      Data from Interview with Mrs. H. L. Munger and Colonel J. P.
          Barney: Notes on Nineteenth and Early Twentieth Century
          Jamestown (24 April 1956).
      Memorandum: Report of Visit to Edenton, North Carolina (27 May
          1934; Interview with Samuel H. Yonge).
      Memorandum to the Historical Division (28 July 1938; Thor
          Borresen's Report on an Old Fortification [Point of Island Bat-
          tery]).
      Record of Interview with Emmett M. Morrison (ca. 1930–1932).
  Jamestown Museum Collection.
      Confederate Fort, Project 100, 1955. Accession 81.
      Elay-Swann, 1937. Accession 7.
      Elay-Swann, Project 235, 1955. Accession 83.
  Superintendent's Monthly Reports, 1931–1975.
Colonial Williamsburg Foundation. Williamsburg, Virginia.
  Cronin, David Edward. "The Vest Mansion: Its Historical and Romantic
      Associations as Confederate and Union Headquarters (1862–1865)
      in the American Civil War."
  Shirley Plantation Collection, 1650–1989.
Fluvanna Historical Society. Palmyra, Virginia.
  Ross Brothers Letters.
Fredericksburg and Spotsylvania National Military Park. Fredericksburg,
  Virginia.
  Wills Papers, 1861–1864.
George C. Marshall Foundation. Lexington, Virginia.
  Brooke Papers. (Private Collection Owned by George M. Brooke, Jr.)
Hollywood Cemetery. Richmond, Virginia.
  Hollywood Cemetery Burial Records.

Library of Congress. Washington, D.C.
    Allen, Samuel E. Letters, 1862.
    Hotchkiss, Jedediah. Papers, 1838–1908.
Library of Virginia. Richmond, Virginia.
    Ambler, John Jaquelin. "The History of the Ambler Family in Virginia."
        Richmond: 1826.
    Confederate Rosters. Virginia.
        10th Battalion Heavy Artillery.
        Confederate Navy, Officers.
    Department of Military Affairs Papers, Adjutant General's Office, Con-
        federate Military Records.
        10th Battalion Virginia Heavy Artillery, "Allen's Battery, Brandon
            Heavy Artillery, Co. D, 10th Battalion, Virginia Artillery" (Box 12).
        52d Virginia Militia (Box 78).
        53d Virginia Infantry (Box 58).
    French, Samuel Bassett. Papers.
    Rowland, James R. Papers, 1861–1862.
    Surry County Records.
        Deed Book No. 13, 1848–1857.
        Deed Book No. 14, 1857–1864.
        Fiduciary Accounts, 1840–1848.
        Militia Records, 1840–1861.
        Order Book, 1862–1877.
        Register of Deaths, 1853–1896.
        Will Book No. 6, 1830–1834.
        Will Book No. 10, 1852–1863.
        Will Book No. 11, 1864–1875.
    Virginia Legislative Petitions, Surry County.
Museum of the Confederacy. Richmond, Virginia.
    Petty, James Thomas. Diaries, 1861–1863.
    Randolph, J. Tucker. Journal. Randolph Papers.
National Archives. Washington, D.C.
    Compiled Service Records of Confederate Soldiers Who Served in Orga-
        nizations from the State of Virginia. Record Group 109. M 324.
        1st Artillery.
        10th Battalion, Heavy Artillery.
        18th Battalion, Heavy Artillery.
        George W. Nelson's Company Virginia Light Artillery (Hanover
            Artillery).
        John D. Smith's Company Virginia Light Artillery (Bedford Light
            Artillery).
        13th Infantry.
        14th Infantry.
        21st Infantry.
        52d Militia.
        53d Infantry.

Confederate States of America. War Department.
 Adjutant and Inspector General's Office. Record Group 109.
  Letters Received, 1861–1865. M 474.
 Military Departments. Army of the Peninsula, May 1861–April 1862.
  Record Group 109.
 General Orders. Chapter 2, Vol. 229.
 Secretary of War. Record Group 109.
  Letters Received, 1861–1865. M 437.
U.S. Census Office.
 7th Census. 1850. M 432.
  Population Schedules.
 8th Census. 1860. M 653.
  Population Schedules.
  Productions of Agriculture During the Year Ending 1 June 1860.
  Products of Industry During the Year Ending 1 June 1860.
  Slave Schedule.
U.S. War Department.
 Record and Pension Office. Record Group 94.
  Compiled Service Records.
   New York.
    1st Mounted Rifles.
   U.S. Colored Troops.
    1st Cavalry.
    2d Cavalry.
  Record of Events. M 594.
   New York.
    1st Mounted Rifles.
    20th Cavalry.
  Volunteer Regiments. Record Books.
   New York.
    16th Heavy Artillery.
     Letter, Order, and Miscellaneous Book.
     Morning Reports Book.
     Order Book.
   U.S. Colored Troops.
    1st Cavalry.
     Regimental Orders, Letters, and Endorsements Book.
New-York Historical Society. New York, New York.
 Cronin, David Edward. Papers.
Private Collection.
 Young, Preston. South Boston, Virginia.
 Geisinger, Michael F. Vernon Hill, Virginia.
  Young, Edward Rush. Diary.

University of North Carolina. Chapel Hill, North Carolina.
  Southern Historical Collection.
      McLaws, Lafayette. Papers, 1836–1897.
University of Virginia. Charlottesville, Virginia.
  Barron, Samuel. Papers. 10134.
  Barron, Waring, and Baylor Family Papers. 10134–c.
U.S. Army Military History Institute. Carlisle, Pennsylvania.
  Civil War Times Illustrated Collection.
      Porter, John A. Papers.
Virginia Historical Society. Richmond, Virginia.
  Archives Accession Book.
  Bagby Family Papers, 1824–1960.
  Berkeley, Henry Robinson. Papers, 1859–1865.
  Cocke Family Papers, 1742–1976.
  Dunlop, James Nathaniel. Papers, 1840–1888.
  Durfey, Goodrich. "Old James Town For Sale," Unidentified newspaper,
      26 November 1844.
  Hankins, Cyrus. Letter to James Ambler Johnston, 15 June 1955.
  Hunter, Alexander. Four Years in the Ranks, 1861–1865: Reminiscences
      of Alexander Hunter.
  Jones, Catesby ap Roger. Report of Ordnance Experiments at Jamestown,
      12 October 1861.
  Jordan-Bell Family Letters, 1861–1864.
  Lee Family Papers, 1824–1918.
  Mason, Charles Tayloe. Papers, 1854–1906.
  Mason Family Papers, 1813–1943.
  Minor Family Papers, 1810–1932.
  Patton Family Papers, 1693–1957.
  Selden, John Armistead. Diary, 1 July 1858–31 May 1864.
  Talcott Family Papers, 1816–1915.
  Talley, Henry M. Papers, 1858–1865.
  Turner Family Papers, 1740–1927.
  Whitcomb, Henry Donald. Letter to Wilfred Emory Cutshaw, 22 April
      1897.
  Williams, John A. Papers, 1861–1865.
Virginia Military Institute. Lexington, Virginia.
  Alumni Biographical File. Class of 1842–Class of 1899.
      Morrison, Emmett Masalon.
Williamsburg-James City County Courthouse. Williamsburg, Virginia.
  Deed Book 2.
  Deed Book 5.
  Plat Book 2.
  Will Book 1.
  Will Book 2.

Yale University. New Haven, Connecticut.
    Alumni Files.
        Ives, Brayton.

MAPS

Colonial National Historical Park. Jamestown, Virginia.
    Archeological Excavations, Unit B & APVA—Jamestown, Part of the Master Plan, Colonial National Historical Park. Map 17. R. A. Wilhelm. National Park Service. Jan. 1941.
    General Plot Plan, Unit A—Jamestown Island, Showing Principal Surface Features and Archeological Explorations of 1934 and 1939. Sheet 1 of 20. J. C. Harrington. National Park Service. 1939.
    Historical Base Map, West Half of Jamestown Island & Portions of Mainland, Including Glass House Point. J. C. Harrington. National Park Service. 16 May 1939.
    Jamestown Island, Part of the Master Plan, Colonial National Historical Park. James M. Knight and Fred P. Parris. National Park Service. Jan. 1937.
    Jamestown: Location & Elevations of Confederate Fort. John L. Cotter & Edward B. Jelks. National Park Service. 30 Jan. 1956.
    Map of Jamestown Island, James City County, Virginia, Showing General Features, Etc. Richmond, Virginia. J. Temple Waddill, Inc., Certified Civil Engineer. 10 July 1930.
    Map of Western End of Jamestown Island Showing Existing Features and Seventeenth Century Shore Line. J. C. Harrington. National Park Service. 19 Feb. 1941.
    Plat of Land Situated on Jamestown Island in James River, Va., Deeded to the Association for the Preservation of Virginia Antiquities by Mrs. Louise J. Barney, Homewood, Va., 22½ Acres.
    Trenches Dug for Water & Sewer Lines, October, 1939. J. C. Harrington. National Park Service. 30 Nov. 1939.
    Western End of Jamestown Island Showing Property of the Association for the Preservation of Virginia Antiquities. 1897.
Library of Congress. Washington, D.C.
    U.S. Coast Survey Office. Military Map of South-Eastern Virginia. H. Lindenkohl & Chs. G. Krebs, Lithographer. [1862?].
National Archives. Washington, D.C.
    U.S. Coast and Geodetic Survey. James River, Chart No. 2, From Point of Shoals Light to Sloop Point. Chart. No. 401B. C. P. Patterson, J. E. Hilgard, R. E. Halter, and J. W. Donn. July 1877.
    U.S. Coast and Geodetic Survey. Topographic Sheet No. 1290. 1873–1874.
    U.S. Coast and Geodetic Survey. Topographic Sheet No. 2693a. 1905.
    U.S. Treasury Department. Jamestown Tercentenary Exposition. Plat of Land Situated on Jamestown Island in James River, Va., Deeded to

the Association for the Preservation of Virginia Antiquities by E. E. Barney, Homewood, Va., 22½ Acres.

Southern Planter and Farmer, new ser. 6 (June 1871): facing 321.
   Preliminary Map of Surry County, Virginia. Jedediah Hotchkiss, Topographical Engineer. 1871.

U.S. War Department. *Atlas to Accompany the Official Records of the Union and Confederate Armies.* Washington, D.C.: Government Printing Office, 1891–1895.

Virginia Historical Society. Richmond, Virginia.
   Map of Eastern and Central Virginia. Chief Engineer's Office, Department of Northern Virginia. J. F. Gilmer, Chief Engineer. 1864?
   Map of New Kent, Charles City, James City, and York Counties. Chief Engineer's Office, Department of Northern Virginia. J. F. Gilmer, Chief Engineer. [1863].

Williamsburg-James City County Courthouse. Williamsburg, Virginia.
   Plat Book. 2:6. 28 Feb. 1907.

PUBLIC DOCUMENTS

U.S. Naval History Division. *Civil War Naval Chronology 1861–1865.* Washington, D.C.: Government Printing Office, 1971.

U.S. Naval War Records Office. *Official Records of the Union and Confederate Navies in the War of the Rebellion.* 30 vols. Washington, D.C.: Government Printing Office, 1894–1922.

————. *Register of Officers of the Confederate States Navy 1861–1865.* Washington, D.C.: Government Printing Office, 1931.

U.S. Surgeon General's Office. *The Medical and Surgical History of the War of the Rebellion (1861–1865).* 6 vols. Washington, D.C.: Government Printing Office. 1870–1888.

U.S. War Department. *The War of the Rebellion: A Compilation of the Official Records of the Union and Confederate Armies.* 128 vols. Washington, D.C.: Government Printing Office, 1880–1901.

Virginia. *Calendar of Virginia State Papers and Other Manuscripts.* Edited by William P. Palmer, Sherwin McRae, Raleigh Colston, and H. W. Flournoy. 11 vols. Richmond: n.p., 1875–1893.

Virginia. Convention. *Journals and Papers of the Virginia State Convention of 1861.* 3 vols. Richmond: Virginia State Library, 1966.

Virginia. Council. *Executive Journals of the Council of Colonial Virginia, 1680–1775.* Edited by H. R. McIlwaine, Wilmer L. Hall and Benjamin J. Hillman. 6 vols. Richmond: Virginia State Library, 1925–1966.

Virginia. Council. *Journals of the Council of the State of Virginia, 1776–1791.* Edited by H. R. McIlwaine, Wilmer L. Hall, George H. Reese, and Sandra Gioia Treadway. 5 vols. Richmond: Virginia State Library, 1931–1982.

Virginia. Council of Three. *Proceedings of the Advisory Council of the State of Virginia, April 21–June 19, 1861.* Edited by James I. Robertson, Jr. Richmond: Virginia State Library, 1977.

Virginia. General Assembly. House of Burgesses. *Journals of the House of Burgesses of Virginia, 1619–1776.* Edited by H. R. McIlwaine and John Pendleton Kennedy. 13 vols. Richmond: Virginia State Library, 1905–1915.

UNPUBLISHED STUDIES

Chapman, Anne West. "Benjamin Stoddert Ewell: A Biography." Ph.D. diss., College of William and Mary, 1984.

Davis, Emma-Jo L. "Mulberry Island and the Civil War, April 1861–May 1862." Fort Eustis Historical and Archeological Association, March 1968.

Goodwin, Mary R. M. "'Kingsmill' Plantation, James City County, Virginia." Colonial Williamsburg Foundation, September 1958.

Hendricks, Christopher. "Land Ownership—Jamestown Island." Jamestown, Virginia: Colonial National Historical Park, Spring 1988.

Kelso, William M., Nicholas M. Luccketti and Beverly A. Straube. "A Re-Evaluation of the Archaeological Evidence Produced by Project 100, the Search for James Fort." Jamestown, Virginia: Virginia Company Foundation, 1990.

Kettenburg, Carol Ann. "The Battle of Williamsburg." Master's thesis, College of William and Mary, 1980.

Melton, Maurice. "Major Military Industries of the Confederate Government." Ph.D. diss., Emory University, 1978.

Riedel, Leonard W., Jr. "John Bankhead Magruder and the Defense of the Virginia Peninsula, 1861–1862." Master's thesis, Old Dominion University, 1991.

NEWSPAPERS

Daily Lynchburg Virginian.
Daily Richmond Examiner.
Fredericksburg News.
Newport News *Daily Press.*
Petersburg Index and Appeal.
Richmond *Daily Dispatch.*
Richmond Daily Whig.
Richmond Enquirer.
Richmond Times-Dispatch.
Smithfield Times.
Suffolk News-Herald.
Washington Post.
Williamsburg *Virginia Gazette.*

PERIODICALS

Civil War History.
Civil War Times Illustrated.
Confederate Veteran.

Historical Magazine.
Jamestown Archaeological Assessment Newsletter.
Journal of Coastal Research.
Proceedings of the American Antiquarian Society.
Quarterly Bulletin Archeological Society of Virginia.
Southern Historical Society Papers.
Southern Literary Messenger.
Southern Planter and Farmer.
Southside Virginian.
Tyler's Quarterly Historical and Genealogical Magazine.
Virginia Cavalcade.
Virginia Magazine of History and Biography.
William and Mary Quarterly.

ARTICLES

"Allen Family of Surry County." *William and Mary Quarterly* 1st ser. 8 (October 1899): 110–12.

Bohannan, Aurelius W. "Jamestown Island and 'The Surry Side.'" *Virginia Magazine of History and Biography* 55 (April 1947): 126–36.

Brown, Marley R., III. "National Park Service Archaeological Assessment of Jamestown, Virginia: Research Plan, 1992–1994." *Jamestown Archaeological Assessment Newsletter* 1 (Fall 1993): 1–5.

Cary, Harriette. "Diary of Miss Harriette Cary, Kept by Her from May 6, 1862, to July 24, 1862." *Tyler's Quarterly Historical and Genealogical Magazine* 9 (October 1927): 104–15.

Clayton, Mrs. Robert B. "Jamestown Island." *William and Mary Quarterly* 1st ser. 10 (October 1901): 142.

"Confederate Letters." *Tyler's Quarterly Historical and Genealogical Magazine* 10 (January 1929): 185–90.

"Council Papers 1698–1702." *Virginia Magazine of History and Biography* 24 (April 1916): 151–57.

Crocker, James F. "Colonel James Gregory Hodges." *Southern Historical Society Papers* 37 (1909): 184–97.

Davis, Emma-Jo L. "Mulberry Island and the Civil War, April 1861–May 1862." *Quarterly Bulletin Archeological Society of Virginia* 26 (March 1972):109–35.

Hackemer, Kurt. "The Other Union Gunboat: The USS *Galena* and the Critical Summer of 1862." *Civil War History* 40 (September 1994): 226–47.

Hall, Virginius Cornick, Jr. "Virginia Post Offices, 1798–1859." *Virginia Magazine of History and Biography* 81 (January 1973): 49–97.

Harrington, Virginia S. "Theories and Evidence for the Location of James Fort." *Virginia Magazine of History and Biography* 93 (January 1985): 36–53.

Hatch, Charles E., Jr. "Jamestown and the Revolution." *William and Mary Quarterly* 2d ser. 22 (January 1942): 30–38.

———. "Robert Sully at Jamestown, 1854." *William and Mary Quarterly* 2d ser. 22 (October 1942): 343–52.

———. "The 'Affair Near James Island' (or, 'The Battle of Green Spring') July 6, 1781." *Virginia Magazine of History and Biography* 53 (July 1945): 171–96.

Hazard, Ebenezer. "The Journal of Ebenezer Hazard in Virginia, 1777." Edited by Fred Shelley. *Virginia Magazine of History and Biography* 62 (October 1954): 400–423.

Hobbs, Carl H., III, Dennis B. Blanton, Robert A. Gammisch, and John Broadwater. "A Marine Archaeological Reconnaissance Using Side-Scan Sonar, Jamestown Island, Virginia, U.S.A." *Journal of Coastal Research* 10 (Spring 1994): 351–59.

Horning, Audrey J., Andrew C. Edwards, and Gregory J. Brown. "1993 Archaeological Investigations in New Towne." *Jamestown Archaeological Assessment Newsletter* 1 (Fall 1993): 8–12.

"Island of Jamestown." *The Southern Literary Messenger* 3 (Richmond: Thos. W. White, 1837): 302–04.

"James City County Petitions." *Tyler's Quarterly Historical and Genealogical Magazine* 2 (January 1921): 177–93.

"James Minge." *Virginia Magazine of History and Biography* 3 (October 1895): 159–60.

"Jamestown Island in 1861." *William and Mary Quarterly* 1st ser. 10 (July 1901): 38–39.

Jones, T. Catesby. "The Iron-Clad *Virginia*." *Virginia Magazine of History and Biography* 49 (October 1941): 296–303.

Kay, William Kennon. "Drewry's Bluff or Fort Darling?" *Virginia Magazine of History and Biography* 77 (April 1969): 191–200.

Kelton, A. S. "Armed Confederates at Jamestown." *Confederate Veteran* 14 (September 1906): 389–90.

"Letter in Dr. Tyler's Scrapbook." *Tyler's Quarterly Historical and Genealogical Magazine* 25 (July 1943): 10–11.

"Letters from a Tyler Collection." *Tyler's Quarterly Historical and Genealogical Magazine* 30 (October 1948): 93–114.

"Letters of Lafayette." *Virginia Magazine of History and Biography* 6 (July 1898): 55–59.

Mardis, Allen, Jr. "Visions of James Fort." *Virginia Magazine of History and Biography* 97 (October 1989): 463–98.

McCusker, John J. "How Much Is That in Real Money? A Historical Price Index for Use as a Deflator of Money Values in the Economy of the United States." *Proceedings of the American Antiquarian Society* 101 (October 1991): 297–373.

Melton, Maurice. "The Selma Naval Ordnance Works." *Civil War Times Illustrated* 14 (December 1975): 18–25, 28–31.

"Nathaniel Bacon's Land at Curles." *Virginia Magazine of History and Biography* 37 (October 1929): 354–57.

"Papers from the Virginia State Auditor's Office, Now in the Virginia State Library." *Virginia Magazine of History and Biography* 25 (October 1917): 376–88.

Rives, Ralph Hardee. "The Jamestown Celebration of 1857." *Virginia Magazine of History and Biography* 66 (July 1958): 260–71.

Robinson, William M., Jr. "Drewry's Bluff: Naval Defense of Richmond, 1862." *Civil War History* 7 (June 1961): 167–75.

Scheips, Paul J. "Union Signal Communications: Innovation and Conflict." *Civil War History* 9 (December 1963): 399–421.

Scribner, Robert L. "With Perry in Japan: A Young Virginian [John R. C. Lewis] Witnessed Historic Events a Hundred Years Ago." *Virginia Cavalcade* 3 (1954): 4–7.

"Sheild Family." *William and Mary Quarterly* 1st ser. 4 (July 1895): 59.

Stone, Doris. "Index to Wills of Surry County, 1800–1900." *Southside Virginian* 6 (October 1988): 156–67.

Thompson, John R. "Celebration at Jamestown." *The Southern Literary Messenger* n.s. 4 (Richmond, Virginia: MacFarlane, Ferguson & Co., 1857): 434–66.

———. "Editor's Table." *The Southern Literary Messenger* n.s. 7 (Richmond: MacFarlane, Ferguson & Co., 1859): 395–97.

"Tombstones at Claremont, Surry County." *William and Mary Quarterly* 1st ser. 8 (October 1899): 112–15.

"Virginia Militia in the Revolution." *Virginia Magazine of History and Biography* 10 (April 1903): 419–20.

"When Ex-President Tyler and Mrs. Tyler Visited Petersburg, Va., in 1854." *Tyler's Quarterly Historical and Genealogical Magazine* 19 (January 1938): 132–39.

Wilkins, Minge. "Minge Family Register." *William and Mary Quarterly* 1st ser. 21 (July 1912): 31–33.

"William H. Ware." *Confederate Veteran* 36 (October 1928): 388.

Wynne, Thomas H. "Jamestown, Virginia." *The Historical Magazine* 2d ser. 3 (Morristown, N.Y.: Henry B. Dawson, 1868): 53.

BOOKS

Barringer, Paul Brandon, James Mercer Garnett and Rosewell Page, eds. *University of Virginia: Its History, Influence, Equipment and Characteristics with Biographical Sketches and Portraits of Founders, Benefactors, Officers, and Alumni.* 2 vols. New York: Lewis Publishing Co., 1904.

Bearss, Edwin C. *River of Lost Opportunities: The Civil War on the James River, 1861–1862.* Lynchburg, Virginia: H. E. Howard, 1995.

Beers, Henry Putney. *The Confederacy: A Guide to the Archives of the Government of the Confederate States of America.* Washington, D.C.: National Archives and Records Administration, 1986.

Berkeley, Henry Robinson. *Four Years in the Confederate Artillery: The Diary of Private Henry Robinson Berkeley*. Edited by William H. Runge. Richmond: Virginia Historical Society, 1991.

Billings, Warren M. *Jamestown and the Founding of the Nation.* Gettysburg, Pa.: Thomas Publications, 1991.

Billings, Warren M., John E. Selby and Thad W. Tate. *Colonial Virginia: A History*. New York: KTO Press, 1986.

Blanton, Wyndham B. *Medicine in Virginia in the Nineteenth Century*. Richmond: Garrett & Massie, 1933.

Boatner, Mark Mayo III. *Encyclopedia of the American Revolution*. New York: David McKay Co., 1966.

———. *The Civil War Dictionary*. New York: David McKay Co., 1959.

Boddie, John Bennett. *Southside Virginia Families*. 2 vols. Redwood City, California: Pacific Coast Publishers, 1955.

Bohannan, Aurelius W. *Old Surry: Thumb-Nail Sketches of Places of Historic Interest in Surry County, Virginia*. Petersburg, Va.: Plummer Printing Co., 1927.

Bohannan, Willis W. *Surry County at War, 1861–1865*. N.p., 1963.

Brooke, George M., Jr. *John M. Brooke: Naval Scientist and Educator*. Charlottesville: University Press of Virginia, 1980.

Browning, Robert M., Jr. *From Cape Charles to Cape Fear: The North Atlantic Blockading Squadron During the Civil War*. Tuscaloosa: University of Alabama Press, 1993.

Bruce, Philip A. *Virginia: Rebirth of the Old Dominion*. 5 vols. Chicago: Lewis Publishing Co., 1929.

Butler, Stuart Lee. *A Guide to Virginia Militia Units in the War of 1812*. Athens, Georgia: Iberian Publishing Co., 1988.

Cappon, Lester J. *Virginia Newspapers 1821–1935: A Bibliography With Historical Introduction and Notes*. New York: D. Appleton-Century Co., 1936.

Chamberlayne, John Hampden. *Ham Chamberlayne—Virginian: Letters and Papers of an Artillery Officer in the War for Southern Independence, 1861–1865*. Edited by G. C. Chamberlayne. Richmond, Va.: Dietz Printing Co., 1932.

Chernault, Tracy and Jeffrey C. Weaver. *18th and 20th Battalions of Heavy Artillery*. Lynchburg, Virginia: H. E. Howard, 1995.

Chesnut, Mary Boykin. *A Diary From Dixie*. Edited by Ben Ames Williams. Boston: Houghton Mifflin Company, 1949.

———. *Mary Chesnut's Civil War*. Edited by C. Vann Woodward. New Haven: Yale University Press, 1981.

Clary, David A. *Fortress America: The Corps of Engineers, Hampton Roads, and United States Coastal Defense*. Charlottesville: University Press of Virginia, 1990.

Clayton, W. F. *A Narrative of the Confederate States Navy*. Weldon, N.C.: Harrell's Printing House, 1910.

Coddington, Edwin B. *The Gettysburg Campaign: A Study in Command.* New York: Charles Scribner's Sons, 1968.

Cormier, Steven A. *The Siege of Suffolk: The Forgotten Campaign, April 11–May 4, 1863.* Lynchburg, Virginia: H. E. Howard, 1989.

Coski, John M. "'All Confusion on the Plantations': Civil War in Charles City County." In *Charles City County, Virginia: An Official History,* edited by James P. Whittenburg and John M. Coski. Salem, West Virginia: Don Mills, 1989.

———. *Capital Navy: The Men, Ships, and Operations of the James River Squadron.* Campbell, California: Savas Woodbury Publishers, 1996.

Cotter, John L. *Archeological Excavations at Jamestown, Virginia.* Washington, D.C.: Government Printing Office, 1958.

Cottrell, James R. "John Mercer Patton, Jr." In *The Virginia Law Reporters Before 1880,* edited by Hamilton W. Bryson. Charlottesville: University Press of Virginia, 1977.

Couture, Richard T. *To Preserve and Protect: A History of the Association for the Preservation of Virginia Antiquities.* Dallas, Texas: Taylor Publishing Co., 1984.

Cowles, Calvin Duvall. *Genealogy of the Cowles Family in America.* 2 vols. New Haven, Conn.: The Tuttle, Morehouse & Taylor Co., 1929.

Crews, Edward R. and Timothy A. Parrish. *14th Virginia Infantry.* Lynchburg, Virginia: H. E. Howard, 1995.

Crittenden, H. Temple, comp. *The Comp'ny: The Story of the Surry, Sussex & Southampton Railway and the Surry Lumber Company.* Parsons, W.Va.: McClain Printing Co., 1967.

Crocker, James F. *Colonel James Gregory Hodges, His Life and Character.* Portsmouth, Va.: W. A. Fiske, 1909.

Cullen, Joseph P. *Richmond National Battlefield Park, Virginia.* Washington, D.C.: Government Printing Office, 1961.

Cullum, George W. *Biographical Register of the Officers and Graduates of the U.S. Military Academy at West Point, N.Y.* 2 vols. New York: D. Van Nostrand, 1868.

Current, Richard N., ed. *Encyclopedia of the Confederacy.* 4 vols. New York: Simon & Schuster, 1993.

Dabney, Virginius. *Richmond: The Story of a City.* Garden City, New York: Doubleday & Co., 1976.

Davis, William C. *Duel Between the First Ironclads.* Garden City, New York: Doubleday & Co., 1975.

DeLeon, T. C. *Belles, Beaux and Brains of the '60s.* New York: G. W. Dillingham Co., 1909.

Dew, Charles B. *Ironmaker to the Confederacy: Joseph R. Anderson and the Tredegar Iron Works.* New Haven: Yale University Press, 1966.

Dickey, Luther S. *History of the Eighty-Fifth Regiment Pennsylvania Volunteer Infantry 1861–1865.* New York: J. C. & W. E. Powers, 1915.

Dictionary of American Biography. 21 vols. New York: Charles Scribner's Sons, 1927–1936.

Dudley, William S. *Going South: U.S. Navy Officer Resignations & Dismissals on the Eve of the Civil War*. Washington: Naval Historical Foundation, 1981.

Dyer, Frederick H. *A Compendium of the War of the Rebellion*. 3 vols. New York: Thomas Yoseloff, 1959.

Eliot, Ellsworth, Jr. *Yale in the Civil War*. New Haven: Yale University Press, 1932.

Eyland, Seth [David Edward Cronin]. *The Evolution of a Life*. New York: S. W. Green's Son, 1884.

Faust, Patricia L., ed. *Historical Times Illustrated Encyclopedia of the Civil War*. New York: Harper & Row, 1986.

Floyd, Fred C. *History of the Fortieth (Mozart) Regiment New York Volunteers*. Boston: F. H. Gilson Co., 1909.

Freeman, Douglas Southall. *R. E. Lee: A Biography*. 4 vols. New York: Charles Scribner's Sons, 1934–35.

———. *Lee's Lieutenants: A Study in Command*. 3 vols. New York: Charles Scribner's Sons, 1942–44.

Gibbon, John. *Personal Recollections of the Civil War*. New York: G. P. Putnam's Sons, 1928.

Gottschalk, Louis. *Lafayette and the Close of the American Revolution*. Chicago, Illinois: University of Chicago Press, 1942.

Grant, Ulysses S. *Personal Memoirs of U. S. Grant*. 2 vols. New York: Charles L. Webster & Co., 1885.

———. *The Papers of Ulysses S. Grant*. Edited by John Y. Simon. 18 vols. (incomplete). Carbondale: Southern Illinois University Press, 1967–.

Graves, Joseph A. *The History of the Bedford Light Artillery*. Bedford City, Va.: Press of the Bedford Democrat, 1903.

Gregory, Eve S. *Claremont Manor: A History*. Petersburg, Virginia: Plummer Printing Co., 1990.

Grimsley, Mark. *The Hard Hand of War: The Union Military Policy Toward Southern Civilians, 1861–1865*. Cambridge: Cambridge University Press, 1995.

Hale, Will T. *True Stories of Jamestown and Its Environs*. Nashville, Tenn.: Smith & Lamar, 1907.

Hall, Edward Hagaman. *Jamestown*. New York: The American Scenic and Historic Preservation Society, 1902.

Hall, Virginius Cornick, Jr. *Portraits in the Collection of the Virginia Historical Society: A Catalogue*. Charlottesville: University Press of Virginia, 1981.

Hardesty's Historical and Geographical Encyclopedia. New York: H. H. Hardesty & Co., 1884.

Hassler, Warren W., Jr. *General George B. McClellan: Shield of the Union*. Baton Rouge: Louisiana State University Press, 1957.

———. *Commanders of the Army of the Potomac*. Baton Rouge: Louisiana State University Press, 1962.

Hatch, Charles E., Jr. *Jamestown, Virginia: The Townsite and Its Story*. Washington, D.C.: Government Printing Office, 1957.

———. *Yorktown and the Siege of 1781*. Washington, D.C.: Government Printing Office, 1957.

Heitman, Francis B. *Historical Register and Dictionary of the United States Army*. 2 vols. Washington, D.C.: Government Printing Office, 1903.

Hummel, Ray O., Jr., ed. *A List of Places Included in 19th Century Virginia Directories*. Richmond, Virginia: Virginia State Library, 1960.

Jamestown Society. *Celebration of the Two Hundred and Fiftieth Anniversary of the English Settlement at Jamestown, May 13, 1857*. Washington: Jno. T. & Lem. Towers, 1857.

Jensen, Les. *32nd Virginia Infantry*. Lynchburg, Virginia: H. E. Howard, 1990.

Jesup, Henry Griswold. *Edward Jessup of West Farms, Winchester Co., New York, and His Descendants*. Cambridge: John Wilson and Son, 1887.

Johnston, Henry P. *The Yorktown Campaign and the Surrender of Cornwallis 1781*. New York: Harper & Brothers, 1881.

Jones, B. W. *Battle Roll of Surry County, Virginia in the War Between the States with Historical and Personal Notes*. Richmond: Everett Waddey Co., 1913.

Jones, Hugh. *The Present State of Virginia*. Edited by Richard L. Morton. Chapel Hill: University of North Carolina Press, 1956.

Jones, Terry L. *Lee's Tigers: The Louisiana Infantry in the Army of Northern Virginia*. Baton Rouge: Louisiana State University Press, 1987.

Jones, Virgil Carrington. *Eight Hours Before Richmond*. New York: Henry Holt and Co., 1957.

Jordan, Ervin L., Jr. *Black Confederates and Afro-Yankees in Civil War Virginia*. Charlottesville: University Press of Virginia, 1995.

Keeler, William Frederick. *Aboard the USS Monitor, 1862: The Letters of Acting Paymaster William Frederick Keeler, U.S. Navy to His Wife, Anna*. Edited by Robert W. Daly. Annapolis, Maryland: United States Naval Institute, 1964.

Koleszar, Marilyn Brewer. *Ashland, Bedford, and Taylor Virginia Light Artillery*. Lynchburg, Virginia: H. E. Howard, 1994.

Kornwolf, James D. *Guide to the Buildings of Surry and the American Revolution*. Surry, Va.: The Surry County, Virginia 1776 Bicentennial Committee, 1976.

Krick, Robert K. *Lee's Colonels: A Biographical Register of the Field Officers of the Army of Northern Virginia*. Dayton, Ohio: Press of Morningside Bookshop, 1979.

Lafayette, Marie Joseph Paul Yves Roch Gilbert du Motier, Marquis de. *Lafayette in the Age of the American Revolution: Selected Letters and Papers, 1776–1790.* Edited by Stanley J. Idzerda, Roger E. Smith, Robert Rhodes Crout, Linda J. Pike, MaryAnn Quinn, Carol Godschall, and Leslie Wharton. 5 vols. (incomplete). Ithaca: Cornell University Press, 1977–.

Lavery, Dennis S. and Mark H. Jordan. *Iron Brigade General: John Gibbon, A Rebel in Blue.* Westport, Connecticut: Greenwood Press, 1993.

Lee, Robert E. *The Wartime Papers of R. E. Lee.* Edited by Clifford Dowdey and Louis H. Manarin. New York: Bramhall House, 1961.

Lincoln, Abraham. *The Collected Works of Abraham Lincoln.* Edited by Roy P. Basler, Marion Dolores Pratt, and Lloyd A. Dunlap. 9 vols. New Brunswick, New Jersey: Rutgers University Press, 1953–55.

Lindgren, James M. *Preserving the Old Dominion: Historic Preservation and Virginia Traditionalism.* Charlottesville: University Press of Virginia, 1993.

Long, E. B. *The Civil War Day By Day: An Almanac, 1861–1865.* Garden City, New York: Doubleday & Co., 1971.

Lossing, Benson J. *The Pictorial Field-Book of the Revolution.* 2 vols. New York: Harper & Brothers, 1851–60.

Luraghi, Raimondo. *A History of the Confederate Navy.* Annapolis, Maryland: Naval Institute Press, 1996.

Mabry, W. S. *Brief Sketch of the Career of Captain Catesby ap R. Jones.* Selma, Alabama: n.p., 1912.

Mahan, D. H. *A Treatise on Field Fortification.* New York: John Wiley, 1863.

Maury, Ann, ed. *Memoirs of a Huguenot Family.* New York: G. P. Putnam's Sons, 1907.

McClellan, George B. *McClellan's Own Story: The War for the Union.* New York: Charles L. Webster & Co., 1887.

————. *The Civil War Papers of George B. McClellan: Selected Correspondence, 1860–1865.* Edited by Stephen W. Sears. New York: Ticknor & Fields, 1989.

McKim, Randolph H. *A Soldier's Recollections: Leaves from the Diary of a Young Confederate.* New York: Longmans, Green, and Co., 1910.

Meade, William. *Old Churches, Ministers and Families of Virginia.* 2 vols. Philadelphia: J. B. Lippincott Co., 1857.

Moebs, Thomas Truxton. *Confederate States Navy Research Guide.* Williamsburg, Virginia: Moebs Publishing Co., 1991.

Morton, Richard L. *Colonial Virginia.* 2 vols. Chapel Hill: University of North Carolina Press, 1960.

Munden, Kenneth W., and Henry Putney Beers. *The Union: A Guide to Federal Archives Relating to the Civil War.* Washington, D.C.: National Archives and Records Administration, 1986.

National Cyclopaedia of American Biography. 13 vols. New York: James T. White & Co., 1892–1906.

Nelson, Paul David. *Anthony Wayne: Soldier of the Early Republic*. Bloomington: Indiana University Press, 1985.

Nichols, James L. *Confederate Engineers*. Tuscaloosa, Alabama: Confederate Publishing Co., 1957.

Norris, J. E., ed. *History of the Lower Shenandoah Valley*. Chicago, Illinois: A. Warner & Co., 1890.

Official Blue Book of the Jamestown Ter-Centennial Exposition. Norfolk, Virginia: Colonial Publishing Co., 1909.

Peckham, Howard H., ed. *The Toll of Independence: Engagements & Battle Casualties of the American Revolution*. Chicago: University of Chicago Press, 1974.

Perry, Milton F. *Infernal Machines: The Story of Confederate Submarine and Mine Warfare*. Baton Rouge: Louisiana State University Press, 1965.

Phisterer, Frederick, comp. *New York in the War of the Rebellion, 1861 to 1865*. 5 vols. Albany: J. R. Lyon Co., 1912.

Plum, William R. *The Military Telegraph During the Civil War in the United States*. Chicago: Jansen, McClurg & Co., 1882.

Porter, John A. *76th Regiment Pennsylvania Volunteer Infantry Keystone Zouaves: The Personal Recollections 1861–1865 of Sergeant John A. Porter Company "B"*. Edited by James A. Chisman, William S. Brockington, Jr., and Michael A. Cavanaugh, Jr. Wilmington, North Carolina: Broadfoot Publishing Co., 1988.

Riggs, David F. *13th Virginia Infantry*. Lynchburg, Virginia: H. E. Howard, 1988.

Riggs, Susan A. *21st Virginia Infantry*. Lynchburg, Virginia: H. E. Howard, 1991.

Ripley, Warren. *Artillery and Ammunition of the Civil War*. New York: Van Nostrand Reinhold Co., 1970.

Robertson, James I., Jr. *Civil War Sites in Virginia: A Tour Guide*. Charlottesville: University Press of Virginia, 1982.

———, ed. in chief. *An Index-Guide to the* Southern Historical Society Papers, *1876–1959*. 2 vols. Millwood, New York: Kraus International Publications, 1980.

Robertson, William Glenn. *Back Door to Richmond: The Bermuda Hundred Campaign, April–June 1864*. Newark: University of Delaware Press, 1987.

Rountree, Helen C. *Pocahontas's People: The Powhatan Indians of Virginia Through Four Centuries*. Norman: University of Oklahoma Press, 1990.

Sanchez-Saavedra, E. M., comp. *A Guide to Virginia Military Organizations in the American Revolution, 1774–1787*. Richmond, Virginia: Virginia State Library, 1978.

Scharf, J. Thomas. *History of the Confederate States Navy from its Organization to the Surrender of its Last Vessel*. New York: Rogers & Sherwood, 1887.

Schiller, Herbert M. *The Bermuda Hundred Campaign*. Dayton, Ohio: Morningside House, 1988.

Sears, Stephen W. *To the Gates of Richmond: The Peninsula Campaign*. New York: Ticknor & Fields, 1992.

Selby, John E. *The Revolution in Virginia 1775–1783*. Williamsburg, Virginia: The Colonial Williamsburg Foundation, 1988.

Selden, John A. "The Westover Journal of John A. Selden, Esqr., 1858–1862." Edited by John Spencer Bassett and Sidney Bradshaw Fay. *Smith College Studies in History*, 6 (July 1921): 251–330.

Sellers, John R., comp. *Civil War Manuscripts: A Guide to Collections in the Manuscript Division of the Library of Congress*. Washington: Library of Congress, 1986.

Shea, William L. *The Virginia Militia in the Seventeenth Century*. Baton Rouge: Louisiana State University Press, 1983.

Silverstone, Paul H. *Warships of the Civil War Navies*. Annapolis, Maryland: Naval Institute Press, 1989.

Stephenson, Mary A. *Old Homes in Surry & Sussex*. Richmond, Va.: Dietz Press, 1942.

Stewart, Robert A. *Index to Printed Virginia Genealogies*. Baltimore: Genealogical Publishing Co., 1965.

Still, William N., Jr. *Iron Afloat: The Story of the Confederate Armorclads*. Nashville, Tenn.: Vanderbilt University Press, 1971.

———. *Confederate Shipbuilding*. Columbia: University of South Carolina Press, 1987.

Stille, Charles J. *Major General Anthony Wayne and the Pennsylvania Line in the Continental Army*. Philadelphia: J. B. Lippincott Co., 1893.

Stowits, George H. *History of the One Hundredth Regiment of New York State Volunteers*. Buffalo: Matthews & Warren, 1870.

Swem, Earl Gregg. *Virginia Historical Index*. 2 vols. Gloucester, Mass.: Peter Smith, 1965.

Swem, Earl Gregg and John W. Williams. *A Register of the General Assembly of Virginia 1776–1918*. Richmond: D. Bottom, 1918.

Symonds, Craig L. *Joseph E. Johnston: A Civil War Biography*. New York: W. W. Norton & Co., 1992.

Thomas, Emory M. *The Confederate Nation: 1861–1865*. New York: Harper & Row, 1979.

Tidwell, William A., James O. Hall, and David Winfred Gaddy. *Come Retribution: The Confederate Secret Service and the Assassination of Lincoln*. Jackson: University Press of Mississippi, 1988.

Travis, Robert J. *The Travis (Travers) Family and Its Allies*. Decatur, Georgia: Bowen Press, 1954.

Tyler, Lyon Gardiner. *The Cradle of the Republic: Jamestown and James River*. Richmond, Va.: The Hermitage Press, 1906.

————. *Encyclopedia of Virginia Biography.* 5 vols. New York: Lewis Historical Publishing Co., 1915.

Van Schreeven, William J., Robert L. Scribner and Brent Tarter, comps. and eds. *Revolutionary Virginia: The Road to Independence.* 7 vols. Charlottesville: University Press of Virginia, 1973–1983.

V.M.I. Register of Former Cadets. Lexington, Virginia: Virginia Military Institute, 1957.

Wallace, Lee A., Jr., comp. *A Guide to Virginia Military Organizations, 1861–1865.* Lynchburg, Virginia: H. E. Howard, 1986.

Warner, Ezra J. *Generals in Gray: Lives of the Confederate Commanders.* Baton Rouge: Louisiana State University Press, 1959.

————. *Generals in Blue: Lives of the Union Commanders.* Baton Rouge: Louisiana State University Press, 1964.

Warner, Pauline Pearce. *Benjamin Harrison of Berkeley, Walter Cocke of Surry; Family Records I.* Tappahannock, Virginia: privately printed, 1962.

Watkins, Lizzie Stringfellow. *The Life of Horace Stringfellow.* Montgomery, Alabama: Paragon Press, 1931.

Weinert, Richard P., Jr. and Robert Arthur. *Defender of the Chesapeake: The Story of Fort Monroe.* Shippensburg, Pa.: White Mane Publishing Co., 1989.

Werlich, David P. *Admiral of the Amazon: John Randolph Tucker, His Confederate Colleagues, and Peru.* Charlottesville: University Press of Virginia, 1990.

Williams, Frances Leigh. *Matthew Fontaine Maury: Scientist of the Sea.* New Brunswick, New Jersey: Rutgers University Press, 1963.

Williams, T. Harry. *Lincoln and His Generals.* New York: Grosset & Dunlap, 1952.

Wise, Jennings Cropper. *The Long Arm of Lee, or the History of the Artillery of the Army of Northern Virginia.* 2 vols. Lincoln: University of Nebraska Press, 1988.

Worsham, John H. *One of Jackson's Foot Cavalry.* Jackson, Tennessee: McCowat-Mercer Press, 1964.

Wright, Marcus J. *General Officers of the Confederate Army.* New York: Neale Publishing Co., 1911.

Wyatt, Edward A., IV. *Along Petersburg Streets: Historic Sites and Buildings of Petersburg, Virginia.* Richmond, Virginia: Dietz Printing Co., 1943.

Yearbook of the Association for the Preservation of Virginia Antiquities for 1898. Richmond: Wm. Ellis Jones, 1899.

Yonge, Samuel H. *The Site of Old "James Towne" 1607–1698.* Richmond, Virginia: L. H. Jenkins, 1952.

INDEX

A

African-Americans. *See* free blacks;
  rebellion, slave; slaves; United States
  Colored Cavalry
agriculture, 11, 13, 14, 17, 18, 39
Aleck (escaped slave), 83, 84, 173n. 6
Allen, Frances Augusta Jessup
        marries William Allen (1828–1875),
        11
        debt of, after Allen's death, 109,
        176n. 5
        and Allen's death, 176n. 7
        burial of, 177n. 8
Allen, William, II (1768–1831)
        death of, 10
        bequest to William Allen (1828–
        1875), 10, 108, 158n. 3
Allen, William (1828–1875)
        birth, 10, 158n. 2
        parents and siblings of, 10, 158n. 2
        changes name to William Allen,
        and legal name of, 10, 158n. 3
        inheritance of, 10, 108
        education and European tour, 10
        acquires Jamestown, 11
        marriage and wife of, 11, 109
        children of, 11, 109, 158n. 5, 177n. 8
        slaves of
              prewar, 11
              used by Confederacy, 25, 31,
              58, 107, 169n. 56
              in Jamestown rebellion, 82–
              86, 108, 172n. 4, 173nn. 7,
              10, 11
              at his funeral, 109
        business of, 12, 62, 159n. 8
        railroad of, 12, 56, 107
        wealth of, 12, 159n. 8
        and Selden, 12, 107–08, 167n. 39

character, 12
interests of, 12
lavish entertainment by, 12, 108
and Jamestown Celebration (1857),
        13–14
in militia, 14
organizes battery and occupies
        Jamestown, 14–15, 23
fort of, 15, 142
and Ambler house, 18, 38–39
furnishes supplies, 21, 29, 40, 107,
        171n. 15, 176n. 2
transfers artillery, 49
provides railroad iron for *Virginia*
        test and for iron plate, 56, 107
and Carter, 58
organizes battalion, 61, 67, 70,
        169n. 59
and Jamestown evacuation, 71–72,
        171n. 15
has vessels near Claremont, 78
praised by Magruder, 82
resignation of, 82, 107
property losses and debt of, 82,
        107–09, 176n. 5
loyalty of Wooten to, 85
friendship with Bohannan, 107
lives at Richmond and Curles
        Neck, 83, 108
returns to Claremont, 108
leases and sells Jamestown, 108,
        109
death and funeral of, 108–09, 158n.
        2, 176n. 7
how remembered, 109
rank and command level, 129
real estate after death of, 176n. 5
Allen Artillery. *See* Virginia artillery
  batteries

197